Marivaux

Three Plays

Translated and Adapted
by Stephen Wadsworth

Great Translations for Actors

SK
A Smith and Kraus Book

Smith and Kraus, Inc.
PO Box 127, Lyme, NH 03768

Marivaux: Three Plays
Copyright © 1999 by Stephen Wadsworth Zinsser
All rights reserved
Manufactured in the United States of America

Changes of Heart Copyright ©1994, 1996, 1999 by Stephen Wadsworth Zinsser.
The Game of Love and Chance Copyright ©1997, 1999 by Stephen Wadsworth Zinsser.
The Triumph of Love Copyright ©1992, 1993, 1999 by Stephen Wadsworth Zinsser.

Cover Photo by T. Charles Erickson
Cover and Book Design by Julia Hill Gignoux, Freedom Hill Design

First Edition: December 1999
9 8 7 6 5 4 3 2 1

Library of Congress Cataloging-in-Publication Data
Marivaux, Pierre Carlet de Chamblain de, 1688–1763.
Marivaux / translated by Stephen Wadsworth.
v. <1 > ; cm.
"Smith and Kraus Book."
Contents: v.1. Three plays.
ISBN 1-57525-148-5
1. Marivaux, Pierre Carlet de Chamblain de, 1688–1763—Translations into English. I. Title.
PQ2003.A288   1998
842'.5—dc21   98-38708
CIP

CONTENTS

Overview vii

Acknowledgments ix

Marivaux in Context, Stephen Wadsworth 1

The France of Marivaux, Christine Pevitt 4

Marivaux on Page and Stage, A conversation between
    Stephen Wadsworth and Janice Paran 11

THE PLAYS

Changes of Heart (The Double Inconstancy), 1723 23

The Game of Love and Chance, 1730 81

The Triumph of Love, 1732 137

POSTSCRIPT

A Marivaux Chronology 191

A List of Marivaux's Plays 195

The Adaptations 197

Pronunciation Guide 198

OVERVIEW

This book invites the reader to savor three major plays by Marivaux and to consider them, briefly, in the context of eighteenth-century history and theatrical tradition. The book includes: an introductory piece, *Marivaux in Context*, which identifies some of the deeper themes and currents in Marivaux's work; a piece by historian and biographer Christine Pevitt, *The France of Marivaux*, offering historical portraits of French rulers and politics before and during Marivaux's career; and *Marivaux on Page and Stage*, a conversation between me and Janice Paran, my dramaturg and editor on these adaptations, touching on Marivaux's literary personality, our approach to the plays on paper and in the theater, and the issue of style. As a postscript we have included a Marivaux chronology, a listing of his plays, a pronunciation guide and further information on these adaptations.

The informational sections of the book all overlap a bit. We hope they will help readers get deeper into these plays, into Marivaux, and perhaps into other glories of the Enlightenment.

ACKNOWLEDGMENTS

Thanks first to Emily Mann of the McCarter Theatre, brilliant producer and friend who asked me to direct a play in the first place and then encouraged me to translate and adapt all three of these plays.

Thanks then to the other stars of her superb McCarter matriarchy—resident producers Loretta Greco and Mara Isaacs and most particularly Janice Paran, dramaturg nonpareil, and my passionate, tough, and beloved editor on these plays and on this book.

Thanks to Nadia Benabid, co-translator and trouble shooter on *The Triumph of Love*, and Pascale Hubert-Leibler, my French editor and conscience on the other two plays—for their luminous affection for Marivaux and respect for his language. Also, to Lionel Gossman of Princeton University, thanks for his thrillingly open mind and his warmhearted support.

And to the actors who brought these scripts to vivid life and who taught me much about dramaturgy and words. Surely the rest of you will understand if I particularly acknowledge John Michael Higgins and Mary Lou Rosato, muses and editors both, and Laurence O'Dwyer, too, because, as one of his colleagues said of him, "If there were a national theater in this country, he would be its leading actor."

Thanks to the designers of the McCarter Marivaux cycle—Tom Lynch and Marty Pakledinaz, exquisite gentlemen and teachers, and lighting designers Chris Akerlind and Peter Kazcorowski. And to the producers who have invited those productions over to their houses and made them welcome—Sharon Ott of the Seattle Rep (and formerly Berkeley Rep), Gordon Davidson of the Mark Taper Forum, and Peter Altman of the Huntington Theatre. Here's to the American regional theater, which really *is* our national theater, for all its vision and courage and unsung excellence.

Thanks to Peter Zeisler and Lindy Zesch, formerly of Theatre Communications Group (TCG), who saw the 1992 production of *The Triumph of Love*, invited me to the TCG conference to talk to the nonprofit theater community about Marivaux and then published the script in *American Theatre* magazine. And to Alvin Klein of *The New York Times*, whose unwavering faith in our work added precious fuel to our fire.

Thank you Charlie Erickson for looking through your camera with such art and perspicacity, and Christine Pevitt for your knowledge and patience.

Thanks to Bruce Ostler and George Sheanshang, Kate Wilson, Claudia Egger, Susie Cordon and Mary Sue Gregson, all McCarter personnel, Paul Mullin, Julia Gignoux and all the helpful hands at Smith and Kraus. Everyone's patience and indulgence are appreciated, particularly Marisa Smith's, Eric Kraus', and Christine Pevitt's, but no one's more than Kurt Ollmann's.

Stephen Wadsworth

MARIVAUX IN CONTEXT
Stephen Wadsworth

A new spirit of intellectual inquiry launched the so-called Age of Enlightenment in eighteenth-century Europe. The seventeenth-century French philosopher Perre Bayle's maxim "Tout connaître pour tout critiquer" ("Know everything to assess everything") and his English contemporary John Locke's assertion that human beings are "by nature all free, equal and independent" encouraged a rational reassessment of centuries-old social, political, religious, and economic systems. Their ideas seized the imaginations of philosophers and peasants alike. In 1789 the French people began, bloodily, to dismantle an archaic monarchy, and the stage was set for modern democracy in Europe.

In the meantime everything was roundly questioned and challenged, from God to gaiters, and the theater was an active arena. During the Enlightenment two great French playwrights—Marivaux and Beaumarchais—stepped forward to make sense of living in a shifting world. Beaumarchais (1732–1799) caught the contentious spirit of the prerevolutionary times in his cutting-edge comedy about equality of the classes and sexes, *The Marriage of Figaro* (better known today as Mozart's opera). Pierre Carlet de Marivaux (1688–1763), writing between 1720 and 1746, relatively untraumatic years for France, had no such dire rumblings to report upon, but he distilled the spirit of his time no less urgently than would Beaumarchais. Marivaux's comedies are really about the agony of change—the aspirations, the uncertainty, the yearning, the fear, the not knowing. In his characters—struggling to understand what is happening to them and to accept the sobering consequences of change at great cost to themselves—we can see the image of Enlightenment Europe.

Marivaux also addressed specific issues of his day, trenchantly and with keen political insight. *Changes of Heart* appeared (as *The Double Inconstancy*) in 1723, at the end of the Regency, a seven-year period during which France was governed by the morally controversial Duc d'Orleans, while the young king-to-be (Louis XV) looked on and learned. Through the character of the Prince, who blithely abducts a woman he desires, intending to break down her resistance with luxury and lovemaking, Marivaux seems to have confronted his audience with a rather provocative, even bleak prediction for their new king, although the playwright ultimately hints that his Prince might learn healing lessons through the experience of love. Marivaux's audiences must have been shaken as well by the idea that a monarch might happily make a commoner his queen, even learn moral responsibility from a pair of peasants. The decadence of French rule and the frivolity of the court, blurring right and wrong at the heart of the nation, seem to have concerned Marivaux. In the very unsentimental education of Harlequin, Silvia, and the Prince, Marivaux foresees the end of an age of innocence—or denial, depending on how you look at it—and a reordering of classes and priorities.

The Game of Love and Chance takes a fairly remorseless look at the way the French were thinking about their social order in 1730, and as usual Marivaux examines class attitudes through both ends of the telescope, in a scenario that is characteristically bold, even racy. By dressing his masters as servants for a day, he exposes all the unthinking snobbery and prejudice of the upper class to public view, and he forces at least one of them to see the folly of his lifelong ways and to leave them behind. By dressing their servants as masters, on the other hand, Marivaux unleashes the rich, conflicted inner life of a much-oppressed people: their barely dreamt-of hopes and a dawning awareness of their own true worth are pitted against old reflexes of fear and shame and a deep, sad sense of inevitable defeat.

In *The Triumph of Love* Marivaux looks as analytically at the rationalist philosophers as they were looking at the world. He was very much caught up in the rationalist worldview himself. He studied human behavior like a scientist and looked with a cold, clear eye at social and political facts of life. But he must have spent time with men who took rationalism to extremes. He parodies them in the too-rigorous, self-denying Hermocrate, whose painful and hilarious emergence as a lover and whose political comeuppance are clear lessons that reason must flow from the heart as much as from the inquiring mind. And intrigues at court are never far offstage in *The Triumph of Love*. The hidden plot of the play is a drama of succession, and the characters speak frequently of a cabal against the current regime: These topics, very hot at the beginning of the century, were still sensitive in 1732. In a provocative reversal of roles, Marivaux casts the exemplar of reason in the role of wrongheaded intriguer and a woman in the role of clearheaded mastermind.

All three plays explore the ramifications of their political situations with a candor and almost cold rationality that were new and probably troubling in the 1720s and 1730s, but irresistible in comedies at least as amusing as they were cynical. All three plays, particularly *The Triumph of Love,* illustrate in a very pure way a classic Enlightenment preoccupation: We must balance passion and rationality, emotion and reason, in order to rule responsibly, in order to grow.

All three plays pit love against reason: Léonide in *Triumph* and Sylvia in *Game of Love* put men to this test, determined that love should prevail, and all the protagonists in *Changes of Heart* find, to their horror as well as to their delight, that the rules of reason do not neccesarily apply in the game of love.

Marivaux wrote most successfully for the Comédie Italienne, a *commedia dell'arte* troupe whose performers recreated stock comic characters in a time-honored tradition of popular improvised comedy. For two hundred years, *commedia* players had amused Paris and influenced its playwrights, notably Molière (1622–1673). Marivaux also wrote for the Comédie Française, where a less natural style of playing prevailed and which at the time favored tragedy over comedy. Here Marivaux would have seen the dramas of Corneille and Racine, two giants of the previous century. Racine's plays—great five-act dramas of inner action, of dilemma and decision—obviously affected Marivaux deeply, but so did the Italians, whose robust style and subversive nature must have relieved him as much as they inspired him: Here was an arena for a newly free, emotionally direct kind of theater not possible "uptown" at the Comédie Française.

Marivaux honored his theatrical forbears in his peculiar and delicious blend of comedy and drama. The characters in these plays are the recognizable grandchildren of Racine's noble, eloquent, long-suffering protagonists, but they're also clearly descended from the mischievous, volatile, lusty *commedia* family. And they share the stage with Harlequin himself—the presumptuous, mercurial, irresistibly histrionic witty idiot, who in Marivaux's time still wore motley and mask in the Italian fashion. The onstage juxtaposition of this unabashed buffoon and men and women in complex, serious predicaments provokes wonderment and delight: Harlequin breathes enlightening humor into them, and they remind him that he is much more than a clown.

Though most of Marivaux's thirty-plus comedies reach boldly across boundaries of class and sex, they are principally about what happens to people who are falling in love. Which might seem frivolous, until you hear the heartbeats of his characters and realize they are going through hell. Love, Marivaux seems to say, gets you in touch with everything—not just the good things, but also the nervousness, the dread, the anxiety, the jealousy, the guilt, the sadness. Love is costly, dangerous, and essential. It is one road to self-knowledge, and to freedom, and it is usually a hard road.

THE FRANCE OF MARIVAUX
Christine Pevitt

THE YOUNG PLAYWRIGHT

Pierre Carlet de Chamblain de Marivaux was born in 1688, the same year as Alexander Pope and three years after Handel and Bach. Racine died when Marivaux was eleven; Benjamin Franklin was born when he was eighteen. Louis XIV, who had ruled France for 72 years, died in Marivaux's twenty-seventh year. When Marivaux died in 1763, Mozart was seven, Voltaire's *Treatise on Tolerance* was published, Frederick the Great established village schools in Prussia, and the first Chambers of Commerce were opened in New York and New Jersey. Seven years later Wordsworth and Beethoven were born. The world had changed shape dramatically, and Europe, its eyes fully open to the impending facts of liberty and equality, awaited the revolution in France, increasingly anxious, increasingly excited.

The society in which Marivaux grew up and developed as an artist informed his plays. In them we see many elements of Parisian life in the early eighteenth century gathered and scrutinized with the rational, analytical delight of a scientist discovering new connections in the natural world and articulating them for the first time. The cynicism and ennui of Louis XIV's last years; the cabals that conspired against Philippe, Duc d'Orleans (who ruled France as Regent for seven years after Louis XIV's death); the atmosphere of intrigue that pervaded Paris during the Regency, and the disingenuousness and manipulativeness of the Regent himself; the breaking down of social barriers precipitated by the collapse of the French banks, and the dissemination of knowledge across the classes; the frank enjoyment and exploitation of sex. The spirit of these times is distilled in the worlds of Marivaux's extraordinary plays.

Marivaux began his career as a playwright in Paris during the last years of the reign of Louis XIV. He came into society in 1710 at the age of twenty-two, having been brought up in a prosperous middle-class family and destined for the study of law. He found Paris bustling with vitality, a city very welcoming to young men of literary aspirations. But, beyond the city, France was a country in dire straits, and the once glorious Sun King was in clear decline.

THE OLD KING

To the majority of Frenchmen in 1700 Louis XIV was the only king they had ever known, and to many he seemed immortal. He had ascended the throne in 1643, at the age of five. He eventually established his court at Versailles, to the southwest of Paris, where he had built a splendid palace with huge and delightful gardens. There he expected the nobility of France to dance attendance upon him in, as Nancy Mitford put it, "a sort of perpetual house-party." The greatest names in the land—the Ducs de Bouillon, de La Rochefoucauld, de Noailles—gave up their great estates and marvelous chateaux to spend their time waiting on the king and quarreling over such issues as who might wear a hat in the royal presence, who might sit on an armchair, or only on a stool, or not at all, and who might have the honor of holding the candlestick at the King's ceremonial Rising and Going to Bed. Louis was a human icon, semidivine, the symbol of the glory of France.

And for many years France was victorious in war and dominant in peace in Europe. Her armies had strengthened and extended her frontiers and cowed her neighbors. Her writers, artists, and musicians—among them Molière, Corneille, Racine, Lully, and Charles Le Brun—celebrated the most cultivated, advanced, and civilized court society in the world. Louis XIV seemed to have created a formidably cohesive and successful France.

But he overreached. In 1689 he entered the War of the League of Augsburg, fighting almost alone against the whole of Europe. Year after year the French armies fought and died in Flanders and on the Rhine, grimly holding on to their frontiers and preventing the English, Austrian, and German forces from breaking through. The country was bled white in order to support the war; in the unjust way of the Ancien Régime, the burden fell mainly on the poorest, who were taxed and levied and worked to exhaustion. Outside Versailles, the mood of the country was sullen. Even in Paris, which benefited from subsidized supplies of grain, and whose middle classes were protected from the worst miseries, opinion hardened against the king.

And in 1709, when the French forces were being battered and defeated, came the worst winter for a hundred years. In the early months of that year a devastating frost destroyed the crops, the rivers froze, even the sea froze. In the provinces thousands died; at court the nobility shivered under sable rugs, and ink froze in inkpots. In Paris the mood was satirical. The theaters were packed and the most popular play, *Turcaret*, by Alain-René Lesage, savagely denounced crooked financiers and opportunists. The king, formerly so revered, was subjected to scornful ridicule. His mistress, very probably his secret wife, certainly his favorite companion, the Marquise de Maintenon, was pilloried as a prude, a bigot, a baneful influence on the nation. The Italian comedians, popular in Paris for many years and a formative influence on Molière, had been banned and banished by the king in 1697 for parodying her in a play entitled *The False Prude*. Rude songs and pamphlets were everywhere. The people were sick of the war, sick of the régime. They wanted a change.

Louis XIV, Madame de Maintenon, and their Jesuit confessor, Père Le Tellier, were regarded as a ruling triad too worn out and repressive to help bring peace and prosperity back to the nation. Even when the Peace of Utrecht was finally signed in 1713, the country remained paralyzed. Louis XIV was unable to launch new initiatives. His thoughts turned to his approaching death and to putting an end to the quarrels in the French Catholic Church. His other main concern, and the obsessive preoccupation of every candlestick-holding hopeful at court, was the succession to his throne.

In 1712 the direct heir to the throne (the Duc de Bourgogne) and his wife and son all died within a few days of each other, probably of scarlet fever, but these being times of elaborate cabals and vast medical ignorance, there were many people who thought that they might have been poisoned. The only surviving member of the Royal family was Louis' three-year-old great-grandson. After him in line of succession was Louis XIV's nephew, Philippe, Duc d'Orléans. A skeptic, freethinker and libertine known for his mistresses, his riotous parties at the Palais-Royal, and his propensity for shocking the nobility, Philippe was widely thought to be the kind of character who could conceivably have arranged the untimely deaths of his relatives. Louis XIV and Madame de Maintenon found him profoundly troubling.

Alarmed by the prospect of the impious Philippe becoming Regent for the boy king, and even more disturbing, succeeding to the throne in the event of the little boy's death, Louis XIV and Madame de Maintenon scrambled to come up with a different plan of succession. Louis set up, for after his death, a Regency council comprised of men who were all hostile to Philippe. He also, to the horror of many, pronounced his sons by his late mistress, the Marquise of Montespan, able to ascend the throne in the event of the deaths of all other members of the royal family. In the final days of his life he worked feverishly to try and control the future. In Paris his subjects counted the minutes to his demise and welcomed any change as an improvement.

Finally, on September 1, 1715, the Sun King died at the age of seventy-seven. Voltaire saw crowds in the streets cheering and laughing. The five-year-old king was installed at the Tuileries. The new Regent, Philippe, Duc d'Orléans, brought the court to Paris and announced that they would remain there, not at Versailles. The whole apparatus of the court arrived in the capital. For the first time in almost a hundred years, French society was united in Paris. It was the beginning of an extraordinary eight-year period of French history.

THE REGENT

Politically the Regent walked a precarious road. He succeeded in having the Parliament of Paris set aside Louis XIV's will and entrust all power to him, but he had many enemies with whom to contend. With the French crown on the head of a frail little boy, the question of the succession still loomed large. If little Louis XV died, the Regent would certainly claim the throne, but his claim was muddied by the existence of another powerful claimant.

In 1701 Louis XIV's grandson, the Duc d'Anjou, had been installed on the throne of Spain as King Philip V, and he considered his claim to the French throne superior to that of the Duc d'Orléans, as indeed it was in terms of strict primogeniture. Even though Philip V had renounced his claims to France, he continued to plot behind the scenes. He recruited many highly placed French supporters and launched a conspiracy to bring down the Duc d'Orléans. The conspiracy was unmasked and the Regent survived. But throughout the Regency, intrigue swirled and plots abounded. It was, quite literally, a very cloak-and-dagger time. Meanwhile, the Regent made every effort, unlike his predecessor, to keep France at peace, and largely succeeded.

The Regency was a glamorous slice of French history, marked by excess and license, tolerance and peace. The aristocracy demeaned themselves in a frenzy of gambling, gluttony, and sex. But along with such grossness, there was also lasting beauty, and artistic achievement. The Parisian neighborhood known as the Faubourg Saint-Germain was embellished with new townhouses, many of which still stand, all designed in the elegant and restrained style that dominated French architecture throughout the century. In a gesture characteristic of the new régime, one of Philippe's first acts as Regent was to invite back to Paris the Italian comedians, the Comédie-Italienne, banished by Louis in 1697. In 1716 they returned to their old theater, and within a few seasons the young Marivaux began his long relationship with them.

Meanwhile, a young artist called Antoine Watteau startled the solemn Académie Française by submitting as his *morceau de réception* the hauntingly beautiful and deeply ambiguous picture *The Embarkation for Cythera*, the first recorded *fête galante* (a genre of paintings depicting melancholy park dalliances). Watteau and Marivaux both fused the refined French court sensibility with the robust, common-man Italian theatrical spirit—Watteau in his dreamy, touching pictures of aristocrats and actors mixing suggestively, Marivaux in genre-bending plays that likewise bring comedians and tragedians into intimate contact.

Making money was another of the entertainments of the age. Philippe's regency is probably best remembered for the adventure of John Law and his "Mississippi Bubble." Law, a Scotsman, brought to France the novel ideas of paper money, a national bank, and investing in far-flung colonies in the Americas. For two years Paris was consumed by a passion to buy shares in Law's "Compagnie des Indes" and then to sell them for huge profits. An ad hoc open-air Stock Exchange was set up in the rue Quincampoix. It seemed to many gullible investors that money was gushing forth from some mysterious stream. In 1721 the stream dried up—the dream of high yield in the new world evaporated, and many in the middle class were ruined.

After the bursting of the Mississippi bubble, the Regent allowed himself to give in to his worst instincts. He had always been self-indulgent, a womanizer and a drinker, and in the depth of his disappointment over the failure of his treasured scheme to make France rich, he caused shock and displeasure with his flaunting of his mistresses. There were even rumors—almost certainly unfounded, but evidence of his dubious reputation—that he slept with his eldest daughter, the outrageously unconventional Duchesse de Berry.

An intelligent man, the Regent ultimately found work more appealing than the wearying pursuit of pleasure. But he had undermined his health in years of dissipation, and his appetite for sober industry came too late. Rather reluctantly, but persuaded that Versailles was the right place for the king to live, he moved the court of Louis XV back to the daunting, drafty, exhausting palace. Once there, to cheer himself up, he had a production of Marivaux's *The Double Inconstancy* (translated here as *Changes of Heart)* performed at court at the end of 1723. Shortly thereafter he dropped dead, at the age of forty-nine. It is pleasing to think that one of the last pleasures of this flawed but amiable prince was to enjoy the subtlety and wit of the new star of his cherished Italian Comedians.

℞

LOUIS XV

Marivaux continued to provide hits for the Italian players through the 1730s. But gradually tastes were changing. With the court at Versailles, the Parisian theater could not rely on a royal or aristocratic audience as much as it had during the Regency. Louis XV rarely came to Paris and showed little interest in the theater (or in any of the arts except architecture). He had grown up to become a rather morose individual, timid and withdrawn, with an unpleasant taste for belittling others. He spent the 1730s in a serial affair with three sisters, Mesdames de Mailly, de Vintimille, and de Châteauroux, while his long-suffering wife, the Polish princess Marie Leszczynska, gave birth to a series of disappointing daughters, and one disappointing son.

In 1745 the king met Jeanne-Antoinette Poisson and was captivated by this Parisian bourgeois, a young woman of delicate beauty and extraordinary force of character. He created her Marquise de Pompadour, and she played an influential role in French politics until her death in 1764. Mainly because of her middle-class origins, she was very unpopular and helped make the king so. She was right to say (if she did), "After us, the deluge." Louis XV failed to make the radical changes that were necessary to France's survival as a monarchy, particularly in the taxation system, and his grandson, Louis XVI, was unable to make them either. In 1789 the Ancien Régime, which had staggered on for so long, finally collapsed in the French Revolution.

☙

MARIVAUX AND THE ITALIANS

The turbulent early years of the century had certainly produced a need for diversion and distraction, for pleasure and fun, but they were increasingly concerned with the burgeoning ideas of the Enlightenment—personal freedoms and the suggestion of social, political, and economic parity among all citizens. Entertainment and serious conversation flourished in the hundreds of cafés in Paris, where newspapers and periodicals could be read and discussed by anyone with enough money for a coffee. Women of means hosted salons where cultivated men and women could discuss the latest books, the current concerns of the rationalist philosophers, and other trends in a fast-shifting society.

At these salons the most sought-after guests were the aged writer Bernard le Bovier de Fontenelle, who had spent his life trying to make the scientific advances of the times accessible to wider audiences, and the playwright Antoine Houdar de la Motte, both standard-bearers of the faction of the "Moderns" in the great literary debate with the "Ancients." (The "Moderns" argued that progress could and should be made in the arts, the "Ancients" that perfection had been reached and could only be emulated.) Among the ambitious young men striving for notice was the future Voltaire, son of a mere notary, bursting with ideas and energy, overflowing with verses and ambition. And of course the young Marivaux.

Parodoxically, Marivaux's career had taken off in the aftermath of John Law's failed financial scheme, of which he was a victim. His wife's substantial dowry vanished. Instead of taking her income for granted, he had to make a living. Already a published journalist, he decided to try his luck at the writing life and particularly hoped for success as a dramatist. He attempted both the prestigious genre of historical tragedy and that of lighthearted comedy. In 1720 he had three plays produced in Paris. His tragedy *Hannibal* was a failure at the Comédie Française, but his comedy *Harlequin Refined by Love* launched his career at the Comédie-Italienne. He was soon the established voice of the Italian comedians and a popular and critical success.

When they first returned to Paris in 1716, the Italian comedians faced stiff competition from the Comédie Française and the Opéra, which were by this time well-established and officially patronized theaters. At the Comédie Française Parisians could see the works of the great seventeenth-century playwrights Racine, Corneille, and Molière, as well as plays by younger authors—Crébillon, de la Motte, and, in his sensational debut in 1718 with *Oedipus*, Voltaire. At the Opéra, in its theater at the Palais-Royal, they could see the established repertoire of Lully's lyric tragedies as well as a new breed of extravagant entertainment, opera-ballets tailored to the more boisterous Regency tastes.

And beyond these official theaters there were popular entertainments that came into town with the fairs. The fairs were surviving remnants of the Middle Ages, gatherings for the sale of livestock, trinkets, foodstuffs, and for the exchange of news and gossip. The fair of Saint-Germain took place from February until Easter in a large area near Saint-Germain-des-Prés, that of Saint Laurent from the end of July to the end of September near the Bastille. The Saint-Germain fair was the classier of the two, but at both acrobats, jugglers, and strolling players performed as they had from medieval times; and in ramshackle buildings troupes of players put on their own brand of theater, usually broad comedy and farce.

The Italians, who had upheld the traditions of the *commedia dell'arte*, came to realize that they had to reinvent themselves in order to survive. The fact that they performed in Italian also hurt them. They needed a new repertoire and new writers in French, and in Marivaux they found their future. In the theatrical cacophony of 1720s Paris, Marivaux and the Italians forged a completely new and distinctive kind of comedy that brought their respective traditions into an unlikely but wonderfully harmonious union.

For almost twenty years their union prospered, with Marivaux producing hit after hit, among them the three plays in this volume—*Changes of Heart* (*The Double Inconstancy*) in 1723, *The Game of Love and Chance* in 1730, and *The Triumph of Love* in 1732. By 1740 cabals were attacking his work so fiercely that he ended his association with the Italians. But Marivaux could afford to rest on his laurels; he had become a member of the literary establishment. In 1742 he was elected to the Académie Française, in preference to Voltaire, which must have caused him some satisfaction. (It certainly annoyed Voltaire.) He died in 1763, in the rue de Richelieu, just after his seventy-fifth birthday.

CHRISTINE PEVITT was born in Lancashire, England. She studied classics at Cambridge University and subsequently worked in publishing in London and New York. She is author of *Philippe, Duc d'Orléans, Regent of France* (Atlantic Monthly Press, 1997) and is writing a biography of Madame de Pompadour.

MARIVAUX ON PAGE AND STAGE
A Conversation between
Stephen Wadsworth and Janice Paran

Janice Paran, Dramaturg and Director of Play Development at the McCarter Theatre, worked closely with Stephen Wadsworth as editor of the adaptations in this volume and as dramaturg of their first productions at the McCarter.

JP: *How did you first become aware of Marivaux? Were you already familiar with his plays when the McCarter approached you in 1991 with the idea of doing one of them?*

SW: I had directed opera for about ten years, and I had gradually zeroed in on the eighteenth century—on Mozart, whose life was contained in the second half of that century, and on Handel, who, writing in its first half, was an exact contemporary of Marivaux. I first encountered references to Marivaux somewhere in my work on Handel, and I felt a clear kinship just seeing his name. The more I read about him and the closer I came to his writing, the clearer it became to me that that we were meant to spend some time together. I read him in translation and saw him in productions that were some of them very interesting and some of them not, but I often had a nagging sense that there were crucial elements missing, that his vision, and the visions of his world, were being reductively adapted to suit ours, or *selectively* represented.

His plays, which seemed to integrate so many concerns, both philosophical and aesthetic, and which are such volatile emotional landscapes, were speaking to some of the most forward-thinking theater artists in Europe, and to a lesser extent in this country—Peter Stein, Patrice Chéreau, Luc Bondy, Anne Bogart. Some of these productions tended to stress that volatile, rather perverse emotional landscape at the expense of a certain frankness of address, a warmth, an ebullient humor—all qualities in Marivaux that fairly leapt off the French page when finally I went there to look for myself.

JP: *Were those qualities entirely absent from the translations you read?*

SW: No, but I realized that in various ways those translations weren't quite capturing the Marivaux I was getting to know. They tended to fall into one of three categories: 1) too British for an American audience to be able to "hear" with immediacy (American English being in many respects its own language); 2) too strictly literal to flow at all or seem real; or 3) too coarsely conceived to be able to represent Marivaux's extraordinary elegance of language or his subtle, complex sensibility.

I was beginning really to learn more about who Marivaux *was,* instead of sitting around and rather grandly and pickily proclaiming what he wasn't! All of my work on these translations, or adaptations, has been a process of getting to know Marivaux, earning his trust somehow, and there have been profound, mysterious moments in the work on the words or with the actors on the shapes, or the designers on certain peculiar details—moments of a contact that feels *actual.* Contact with Marivaux, the Italian comedians, Harlequin in particular, with the French stage, and with peculiar details of French life in the Regency and beyond. Perhaps it is all misplaced enthusiasm, but in any case it became a sort of passion that is hard to explain.

JP: *I'm going to press you to try to explain anyway. What is the magic of Marivaux for you?*

SW: He had brilliantly lucid vision when he looked at the world around him. He caught that deep Zeitgeist-y moment. He captured the fallible, changeable, scheming, rapturous heart of any lover in any time. He struck a unique theatrical spark throwing, as it were, the Italians through a classical French proscenium. He plotted life's wicked ironies beautifully. He wrote a rich, intriguing, often gorgeous prose. For me the big draws are the complex emotional transactions, all limned with subtlety and a scientist's precision, and that wonderful sort of mashing together of hilarity and heartbreak into the same instant. I'm very drawn to material that is both funny and emotionally dire, and perhaps also to a mix of the highly cultivated and the colloquial. And I find the period itself exciting from virtually any angle.

There's a fascinating irony in eighteenth-century art. All elements of craft had achieved a thrilling finish and refinement; the forms of art were at a sort of peak, ready to give exquisite articulation to a newly ambivalent Zeitgeist. Times they were a-changing, and hugely unsettling visions of change found startlingly clear expression, startlingly beautiful expression. The pain of change in an image of melting beauty—when I look at these plays I see that irony everywhere, and my response to it is, well, visceral.

JP: *So in 1991—*

SW: In 1991 Emily Mann asked me to direct a play for the first time; I'd directed only opera before that. The first title we settled on was *The Triumph of Love*, and I had no clue that I would also be *adapting* it, but I was so particular about the various things I felt an adaptation must do that in the end Emily said, "Well *you* do it then, and do it fast, because we're running out of time!"

JP: *We had a very clear mandate for you, too. We wanted the adaptation to be easily, naturally speakable by American actors, and easily, immediately "hearable," as you say, by American audiences.*

SW: And that mandate was the focusing discipline for my work, and almost always got me out of my writer's logjams. Whenever I looked at the baleful circles you drew around some of the lines or speeches in my early drafts, I'd think, "clarity," or "ease," or "immediacy," and I'd be able to get on with it. Marivaux's writing has long been called untranslatable because its undeniable subtleties were thought to be inextricably linked to sounds made only by the French tongue, but he is just as often a very direct, frank writer, and he seemed to be asking for the same thing you asked for.

JP: *How did you go about adapting* The Triumph of Love? *You had never translated a play before.*

SW: I had made singing translations of a number of operas, including three by Handel from the same decade as *Triumph*, but I had worked only from Italian and German. We commissioned a so-called literal translation of *Triumph*, but it became immediately clear that there couldn't be any such thing as a literal translation of Marivaux.

JP: *Why is that?*

SW: So much of the meaning of the speeches, of what the characters really mean, is implied or suggested, and not said in words. There are not a lot of complicated words in these plays, but the situational complications give the words layers. It's rarely about what this character actually says to that character, it's usually about how the characters are leading one another deeper into the trick of the play. I mean, in all three of these plays characters pretend to be people they are not. They do a lot of talking, but they don't always say what they mean. Although they do usually mean what they say! Marivaux is a master of double-entendre, of double speak.

JP: *Yes, that elusive* marivaudage. *In one of our first conversations we tried to come to terms with that word. As I understand it,* marivaudage *is a term the French* *coined in response to Marivaux's particular use of language, the way "Pinter-esque" has taken on a connotative life of its own in the English-language theater. Marivaux had an extraordinary ability to characterize incredibly nuanced layers of emotion through minuscule pulses of discovery, thought, and perception—moment by moment.*

SW: You've said it beautifully. I'm not sure that the term wasn't originally coined to denigrate Marivaux, of whom Voltaire dismissively said that he spent all his time weighing fly's eggs in cobweb scales, or some such image. Meaning that Marivaux's concentration on love, and on subtle changes of heart, was insubstantial. To me *marivaudage* means first the way the words move, that *flow* of language that is peculiar to this writer, and its mercurial elegance. I remember an elderly actor who read for me in San Francisco recalling a Marivaux play he'd seen when the Comédie Française visited New York in the 1950s. He said, "The words flowed back and forth between them like water."

To me *marivaudage* also means the games people play with each other using that language. Marivaux's characters *need* the language to be mercurial, because almost always they know something their scene partners don't, or they are trying covertly to discover what their scene partners know and they don't. And they are invariably prevaricating. Often, ironically, they prevaricate in order to discover the truth.

JP: *How, then, does Marivaux's unique style manifest itself, if not through vocabulary, through the actual words?*

SW: He does his implying and suggesting with the *flow* of words, as I've said; sometimes with their beauty (there are some passages of real lyric beauty), and always with his manipulation of grammar, or his transcendence of grammar, you might say. He was partial to a sort of grammatically open, stream-of-consciousness run-on sentence, with erratic use of commas, dashes, dot-dot-dots, and semicolons galore. There are speeches that take off in this direction that are masterpieces of suggestive intention.

JP: *So where does translation begin to be adaptation?*

SW: One example. In I,3 of *Changes of Heart* Flaminia spins for her sister Lisette a rapturous description of Lisette's arsenal of coquettish mannerisms, all in the interest of criticizing it. When I felt I had gotten it to flow and sound, and *suggest*, like Marivaux's original, I realized that I had changed the order of the sentences in the speech, reshaped its grammar, and, if I recall rightly, slightly expanded on a couple of Flaminia's images.

In working on *Triumph* I had done very little of this sort of thing, I'd generally stuck much closer to the original. Yet I felt that this Flaminia speech was in a way the most accurate translation—of words, of grammar, of intention, of Marivaux's literary style—that I had yet done. The most important thing was to make these superb Marivaux complexities *clear*, and, in as many ways as possible, to make the adaptations read and sound like his writing.

I took another, even more invasive step in that play, adaptation-wise, by writing Lisette deeper into the plot. I actually developed her function in the play—II,10 of *Changes of Heart* is as much my writing as Marivaux's, with help from the actresses who played the scene in three productions[1]. Not standard scholarly practice, I confess, but in the original Lisette fades away somewhat inexplicably, and her function in this scene in particular was so ambiguous that none of the scholars I turned to could explain it. I knew the play would work better if her own purpose in this scene was clearer. So adaptation doesn't mean just words.

JP: *For one thing, it seems to have meant transporting ideas of that mind in that time into the minds and hearts of people in a different time.*

SW: Yes, and ideas that were intuited, or *had*, in a certain time for the manifold *reasons* of that time. There are certain basic structures of life in Marivaux's world, for instance, on which the plays are partially or wholly based but with which we have either no familiarity or a radically different way of thinking.

JP: *Such as?*

SW: Such as class, which became the defining issue of the eighteenth century and its ultimate bone of contention. The basic situation and theme of *The Game of Love and Chance* is class—the supposed differences between the moneyed class and the servant class, and the supposed unmixability of the two. Now, doing this play for a late twentieth-century audience that mostly fancies itself very particularly a *classless* society, how are we going to get that audience to understand and buy into a premise that is so *other* and that they might even find tiresome? The moneyed boy, Dorante, agonizes for an entire play over whether he can bring himself to marry someone from a different class. Certainly, there are many classic plays that trade on long-dead or distant social orders or customs, but I felt that for this play really to work, and still remain a fleet-footed, joyous comedy, I needed to help the audience understand certain things, to make clearly manifest for the audience things *im*plicit in the original. I took the appalling liberty of adding a scene to the play, the last section of Act I.

---

[1] *Kathryne Brown, Maria Canals, Francesca Faridany, Miriam Laube, Natacha Roi, Sheryl Taub

I imagined an encounter Marivaux did not write—the servant-as-master meeting the maid-as-mistress, in which the two converse self-consciously about class because each thinks the other is his/her social better. We hear from Marivaux about this encounter after the fact, and I thought that it would help us at this point in the evening if we watched these two people jump through this high-anxiety, high-risk hoop: We could learn firsthand about their hopes and dreams, and also about their low expectations of happiness and *choice* in a class-dominated world. I also felt we would enjoy seeing what actually happened when they met. Later, I also added a second scene Marivaux did not write—the maid-as-mistress meeting the real master dressed up as his servant (II,2).

So that's rather fanciful adapting, to say the least. But I don't think I do violence to this text in adding these scenes. They slot in, I didn't have to change anything significant in the text as it stands, and their premise is the premise of every scene in the play—ironic debate of class differences. I wrote them so that the heart of the play would be further elucidated, more real and more fully imposing for an audience in another place and time. Of course, my fantasy is that both of these scenes will be found, in the original French, in a cupboard somewhere in the Palais-Royal.

JP: *Audiences and critics have, for the most part, responded very warmly to your work with Marivaux. Given how free you've been in some of your adapting choices, has the response of the academic establishment been equally warm?*

SW: Not always, no. Some French purists have gotten very edgy, at least the ones who are more interested in the Marivaux tradition than they are in Marivaux. The French had no use for Marivaux for a very long time after his lifetime, but now France celebrates Marivaux as *necessarily* and quintessentially French, so the idea that he had linguistic and theatrical intercourse with a bunch of Italians of whom all but one are known to have spoken French with a very strong foreign accent—this idea is not at all appealing to many French scholars and theater artists! And for some reason the idea that Harlequin wore his black mask can be very upsetting to them.

Critics have certainly reprimanded me from time to time. I think there's a lot of room for criticism of my work on these plays, but I've worked hard to capture the essential qualities of Marivaux in spirit and word, even if the word is sometimes different in English from what it is in French. I remember that, having translated *Changes of Heart* before the movie *Clueless* came out, I'd used the word "whatever" several times in very much the way the kids in that film used it, to suggest, and even to retreat from, unsayably complex things. When we did the play in L.A. some of the critics produced a nice juicy paragraph on how tasteless and trendy I was to imitate Alicia Silverstone in a classic play. Oops. This was not a confusion that interested me, so I rewrote.

JP: *Your "fanciful adapting" notwithstanding, it seems to me one of the things that distinguishes your work on these texts is that your point of departure is Marivaux's world, not ours. What are some other ways these three plays reveal Marivaux's world? Would you talk in terms of both style and subject matter?*

SW: Style first. All of them were written for the Italian comedians, who were performing in French, and the diction of the plays is attributable, in my view, as much to the influence of the Italians as to the examples of Marivaux's French role models, notably Racine. That frankness of address, that warmth and humor I spoke about before, was the Italians', and it collides in all three plays with that very Gallic refinement of language and emotional restraint that came from the French tradition. The Italian theatrical tradition was still an oral, improvisatory tradition, while the French theater was already a *literary* tradition. The scenes in *The Triumph of Love* in which Harlequin aggressively needles the infinitely proper, grand-manner spinster Léontine are almost surreal. Just the fact that Monsieur Patchwork Clown is on the same *stage* as Madame Long-Suffering Tragedienne is radical, but then he is also ruthlessly perceiving and broadcasting her private moral dilemma and causing her to see her own desires! This I believe is the deepest use of this collision of traditions and temperaments. This image of the *commedia dell'arte* players mingling with the French nobility completely seized the imagination of Paris in the 1720s and 1730s; Watteau's paintings and Marivaux's plays envisioned and reenvisioned it.

JP: *What was the fascination?*

SW: I think it was that in the image of Harlequin in an intimate stolen moment with a finely dressed woman of the court there was the implication of the classes sexually and therefore irrevocably mixing. Here was an expression of the headiest change in the air, a distilled image of the deepest concern of the Enlightenment.

So this is a huge revelation of Marivaux's world. In *Triumph*, the first of the plays we did, Harlequin impinges on the the private worlds of the high-class French protagonists. Then we moved into *Changes of Heart*, in which Marivaux actually takes Harlequin all the way to the royal palace, and in which the "French" prince reaches out lustfully, then passionately, and finally politically, as it were, to the "Italian" comedienne playing the farm girl (Silvia was the name of both actress and character). In *Game of Love* the "French" and "Italian" roles, the wealthy romantic leads and the unruly comics, utterly confuse the scheme by dressing up as one another and, in a very real sense, *becoming* one another for a while—long enough for a few hundred years of class notions to explode around them. Harlequin reverted to his traditional motley at the end of our production, but Lisette still wore her mistress' dress, so there was that Watteau image suddenly—the suggestive cross-class dalliance under a tree.

All the plays are deeply predicated on Marivaux's keen sense of imminent change in the social and political structure of his world.

JP: *Style and subject matter don't seem to be separable.*

SW: No! It's hard for me to separate them. But of course there are lots of examples of how Marivaux's subject matter reveals the Enlightenment world, indeed cuts right into its core.

The Triumph of Love parodies the rationalist philosophers, whose explorations brought the Enlightenment to the surface of eighteenth-century life, and whose company Marivaux was delighted to keep. As they taught the world to think rationally about subjects church and state had always dealt with irrationally, Marivaux in this play goes about teaching *them* that there's a limit on their rationalist passion. Hermocrate assumes that he can reject emotion and particularly love as an irrational and destructive notion, but Léonide (as vivid and proactive a woman as exists in eighteenth-century literature) shows him that he must accept emotion to live and that he must moreover *balance* emotion and rationality to be truly wise. This is a key equation in early Enlightenment art—learning to temper passion with reason—and Marivaux is turning it around delightfully. In 1732 France herself was like a young person in rebellion who saw a chance to break free from a repressive, limiting tradition. She pushed many new envelopes, some too didactically, some too passionately. In *Triumph* Marivaux may have been warning her to balance even as he encouraged her explorations.

JP: *How did the* commedia *influence otherwise come into play?*

SW: Well, clearly I believe that, in the style of playing, it was an equal partner with the classical seventeenth-century French tradition in the style of playing. Marivaux was writing for all-Italian casts of actors who only recently had started to perform scripted material—and in a foreign tongue! The newness of the language probably kept them quite close to the script, but as I worked on the plays I felt and even heard the comic actors wanting to digress when the scene presented them with an opportunity for a *lazzi* (a sort of vaudeville turn in character). Tomasso Vicentini, called Thomassin, the original Harlequin, was quite noisy sometimes when I was writing *Changes of Heart*, and I had to make a decision about how to deal with him. I mean, it didn't seem right to lock him out of my study, considering what I was working on, plus Marivaux himself seemed interested in giving him the floor.

Thomassin *was* Harlequin; he played only that role, ever, as far as is known, banging irreverently into a host of plots and plays with the same relentlessly paradoxical profile, and always dressed in the same motley and mask. After Thomassin died Marivaux never wrote another Harlequin play. Harlequin relied on Thomassin for life and when Thomassin spoke, Harlequin spoke. I decided to listen. Some of the verbal *lazzi*, including sections of *Changes of Heart* I,4, for example, were dictated to me, as it were.

John Michael Higgins, the first Harlequin of our revivals, instinctively understood the qualities of this Gallicized Italian clown—the effortless physical grace, the joyfully anarchic sensibility, the verbal acrobatics, the dangerously vulnerable heart. I remember when he first put on the mask. Something inexplicable happened. The mask had lots of information in it, as masks are supposed to have. That was a defining moment in my artistic life—it was for both of us, I think.

And so was the moment when Michael's Harlequin squared off with Mary Lou Rosato as Léontine in *The Triumph of Love* [*Plate 36*]. Mary Lou understood the qualities of the French tradition—the exquisite restraint barely masking a grand passion, the sovereign control of language, the spinning out of words, the impassioned declamation, the flawlessly erect posture [*Plate 32*]. The twain met, and we all knew we were in the ballpark. Both Mary Lou and Michael are also very grounded actors, in the American sense of being grounded in emotional honesty and directness. Their performances bridged those two centuries and were cornerstones in our rediscovery of this style, to use Michel St. Denis' phrase.

JP: *Style is a word that crops up frequently in your conversation. How would you define it, and why is it important?*

SW: Perhaps style is how form and content merge. How the *way* of doing a thing, or of saying a thing, is the same as the thing itself. Style is often thought to be something different from emotional truth, but the fact is that style *is* content, there is no difference between the two things. A physical gesture, for example, *is* an emotion, must be, and the actor must be able to understand how it might even be the very truest, most vivid way of accessing the emotion in question. If it is a gesture only, you've got it wrong, or you're not there yet. If you can understand how someone can do this [*Wadsworth casts his hand up into the air, fingers articulated, wrist bent back*] and be asking something of heaven, then maybe you are ready to use the gesture and play the material. If you can understand how the so-called "externals" are totally not external, and how to work from the outside in, as well as from the inside out, then maybe you are ready to deal with style. And you'd better be, because style is not something peculiar to weird old French plays, *everything* has a style.

You might also say that style is the way in which a particular artist theatricalizes reality. Theater is not reality, it is reality theatricalized, styled, encoded in ways of behaving and speaking and moving. Often we think that because contemporary writers are writing scenes from our lives, and because we know so much about how those scenes play out in life, that their work doesn't have as specific a style as the plays of dead writers or writers from times and cultures less familiar to us. But just wait another twenty or thirty years! Think of Noël Coward, Tennessee Williams, and Samuel Beckett, to name three wildly different worlds of style. Or coming forward in time: Joe Orton, Sam Shepard, Suzan Lori Parks, Beth Henley. All of these are artists who have created recognizable and widely varying styles from various positions, who have *invented* a style that is as much the message as the message itself.

More broadly, of course, you could define style as the language in which you choose to speak the truths of the play—a language not just of words but of physical life and rhythm and visuals and so on. And so, in this sense, style doesn't have to mean a style the playwright dreamt in, imagined, or ever saw. It can be your language and still be very revealing of qualities in the play. Though sometimes at a steep cost to the play. An aesthetic comes into existence to be able to articulate a certain world, an adopted aesthetic will speak the play very differently and inevitably result in tensions that can blur essences in the material. It can be interesting to hear a smart artist sort of dialogue with a work of art, but if it's a great classic play, say, that your audience hasn't seen in a long time or ever, they can end up seeing a *treatment* of the play, even if it is a loving one, and when will they next have a chance to see that play? It seems to me you have to be very clear with the audience about how and why you are departing from the play, it's part of being a responsible curator of art.

JP: *Good or bad, style is something often seen as extrinsic to the emotional truth of a play, at least in the American theater.*

SW: The glory of the American acting tradition is working from the inside out—finding the emotional truth for the character and the moment. The theory is: Find a physical shape that suits that inner truth, and this becomes the shape of your scene. The Method was the most hard-core, aggressive manifestation of that trend in this century. We gradually offloaded all the "externals"—we got rid of all the *scenery* even, and sat around on boxes and waited, sincerely, for those shapes to come, and if they didn't, we just talked to each other. And eventually, when we did *King Lear*, or *The Seagull*, or even *Streetcar Named*

Desire, something was missing. Lots was missing, especially if the acting wasn't absolutely galvanic. Style had been sidelined, and we were left with some pretty mundane evenings, all earnest searching and not much physical or visual grace, not much musicality, little evidence of the plastic arts, the all-important "externals." In being stripped of their externals, the plays had been stripped of so much of their *internals*—essential elements of character, intention, and deepest purpose that actors *cannot make up*. Most often *some* of these things, these physical manifestations of truth, get found, you know, by *some* of the cast, in *some* of the scenes. But responsible curating of art does not mean getting a few things right and asking the audience to indulge you while we all sit there waiting for the next useful image to arrive.

I'd love to see more classical work that uses the style of the play to speak its truths and that brings the period in question alive as something *actual*, and tangible. "Actual" meaning: That is the way it was, and it has immediacy, it is real, as real as or even realer than—for at least a thrilling couple of hours—our reality. Period, and by extension style, are often considered to be things standing *between* audience and play, but I think they are aspects of a metaphor we all crave—the metaphor that dresses up the most serious messages in clothes other than ours and then socks them to us. With if anything *more* power for their otherness.

JP: *You're talking like a director now. It's not wrong to assume that your work as a translator/adapter is strongly informed by the director in you, is it?*

SW: Heavens no. What I've learned over the years as a director—about dramaturgy, character, language, all of it—has made it possible for me to write for the theater. I could never have thought of approaching these plays as a writer had I not come armed with that knowledge, or perhaps I should say that gradual cultivation and disciplining of *instinct*. I also first came to the eighteenth century as a director. Actually, I came first as a child, looking at and hearing its beautiful sights and sounds, and it was only after years of enjoyment of it and later work on it that I even asked why I was drawn to it. I've tried increasingly, as a director, to realize "classic" art works on their creators' terms—the cultural, historical, aesthetic contexts that gave them birth. We are curators when we touch this art, and we must be responsible, however we choose to work on it. We must know where it's coming from and why it came.

There has been a trend, in the last twenty years or so, of resetting classic plays and operas in places and times their creators did not set them in or even know about. I've certainly done it. Not surprising, I suppose, that as the first generation of TV children came of age and went to work in the theater, in the 1970s, visuals started to take the wheel and drive theater in a new, less linear direction. Before long we learned to look at storytelling in some new and often highly fanciful ways, and some of them were important and arresting and gave new life to the idea of theater and to the plays in question. I have had deep use, as an audience member, for many of the images I've inhaled from productions in postmodern styles, and I buy the deep need of some artists to create them and to explode or examine notions of storytelling. But I have different artistic needs, and when I look back in time my vision tends to adapt to its surroundings.

I just want people to know that you can construct an elegant, visually "traditional" production in period dress and still do *really* aggressive, radical, invasive work. Radical classics doesn't mean only visually extreme; it can be emotionally extreme, morally extreme, intellectually hot, verbally and rhythmically *wild*. I want to encourage others to turn to the *plays* for aesthetic direction instead of to prevailing fashions, to see as clearly and truly as possible the incredibly exciting and sometimes dangerously real worlds from which they cry out to us. Aesthetically and politically, it is pretty hard to find hotter material. The realities of early-Enlightenment France are so fabulously interesting, and the aesthetic of Marivaux's theater so exquisite, that I see no reason, for my own part, to depart from them.

Although of course I do, inevitably, and in some respects perhaps radically, because in fact I am at best channeling it, and no matter how much I learn or imagine about the period, my vision is blurred by the intervening centuries. So what I have to do is re-envisage, re-imagine, rediscover a style for playing these plays—as adapter, too, not just as director—which honors both where they came from and where they are headed, i.e., into the hearts and minds of an over-complicated, media-drunk, hungry-for-meaning fin de siècle culture.

Changes of Heart
(The Double Inconstancy)

1723

℗

For Kurt
in memory of Lukie and his canine harlequinade

ORIGINAL PRODUCTION

La Double Inconstance was played for the first time by the Comédie Italienne in Paris on April 6, 1723. Zanotta Benozzi, called Silvia, moved up in the ranks to take the leading role. The troupe's leader, Luigi Riccoboni (aged 49), who never lost his strong accent, took the role of the Prince, and his wife, Elena Balletti Riccoboni, was Flaminia. Elena's brother Antoine Balletti, who stammered, was the Lord. Tomasso Vicentini, Marivaux's only Harlequin, had the starring role this time, and his wife, called Violette, was Lisette. Domenico Biancolelli, called Dominique, himself the son of a great Harlequin, played his signature role, Trivelin.

This adaptation was originally commissioned and produced, as *Changes of Heart,* by the McCarter Theatre in Princeton, N.J., May 6, 1994, with the following cast and creative contributors:

TRIVELIN . . . . Laurence O'Dwyer
SILVIA. . . . . Natacha Roi
THE PRINCE. . . . . Robert Sean Leonard
FLAMINIA . . . . Mary Lou Rosato
LISETTE. . . . . Sheryl Taub
HARLEQUIN . . . . John Michael Higgins
A LORD. . . . . Nicholas Kepros

Director . . . . Stephen Wadsworth
Set Designer . . . . Thomas Lynch
Costume Designer . . . . Martin Pakledinaz
Lighting Designer . . . . Christopher Akerlind
Production Stage Manager. Susie Cordon
Artistic Director, McCarter Theatre. . . . . Emily Mann
Staff Producer. . . . . Loretta Greco
Dramaturg . . . . Janice Paran

Changes of Heart was developed further in 1996 productions at Berkeley Repertory Theatre, Sharon Ott, Artistic Director, and the Mark Taper Forum, Gordon Davidson, Artistic Director.

CHARACTERS

HARLEQUIN
SILVIA: who loves Harlequin
THE PRINCE: sometimes disguised as a guardsman
TRIVELIN: a servant of the Prince
FLAMINIA: a woman of the court, daughter of a palace servant
LISETTE: Flaminia's sister
A LORD

SETTING

The action takes place in the palace of the Prince. The play can be performed on one set.

ACT I
SCENE I

(Trivelin pursues Silvia with a sumptuous breakfast. Silvia is in a rage.)

TRIVELIN: But Madame, hear me out.

SILVIA: You annoy me.

TRIVELIN: Oughtn't one to be reasonable?

SILVIA: *(Provoked.)* No, one *oughtn't,* and I'm certainly not about to be.

TRIVELIN: Nevertheless…

SILVIA: *(Interrupting.)* Nevertheless, I absolutely do not *wish* to be reasonable, and if you start up again with your endless "neverthelesses" I will *never* wish to be reasonable. So there.

TRIVELIN: You ate so lightly yesterday that you will fall ill if you take nothing this morning.

SILVIA: Well I'd just as soon be dead as alive, so you might as well take back that whole spread, because I don't want breakfast, lunch, or dinner today, and the same goes for tomorrow. *You took me away from Harlequin!* All I want is to be angry, and to hate you all, whoever you are, until I see him again. That's where I stand, and if you wish me to go *mad,* you have only to keep telling me to be reasonable, and I *will* go mad.

TRIVELIN: Well then I *won't,* because I can see you *would.* But I would just beg you to consider…

SILVIA: Why can't you get it through your head that what you would beg me to consider does not *suit* me, in fact has nothing whatever to do with me?!

TRIVELIN: *(Continuing.)* …to consider *that it is your sovereign prince who loves you!*

SILVIA: Well I cannot stop him doing so, he *is* in charge, but does that mean that I should love *him?* No. And I can't encourage him to love me, because I can't and *don't* love him—that's easy to see, a child could see it, but you can't.

TRIVELIN: Bear in mind that he could choose any one of his subjects to be his wife—and he has chosen *you!*

SILVIA: Well who told him to choose me? And did he consult me? If he had said to me, "Silvia, do you want me?" I would have said to him, "No, dear Prince, an honest woman should love her husband, and I could never love you." Now that is simple logic, but no, not at all, he loves me, and boom, he *abducts* me, without even asking my *permission!*

TRIVELIN: He abducts you only to offer you his hand…

SILVIA: And what does he wish me to *do* with his hand, if I am not disposed to clasp it in mine? Does one force people to accept gifts they do not want?

TRIVELIN: But look how he's regaled you in the three days you have been here!

The honor he shows you, the women who attend you, the amusements they all scramble to provide you with! What is Harlequin compared with a *prince,* who would defer utterly to you, and who does not wish even to show himself to you until such time as you *might* be disposed to clasp his hand in yours? Compared with a young, beautiful prince who is full of desire? For that is how you will find him. Ah, Madame, open your eyes, see your fortune, and profit from his interest.

SILVIA: Tell me, does he pay you to annoy me? To spew this absolutely pathetic nonsense at me?

TRIVELIN: *(Aside.)* Oh for God's sake, she exhausts me, I'm just not up to it, I'm losing hope.

SILVIA: You'd be much better off simply giving up *all* hope.

TRIVELIN: But Madame, deign, if you would, to show me where I have gone wrong.

SILVIA: *(Turning sharply on him.)* I'm going to show you *exactly* where!

TRIVELIN: Easy does it Madame! The last thing I mean to do is vex you.

SILVIA: Then you really are an idiot.

TRIVELIN: Your servant, Madame.

SILVIA: Very well, *my servant,* you think so highly of the honor shown me here—what do I need idle ladies-in-waiting spying on me for? They take away my lover and replace him with *women?* Hardly adequate compensation! And what do I care about all the singing and dancing they force me to sit through? A village girl happy in a little town is worth more than a princess weeping in a gorgeous suite of rooms. If the prince is so young and beautiful and full of desire, it's not my fault. He should keep all that for his equals and leave me to my poor Harlequin, who is no more a man of means than I am a woman of leisure, who is not richer than I am or fancier than I am, and who doesn't live in a bigger house than I do, but who *loves* me, without guile or pretense, and whom I love in return in the same way, and for whom I will die of a broken heart if I don't see him again soon. And what have they done to *him?* Perhaps they are mistreating him… *(Silvia's rage peaks.)* I am so angry! This is so unfair! You are my servant? Get out of my sight, I cannot abide you!

TRIVELIN: I will go. Nevertheless…

SILVIA: *(Interrupting at a scream.) No!* Just go!

TRIVELIN: Nevertheless *Harlequin…*

(Silvia turns immediately to him.)

TRIVELIN: …will be here presently. He's been sent for.

SILVIA: I'll see him then!

TRIVELIN: And speak to him as well.

SILVIA: *(Starting off.)* I shall go watch for him. *(She suddenly stops and spins on*

Trivelin.) But if this is a trick, if you *don't* let me see him, I shall neither see, nor speak to, *anyone*. I will make your life miserable.

(She dashes away. The Prince and Flaminia sweep in and witness her departure.)

SCENE II

THE PRINCE: *(To Trivelin.)* Well! Can you offer me any hope? What does she say?

TRIVELIN: What she says, My Lord, I assure you, really doesn't bear repeating. I have nothing to report that would merit your interest

THE PRINCE: Tell me anyway. Every word.

TRIVELIN: I think not, My Lord. To tell you all of it would simply bore you; they are trifles, mere trifles—tenderness for Harlequin, impatience to rejoin him, zero interest in making your acquaintance, a violent desire in fact *not* to meet you, and *quantities* of rancor for all of *us*. That is a brief précis of her feelings at this point. I am sure you will agree that this is hardly cause for rejoicing; and frankly, if I may make so bold as to speak my mind, it would be best to put her back where you found her.

FLAMINIA: I've already told him the same thing, but it's useless, so we must forge ahead.

(The Prince muses sadly.)

FLAMINIA: I think we should concentrate on destroying her love for Harlequin.

TRIVELIN: It is my personal opinion that there is something a little unusual about this girl. To refuse what she's refusing, it's not at all natural. This is no woman, but a creature of a species unknown to us. With a woman, everything would be going swimmingly, but we're getting nowhere. Clearly, she is a phenomenon. Let us go no further.

THE PRINCE: She *is* a phenomenon, and that makes me want her even more.

FLAMINIA: My Lord, don't listen to Trivelin. I know my sex, and the only truly phenomenal thing about it is its vanity. Now then, let's be sensible. Silvia has no interest in rising in the world, so she is not vulnerable to us on that point; but she does have a heart, and consequently also…some vanity. And it is on this point that I shall be able to…remind her of her duties as a woman and bring her into the fold. *(Getting down to business.)* Have they gone to look for Harlequin?

TRIVELIN: We are expecting him.

THE PRINCE: *(Unsettled.)* I must say, Flaminia, we risk a great deal in allowing her to see him. Her…fondness for him is bound to grow *stronger*.

TRIVELIN: Yes but if she doesn't see him, she'll go mad. I have her word for it.

FLAMINIA: And if she *does* see him we shall get somewhere. My Lord, I thought I had convinced you that Harlequin is necessary to us.

THE PRINCE: He is, I know, but let us keep him in the wings for as long as possible. *(A sudden idea.)* You can promise him that I'll shower him with money and titles if he agrees to marry someone other than Silvia.

TRIVELIN: And we have only to force him into submission if he refuses.

THE PRINCE: No. The law that allows me to marry a commoner forbids me to use any coercion in winning her.

FLAMINIA: Exactly, but you needn't worry, everything will be resolved amicably. Isn't it true after all that Silvia has already…met you?

THE PRINCE: Yes. *(A beat. The Prince remembers.)* One day at the hunt, separated from the others, I happened to see her, near her house. I was thirsty; she found me something to drink. I was enchanted by her beauty, and by her simplicity, and I confessed as much to her. But somehow I could not tell her who I was. I met her five or six other times, in the same way, with the same alias—an officer, a guardsman, with a commission at court. But, for all that she behaved toward me with great gentleness, I could never make her renounce Harlequin. Who actually surprised me with her on more than one occasion.

FLAMINIA: We must profit from her ignorance of your true rank. She has been told that she will not see the Prince for a while, and at the moment that suits her. I shall now take charge of the rest, but I must do as I see fit, and you must do as I tell you.

THE PRINCE: Very well, I shall. If you win Silvia's heart for me, my gratitude will be…beyond measure. There is no sign of favor you might not expect from me. *(He leaves swiftly.)*

FLAMINIA: Trivelin, go tell my sister she is late.

TRIVELIN: No need, for she is here. I shall await Harlequin.

(He goes. Lisette enters.)

SCENE III

LISETTE: I'm here to receive my orders.

FLAMINIA: Come closer, let me look at you.

LISETTE: Gladly. I love to be ogled.

(Flaminia inspects Lisette.)

FLAMINIA: My my *my* but you are pretty today.

LISETTE: I am hoping the Prince will think so.

FLAMINIA: That beauty spot is quite exciting. *(Flaminia studies Lisette's face.)* But you must remove it.

LISETTE: Oh I couldn't possibly; my mirror *insisted* on it.

FLAMINIA: Do as I say.

(Lisette produces a small powder box, looks in the mirror, and removes the beauty spot.)

LISETTE: *(Looking at her reflection* sans *spot.)* What a crime. *(She puts the box away.)* So what do you have against my beauty spot?

FLAMINIA: Lisette, we have no time to waste, now listen to me. You are in your prime, you have a good figure, and you are quite...pleasing.

LISETTE: So it is said.

FLAMINIA: And you like to please.

LISETTE: That is my weakness.

FLAMINIA: Do you think you could please a man—make him love you, even— and let him know that he pleases you?

LISETTE: Of course.

FLAMINIA: But could you do this and seem modest, and absolutely without guile?

(A beat.)

LISETTE: We must speak again of my beauty spot; it might be necessary to the business you propose.

FLAMINIA: *(Incisive.)* Will you for once forget your beauty spot? It is *not* necessary, quite the contrary. The person in question is a simple man, a villager, a sort of...rustic, with no experience of worldly things, who imagines that we women from, shall we say, this side of the fence, must be as simple, and as unpretentious, as the girls in his village. And you know, these people have an idea of modesty which is in fact very different from ours. In the city, in the court, we claim certain...exemptions that would scandalize them. So think no more of beauty spots, and let us speak instead of your *manner.*

LISETTE: But my manner has not failed me yet. *(Coy.)* You said yourself that I am pleasing.

FLAMINIA: But you must realize that anyone can see that you are bent on being so, and that just won't *do.* One sees it in your exquisite little hands as they wander suggestively about...and in those great big adorable eyes, which are so shy one moment, so rapacious the next, full of promises...full of ideas. And in the way you move, with a certain nonchalance, an elusive something that suggests both indifference and tenderness—your head insouciantly atilt, your chin floating lightly, your shoulders inviting the touch of a passing finger. And in the way you speak, plucking from the vine the words most apt, pausing ambiguously, and delicately building toward an extravagant flash of wit or a calculatedly rash outburst of passion. In short, you have mastered the ever so slightly dissipated elegance so de rigueur at court, which is fine here, where it is considered just the thing, and essential to the conquest of a man. But for the sake of our green country boy you'll have to do without these finer points, he simply isn't up to them. He's rather like a man who's never drunk anything but pure, clear water; absinth is hardly going to agree with him.

LISETTE: *(Sobered.)* The way you have…rearranged my charms, they seem somehow less pleasing than you say.

FLAMINIA: If they seem a bit ridiculous, it is perhaps because I have subjected them to such close scrutiny. But you don't have to worry; *cultivated* men won't figure any of this out…

LISETTE: With what, pray tell, am I supposed to replace all these "finer points"?

FLAMINIA: With nothing, don't replace them. Just let your glances fall where they may, if your hunting instinct can be suppressed. Keep your head still, if you can possibly imagine denying it its featherbrained meanderings. Leave your face exactly as it is when *no one* is looking at you. Now look at me *ingenuously.*

LISETTE: Ingenuously?

FLAMINIA: *(Nodding assent.)* Mmmm.

(Lisette composes herself then turns to Flaminia with a look on her face.)

LISETTE: How's this?

(Flaminia regards her and chuckles.)

FLAMINIA: But you must practice.

LISETTE: Oh for God's sake, you are a *woman,* is that supposed to inspire me? I'm not going to play my juiciest scene for *you. That* is for the bumpkin.

FLAMINIA: And may he enjoy it.

LISETTE: Poor thing, if I don't love him I shall be deceiving him, and I am a woman of honor. I do have some qualms about it. And in any case I want the *Prince,* and I believe he is not indifferent to me.

FLAMINIA: Well you will not *get* the Prince, and if you ever did appeal to him, you don't anymore, I can assure you—not since *she* appeared on the scene. But if this Harlequin comes to love you, you'll marry him, and that will make your fortune. Woman of honor indeed! We are nothing more than the daughters of a palace servant. But you could become a great lady. Now, do you still have qualms?

(A beat.)

LISETTE: *(With a sigh.)* My conscience rests. Under the circumstances it isn't necessary for me to love him to marry him. *(A beat. She smiles.)* And maybe I could have the Prince…as well. *(A beat.)* I'll go practice.

FLAMINIA: *(Seeing Harlequin in the distance.)* We must fly. The little man is coming.

LISETTE: *À bientôt!*

FLAMINIA: *À bientôt!*

(Lisette hurries off. Flaminia hides.)

SCENE IV

(Trivelin escorts Harlequin through the hall. Harlequin looks all around him, and at Trivelin, with suspicion. Flaminia looks on with interest.)

TRIVELIN: Now then, Lord Harlequin. Do you like what you see? Is this not truly a splendid house?

HARLEQUIN: What *is* going on here? Who are you, what do you want, and how much further are we going? Because my feet are killing me.

TRIVELIN: I am an honest man who is, at present, your servant. I want only to serve you, we are not going too much further, and I shall do everything in my power to improve your feet.

HARLEQUIN: Well, servant, you can take the day off. I have to find Silvia. *(Harlequin cocks his hat and sets off.)*

TRIVELIN: *(Stopping him.)* Not so fast.

HARLEQUIN: You are impertinent indeed to your master. Explain yourself!

TRIVELIN: It is a greater master than you who makes *you my* master. *(A beat. Harlequin puzzles this out, scratching his head.)*

HARLEQUIN: Pray, who is this peculiar person who gives me valets whether I like it or not?

TRIVELIN: When you find out, you will change your tone. But let's not get ahead of ourselves.

HARLEQUIN: How can I get ahead of myself if you're standing in my way? *(Harlequin cocks his hat and sets off again. Trivelin stops him again.)*

TRIVELIN: There are things we must talk about…

HARLEQUIN: But we have nothing to say to each other!

TRIVELIN: We could talk about Silvia.

HARLEQUIN: *(Suddenly transported.)* Ah, Silvia! Alas, I humbly beg your pardon, for you see—and this is the truth—I didn't realize I had to speak to *you* about her.

TRIVELIN: When did you see her last?

HARLEQUIN: The day before yesterday. Thieves tore her from my breast!

TRIVELIN: Those were not thieves.

HARLEQUIN: *(Stentorian pronouncement.)* Call them what you like, I say they're good-for-nothing scum!

TRIVELIN: I know where she is.

HARLEQUIN: *(Carried away again, caressing Trivelin.)* You know where she is! My friend, my valet, my master, my whatever-you-want-from-me person, my name-your-price person! Ah, how sorry I am not to be rich as the Prince, I'd give you the crown jewels for a tip! Tell me, honest man, which way do I go? To the left? To the right? Or down the middle?

TRIVELIN: She will come to you.

HARLEQUIN: *(Enchanted, rapturous.)* She will come to me? Ah, but you are really too good, too kind, to have brought me here as you have done. *(He hurls himself to the ground.)* I grovel, I toady, I kowtow. I hang on your skirts, I scratch your back, I polish your apple! I am your doormat. *(A change comes over him.)* Silvia, Silvia, adored child of my heart, my pet, I weep for joy! *(He weeps for joy and embraces Trivelin as if Trivelin were Silvia.)*

TRIVELIN: *(Aside.)* If this idiot plays every scene this way, it could be a long evening. *(He addresses Harlequin.)* But listen, there's something else.

HARLEQUIN: All right, but let's go see Silvia first, please! *(He squeezes Trivelin amorously.)* You see how…*eager* I am.

TRIVELIN: *(Disengaging himself.)* Do you remember a certain guardsman who paid several visits to Silvia, and whom you saw with her?

HARLEQUIN: Yes, but I think he was just *pretending* to be a guardsman. To impress her.

TRIVELIN: That man found your Silvia *extremely* attractive.

HARLEQUIN: Well he didn't find anything that hadn't been found before *he* started looking for it!

TRIVELIN: And his description of her utterly captivated the Prince.

HARLEQUIN: Blabbermouth!

TRIVELIN: The Prince wanted to see her and ordered that she be brought here.

HARLEQUIN: But he took her from *me!* Is that fair?!

TRIVELIN: And there is a little problem: The Prince has fallen in love with her and hopes to be loved, in his turn, by her.

HARLEQUIN: Well it's not his turn, and it never will be! It's *me* she loves.

TRIVELIN: *(Tiring of Harlequin's objections.)* You're not getting the point at all. Hear me through to the end of it.

HARLEQUIN: *(Raising his voice.)* This *is* the end of it. And that *is* the point. Are you trying to trick me out of what is rightfully mine?

TRIVELIN: Are you not aware that the Prince has the right to take himself a wife from anywhere in the realm?

HARLEQUIN: That's news to me, but it's *beside* the point.

TRIVELIN: *(Sharp.)* It's news that could affect you.

HARLEQUIN: *(Sharper.)* Well no news is good news.

TRIVELIN: The Prince likes Silvia, and he would like her to like him before he weds her. The love *she* has for *you* presents an obstacle to the love *he* has for *her*.

HARLEQUIN: So he should go make love to someone else! *(Demonstrating with his hands.)* Because as it stands now he has only her body, while I have her heart, so we're both lacking something important, and all three of us are very uncomfortable.

TRIVELIN: But don't you see that if you were to marry Silvia the Prince would *remain* uncomfortable?

(Harlequin considers this.)

HARLEQUIN: It's true, he'd be a little sad at first, but he would have done his duty as a man of honor, and that would console him. And you see, if he *did* marry her, *he'd* be happy, but he'd make *her* so sad she'd cry all the time, and *I'd* cry all the time too, which would leave only him laughing, and there's no pleasure in laughing all alone! *(He laughs an insolent, empty laugh and sets off again.)*

TRIVELIN: *(Firm.)* My Lord Harlequin, you must do what you can for your sovereign. And believe me, he's not going to give her up, she just *will* be his wife. The astrologer has predicted it, and the prediction will be fulfilled.

HARLEQUIN: No such ridiculous things are written in the stars. Let me put it to you this way: *I* have predicted that I will beat you to death by tearing your derrière to shreds with this bat. How would you like me to fulfill *that* prediction?

TRIVELIN: Please don't! Why should you do *me* harm?

HARLEQUIN: Because you have predicted for me *terrible* harm—no Silvia, misery, *death!* *(Sensible.)* Well I'm not *going* to die, so if someone must, it might as well be the astrologer. *(Starting off and reaching for his bat.)* Where is he?

TRIVELIN: Now for heaven's sake, *no one* here means you harm. We have lovely girls here; marry one, and make your fortune.

HARLEQUIN: Oh, wonderful! I get tangled up with some other girl, and Silvia gets furious and takes her love elsewhere! You imbecile, you *booby,* how much have you been paid to entrap me?! Go away! Keep your girls! We will never come to terms!

TRIVELIN: You understand that what I'm proposing will win you the Prince's friendship?

HARLEQUIN: What kind of friendship would that be, with him being so much wealthier and more powerful?

TRIVELIN: But you might share in that power and wealth…

HARLEQUIN: But if you have your *health,* and an appetite, and enough to scrape by on, you don't need *things,* by God!

TRIVELIN: You don't know the value of what you're refusing.

HARLEQUIN: Right. So I have nothing to lose!

TRIVELIN: A house in town, a house in the country.

HARLEQUIN: Lovely, but who lives in my townhouse when I'm in the country?

TRIVELIN: Why, your servants, of course.

HARLEQUIN: Why should *they* get to live there? It's my house.

TRIVELIN: *(Growing impatient.)* Well you can't be two places at the same time.

HARLEQUIN: Exactly, you fool! Until I learn that trick there's no point in having two houses!

TRIVELIN: But you could go from one to the other on weekends.

HARLEQUIN: Give up the woman I love for the pleasure of moving all my furniture twice a week?!

TRIVELIN: *(Exasperated.)* But anyone else would be thrilled to have beautiful chateaus and lots of servants!

HARLEQUIN: I need only one room, I don't like to encourage idlers, and I will never find a valet as faithful or as affectionate as myself!

TRIVELIN: But you'd never get a vacation.

HARLEQUIN: *(Triumphant.)* I *am* a vacation!

TRIVELIN: *(At his wits' end.)* But wouldn't you enjoy having good horses, a fine carriage, exquisite furnishings?

HARLEQUIN: My friend, I tire of your cock-and-bull. You promised to show me Silvia, and a man is only as good as his word.

TRIVELIN: *(Desperate.)* Wait. You have no interest in titles…

HARLEQUIN: No.

TRIVELIN: …wealth…

HARLEQUIN: No.

TRIVELIN: …stately homes…

HARLEQUIN: No.

TRIVELIN: …luxury…

HARLEQUIN: No.

TRIVELIN: …influence…

HARLEQUIN: No.

TRIVELIN: …or servants?

HARLEQUIN: No.

TRIVELIN: What about a cellar of the most exquisite wines?

(*Harlequin makes a noise.*)

TRIVELIN: A kitchen ready to cater to your every hunger pang? In short, what about *food?!*

(*Harlequin drops his bat. Trivelin casts a spell.*)

TRIVELIN: Oysters, pheasants, lamb chops, sweetbreads, jellies, custards, cherries, figs, and wheel after wheel of runny cheese...

(*Harlequin considers this.*)

HARLEQUIN: What you now propose...is tempting. Because I am...a pig. But still, I crave love even more than I crave food.

TRIVELIN: (*Trying to reason.*) Well you can still have both! Come on, dear Master, this is your chance to improve your lot. It is simply a question of giving up one girl for another.

HARLEQUIN: I really am rather sorry about it, but there's no point in discussing it. I'm telling you, Silvia's meal enough for me! Now, are you going to bring her here or not?

(*Lisette appears suddenly.*)

SCENE V

LISETTE: (*Sweet.*) I've been looking for you everywhere, Trivelin. The Prince wants you.

TRIVELIN: The Prince! I must run. But pray keep My Lord Harlequin company during my absence.

HARLEQUIN: Oh, don't trouble yourself, I can keep myself company.

TRIVELIN: Yes, but that might get boring.

HARLEQUIN: I never tire of myself. Begone!

(*Lisette and Trivelin look at each other as Trivelin hurries away. Harlequin retreats to a corner.*)

SCENE VI

HARLEQUIN: *(Aside.)* I'll bet this little sweetmeat was sent here to tempt me away from Silvia. Not on her life!

LISETTE: *(Gentle.)* Is it you then, Monsieur, who is the lover of Mademoiselle Silvia?

HARLEQUIN: *(Cold.)* Yes.

LISETTE: She is a very pretty girl.

HARLEQUIN: *(Again cold.)* Yes.

LISETTE: Everyone loves her.

HARLEQUIN: *(Gruff.)* Everyone shouldn't.

LISETTE: But why, since she obviously deserves their love?

HARLEQUIN: *(Again gruff.)* Because she loves only me.

LISETTE: I don't doubt it. And I can understand her interest in you.

HARLEQUIN: And what is that supposed to mean?

LISETTE: I mean to say that I am no longer as surprised as I was, before I met you, at her obstinate determination to love you.

HARLEQUIN: *(Contentious.)* And by virtue of what were you, before you met me, surprised at that, may I ask?

LISETTE: Why by virtue of the fact that she refused a *prince,* and a very attractive one at that.

HARLEQUIN: And because he is attractive I cannot also be attractive?

LISETTE: *(Peaceable.)* No! But he is after all a prince.

HARLEQUIN: So what? Where women are concerned at least, this prince is not more privileged than I.

LISETTE: Good for you! It's just that he has land, palaces, subjects. And attractive as you are, you don't.

HARLEQUIN: Oh please. I may not have any subjects, but at least I'm not beholden to anyone for anything, and it's not my fault when things go wrong. And palaces don't make one prettier, and as for land—whether you have it or not, you still take up the same amount of space. So all things considered, you were wrong to be surprised that I'm loveable, weren't you?!

LISETTE: *(Aside.)* Nasty little man: I compliment him, and he quibbles.

HARLEQUIN: Did you say something? Who are you talking to? *(Harlequin looks around the theater.)*

LISETTE: *(Trying to keep things afloat.)* I seem to have said something that offended you; and I confess that before I spoke to you, from your *appearance,* I expected a more…*pleasant* conversation.

HARLEQUIN: Well that's me, and there's no fixing it. I shall always be like this.

LISETTE: Undoubtedly you shall.

HARLEQUIN: *(Pretending to flirt, to entrap her.)* Which is just as well, because I'm not interesting to *you*, anyway.

LISETTE: *(Responding immediately to his lure.)* Why do you say that?

HARLEQUIN: Because I assume it's the truth.

LISETTE: I would be foolish to tell you the truth on that point. And anyway, a girl should keep quiet.

HARLEQUIN: But should a woman?

LISETTE: *(Getting warm.)* That depends on the man.

HARLEQUIN: And if I were the man?

LISETTE: *(Coquettish.)* *Are* you the man?

HARLEQUIN: You…are a coquette!

LISETTE: Me?

HARLEQUIN: A rampant, harum-scarum coquette.

LISETTE: *(Appalled.)* Don't you know that such things aren't said to a woman? You've insulted me!

HARLEQUIN: There's nothing insulting in seeing what people choose to show us about themselves. I am not wrong to call you a coquette, Mademoiselle, you are wrong to be one!

LISETTE: *(Spirited.)* But how would *you* possibly know if I am one?

HARLEQUIN: Because for the past ten minutes you've been taking great pains to butter me up and hint that you might love me. Listen, if you really *do* love me, leave, fast, so it'll go away, because I am already taken. And if you really *don't* love me, then all this is part of a plot, or sheer vanity, or *both!* Have you no qualms about leading me on? Have you no conscience?! Fie fie, Mademoiselle, *fie fie!*

LISETTE: *(Angry.)* You're raving.

HARLEQUIN: How can the fools at court *tolerate* these affectations in their mistresses?! Because women are really ugly when they play the coquette.

LISETTE: *(Smarting.)* You don't know what you're talking about.

HARLEQUIN: You mentioned Silvia, now *she's* loveable! I should tell you about her modesty during our courtship; you would throw yourself at her feet in admiration. You should have seen how shy she was when we first met—she left the room! And then she left the room more slowly, and then less often, and then eventually she stopped leaving the room; and only then, after that, did she sneak a look at me, and then she was bashful when I saw her do so, and I was happy as a *prince* to see her bashfulness! And then, but only then, we actually looked at each other! At the same time! And then soon after that I took her hand in mine, and she let me take it, but she was still completely abashed; and so then, finally, I spoke to her. Well then she said absolutely nothing at all but didn't seem to think less of me, and then little by little *she* started speaking to *me,* at first with her eyes and then with a flood of words, because her heart was ahead of her tongue! And then the spell was cast forever, and I myself was abashed. I was…beside myself. And that's what I call a woman! *(A beat.)* But you're not like that at all.

LISETTE: *(Humiliated.)* I must say, you amuse me, you make me laugh.

HARLEQUIN: Well I'm bored with making you laugh at your own expense. I'd better be going; I mean, if you spent all your time with people like me, you'd sooner find a snowball in hell than a suitor!

(Harlequin turns to go. Trivelin enters. The Prince and Flaminia, following him, eavesdrop, unseen by Harlequin.)

SCENE VII

TRIVELIN: *(To Harlequin.)* You're leaving?

HARLEQUIN: Yes, for some reason this young spinster is after me, but there's no way she'll get me. She bores me.

(Harlequin starts to leave. Trivelin reroutes him to avoid the Prince and Flaminia.)

TRIVELIN: Come come, let's go *this* way, and have a walk around the grounds before dinner. It will relieve your boredom.

(They go out. The Prince and Flaminia enter.)

SCENE VIII

FLAMINIA: *(To Lisette.)* Well then, are things proceeding as planned? Did you arouse his interest in you?

LISETTE: *(Aggrieved.)* He *has* no interest in me.

FLAMINIA: I take it you met with a poor reception.

LISETTE: "You are a rampant, harum-scarum coquette, and you'd sooner find a snowball in hell than a suitor."

THE PRINCE: If *you* can't win Harlequin, Lisette, he can't be won. *(Turning to Flaminia.)* And Silvia will never love me.

FLAMINIA: Well perhaps it's up to *me* to try my luck. My Lord, I don't mind telling you that I have seen Harlequin, and that… *(A beat.)* …I rather like him! Furthermore, I have taken it into my head to make you happy, and I promise you will be, and I shall be as good as my word.

(The Prince isn't sure.)

FLAMINIA: Oh but you do not know what I'm capable of! What, My Lord, do you think Harlequin and Silvia can hold out against me? I who have made a promise, who have set my sights, who am determined, persistent, unyielding? I can handle these two, with their simple hearts, I would be a disgrace to my sex if I couldn't. My Lord, you can order your wedding clothes with complete confidence, and today. You can actually get dressed in them if you like. You will be loved, and you will be married; Silvia will give you her heart, and after that her hand. I can hear her now in my ear, murmuring into yours, "I love you." I can see the wedding in my mind's eye… *(After a brief pause.)* Harlequin will marry me, you will show us your favor, and that will be that. The end.

LISETTE: *(Incredulous.)* The *end?* You haven't even started.

FLAMINIA: Have a little imagination.

THE PRINCE: You encourage me to hope, but I have to say, as things stand now I have nothing to go on.

FLAMINIA: You soon shall. Lisette, you were so good at provoking Harlequin, how would you like to dress up as a proper lady and provoke Silvia? You will insult her, and the Prince will come to her rescue…in his disguise as the guardsman!

THE PRINCE: *(Excited by this idea.)* Yes!

FLAMINIA: *(To Lisette.)* Can you do that?

(Lisette looks at the Prince, then at Flaminia.)

LISETTE: If I must.

FLAMINIA: And I shall also prevail upon members of the court to help us. But first, the lovers must be reunited.

LISETTE: When those two see each other, I'm afraid all your talents may fail you, and the Prince will have to choose…someone other than Silvia.

THE PRINCE: That's what I'm afraid of, too.

FLAMINIA: *(Cheerful.)* There's nothing to fear. We shall, from all sides, seduce the lovers away from each other. And strangely enough, nothing will be so useful in separating them as letting them, in the meantime, occasionally be together. There are many tricks in this game, and it is with this card…that we shall take them. *(A beat. She turns to the Prince.)* How else would you acquire the object of desire?

THE PRINCE: Indeed. So. Place your bets!

LISETTE: *(Seeing Harlequin offstage.)* He's back! I can't stay.

FLAMINIA: *(To the Prince.)* Shall we go?

(They rush away.)

SCENE IX

(Harlequin and Trivelin enter, attended by valets.)

HARLEQUIN: By the way, tell me something. I've been trying to figure it out since I got here. *(Indicating the valets.)* These great purse-lipped persons who follow us everywhere—what are they *for?* What do they *mean?* They are just *too* peculiar.

TRIVELIN: The Prince wants to give you evidence of his good intentions. He shows you *honor* by ordering these persons to attend you.

HARLEQUIN: Oh, so this is a mark of honor?

TRIVELIN: Yes, absolutely.

HARLEQUIN: And tell me—these persons who attend me, who attends *them?*

TRIVELIN: No one.

HARLEQUIN: And you, no one attends you either?

TRIVELIN: No one.

HARLEQUIN: So no one shows you honor, you and the persons here?

TRIVELIN: *(Obsequious.)* We do not deserve such honor.

HARLEQUIN: *(Suddenly enraged, brandishing his bat.)* Well that's it then, get out!

TRIVELIN: What's the matter? What has upset you?

HARLEQUIN: Do you expect me to tolerate having in my employ dishonorable persons who plainly admit to being undeserving?!

TRIVELIN: You misunderstood what I said!

HARLEQUIN: *(Smacking Trivelin mightily with his bat.)* Get thee behind me, *cretin!!*

TRIVELIN: *(Fleeing Harlequin.)* Stop! Stop! What are you *doing?!* Are you *mad?*
(Harlequin chases Trivelin and the valets around the room and into the wings, smacking at them violently with his bat. Sounds of confusion and ruin emanate from offstage.)

SCENE X

(Harlequin bounds back onto the stage almost immediately.)

HARLEQUIN: Villains! Curs! It certainly is a strange way to honor someone!
(Trivelin drags himself back onto the stage holding his rear end.)

TRIVELIN: Listen, when I said to you that we do not deserve such honor, I meant that we are not *entitled* to have people attending us. Not because we are *dis*honorable, or *lack* honor, but because only rich or influential people are honored in this way.

HARLEQUIN: *(Pleasant.)* Oh, I see.

TRIVELIN: If it were enough simply to be an honorable man to be honored, I would have an *army* of valets attending me.

HARLEQUIN: Well why didn't you say that in the first place?

TRIVELIN: You really hurt me.

HARLEQUIN: That was the idea. Luckily for you this was only a misunderstanding and you're innocent, because the beatings are much worse when you really do something wrong.

(Silvia races in, followed by Flaminia, and interrupts him.)

SCENE XI

SILVIA: Harlequin! *(She runs joyfully to Harlequin.)* Oh Harlequin, it's really you! I thought I'd never see you again! My poor little thing, I am so relieved.

HARLEQUIN: Me too! Me too! I shall die of happiness!

SILVIA: He loves me! How sweet to be loved like this!

FLAMINIA: *(Watching them.)* You are so delightful, my dears! And it is truly touching that you are so devoted to each other. *(Confidentially.)* If anyone were to hear me say this I would be lost…but, from the bottom of my heart, I admire you, and I feel for you.

SILVIA: That's because you have a good heart. *(To Harlequin.)* I can't tell you how much I missed you, my sweet Harlequin.

HARLEQUIN: *(Tenderly, taking her hand.)* Will you love me always, no matter what?

SILVIA: Will I love you always? How can you ask such a thing?

FLAMINIA: I can vouch for her. She was in a despair in your absence, she wept for you. I was so touched by her grief that I longed to see you reunited. And now you are. *(A beat.)* Good-bye my friends, I must leave you, for I am moved. You've made me remember my great love, who is no longer with us, and I feel such sadness. I shall never forget him. He was so like you, Harlequin. Silvia, they gave me the privilege of serving you, and I would never do you a *dis*service. Always love Harlequin, he deserves it. And you, Harlequin, whatever happens, look upon me as a friend. There is nothing I would not do for you.

HARLEQUIN: *(Gentle.)* Well, Mademoiselle, you are an honest woman. And I am *your* friend too. I am sorry about the death of your lover. It's too bad you are in such a state. *(Looking at Silvia.)* It's too bad *we're* in such a state. *(Exit Flaminia.)*

SCENE XII

SILVIA: *(Plaintive.)* Well, my boy?

HARLEQUIN: Well, my angel?

SILVIA: We are really in a pickle.

HARLEQUIN: Let's be patient and love each other always; that will give us strength.

SILVIA: Yes, but our love—what will become of it? I am worried about what is happening.

HARLEQUIN: Alas, my love, I'm telling you to be patient, but I'm just as worried as you are. *(He takes her hand in his.)* My poor little treasure, my own beloved girl. It's been three *days* since last I saw these beautiful eyes; look at me forever, to make up for those three days.

SILVIA: *(Anxious.)* Oh, I have so much to tell you. I am afraid of losing you. I am afraid that they might hurt you. I am afraid that if you didn't see me for a long time, you would get used to doing without me.

HARLEQUIN: Dear heart, if I didn't see you for a long time I would be miserable, and I could never get used to being miserable.

SILVIA: I really don't want you ever to forget me. I really don't want you to suffer because of me. I really don't know how to say what I want, I love you so much. I'm sorry I'm so confused. Everything makes me sad. *(Harlequin cries loudly.)*

SILVIA: Oh dear, now you're going to make me cry too. Don't cry.

HARLEQUIN: How do you expect me to keep from crying when you insist on being so sad? If you would be less sad, then I wouldn't cry, and then you wouldn't cry, and then you'd be happier.

SILVIA: Then you stop crying, and I won't talk about being sad.

HARLEQUIN: Yes, but I shall know that you are. You'll have to promise me that you *won't* be anymore.

SILVIA: Yes, my little one, but then you must promise *me* that you will always love me.

HARLEQUIN: *(Stopping short to look at her.)* Silvia, I am your lover, and you are my mistress, and I adore you. Remember this always, for it is the truth, and as long as I live it will always be true—unshakably true. I will die with it in my heart, on my breath. *(A beat.)* I could swear you an oath if you want.

SILVIA: I feel better now, and anyway I don't know any oaths. You are an honorable man. I have your love, and you have mine, and I will not ask for it back. Who would I ever need it back for, aren't you the handsomest fellow in the world? And is there any woman who could love you as much as I do? Certainly not. What more do we need? We have only to be who we are, and there will be no need of oaths.

HARLEQUIN: Your words…are like honey.

SCENE XIII

(Flaminia returns with Trivelin.)

TRIVELIN: *(To Silvia.)* I am terribly sorry to interrupt you, but your mother has just arrived, Madame, and she is most eager to see you.

SILVIA: My mother?

TRIVELIN: Your mother.

SILVIA: Harlequin, come with me. My mother is your mother.

HARLEQUIN: *(Taking her arm.)* We're off, my dove.

FLAMINIA: My dear Silvia, shouldn't you really visit alone with your mother?

(Silvia and Harlequin hesitate.)

FLAMINIA: But you two have nothing to fear, you're free to see each other whenever you please. *(So Trivelin doesn't hear her.)* You have my word for it, and you know I would never wish to deceive you.

(Silvia and Harlequin wonder what to do.)

HARLEQUIN: No, you're one of us, you are.

SILVIA: Well then adieu, my boy, I'll be back soon. *(Silvia kisses Harlequin and rushes away.)*

HARLEQUIN: *(To Flaminia.)* Dear friend, why not wait here with me while Silvia is off with her mother? To keep me from getting bored. *(Pointedly, so Trivelin can overhear.)* You're the only one around here whose company I can bear.

FLAMINIA: *(Confidential.)* As you know, my dear Harlequin, your company gives me pleasure as well; but I'm afraid my affection for you might be discovered.

(Harlequin looks at Flaminia.)

TRIVELIN: My Lord Harlequin, dinner is served.

HARLEQUIN: *(Starting off, delighted.)* Oh! *(He stops in his tracks. A beat.)* But I should wait for Silvia. And then we'll go home.

FLAMINIA: *(Intimate.)* I want you to eat, you *must* eat.

HARLEQUIN: You think so?

FLAMINIA: Yes.

HARLEQUIN: *(Uncertain how to proceed.)* I'm not sure. *(To Trivelin.)* The soup—is it good?

TRIVELIN: The soup…is divine.

(A beat.)

HARLEQUIN: Well...I'm not that hungry. And I should wait for Silvia, she just *loves* soup.

FLAMINIA: Surely Silvia will be dining with her mother. Of course, you can do exactly as you wish, you are the master, but I'd say give them time alone together. Don't you think? You'll see Silvia *after* dinner.

HARLEQUIN: Very well... *(Uncertain again.)* But...I'm still not that hungry.

TRIVELIN: There's lots of wine.

(Harlequin hesitates.)

TRIVELIN: It's free.

(Harlequin is very torn.)

TRIVELIN: The roast is ready.

HARLEQUIN: *(More and more torn.)* Tell me about the roast.

TRIVELIN: It's pink and juicy.

HARLEQUIN: *(The quandary deepens.)* Pink and juicy. And all this...

TRIVELIN: Is on your very plate.

HARLEQUIN: Oh. *(After a final hesitation.)* Well...we'd better go and eat it then. Or it'll just go to waste.

(Harlequin sets off, Trivelin falls in behind him.)

FLAMINIA: Don't forget to drink to my health.

HARLEQUIN: Come drink to mine, to our acquaintance!

FLAMINIA: Why... *(A beat. She appears to be on the verge of a decision.)* ...not?! Gladly. I have a half an hour.

HARLEQUIN: *(Merry.)* Good! You please me.

(Harlequin offers Flaminia his arm. He whispers to Flaminia so Trivelin doesn't hear, confidential, pleased with himself.)

HARLEQUIN: I was really hungry the whole time.

(Harlequin escorts Flaminia off to dinner. Trivelin follows.)

(Blackout.)

ACT II
SCENE I

(Flaminia and Silvia are in the middle of a conversation.)

SILVIA: You're the only person around here I can tolerate, and you seem to have my interests at heart. I don't trust the rest of them. Where is Harlequin?

FLAMINIA: He's still eating.

SILVIA: You know, this place is really dreadful. I've never seen people so... *polite.* There are *so* many curtseys, *so* many pretty speeches—you'd think they were the best people in the world, that they're full of integrity and good intentions. But no, not at all. There's not one of them who hasn't come to me and said oh-so-discreetly, "Mademoiselle, believe me, you're better off forgetting Harlequin and marrying the Prince." And they say this to me absolutely without a qualm, as if they were encouraging me to do the right thing! "But," I say to them, "I gave my promise to Harlequin. What about fidelity, honor, good faith?" They don't even know what I'm talking about. They laugh in my face and tell me I'm being childish, that a proper young lady ought to be reasonable, isn't *that* nice! To hold nothing sacred, to cheat one's fellow man, to go back on one's word, to be two-faced and to lie—*that's* how to be a proper young lady? Who *are* these people? Where do they come from? What dough did they make them out of?

FLAMINIA: The same dough they used to make us, my dear. You know, it really shouldn't surprise you if they think you should be happy to marry the Prince. I mean, he's the *Prince.*

SILVIA: But don't I have to be true to Harlequin? Isn't it my duty to be an honest woman? And if I failed in that duty, would I be *happy?* Also, isn't my constancy part of my appeal? Doesn't it make me attractive? They have the audacity to tell me, "Go ahead, do something bad," when only bad things would ever come of it. And because I don't want to do as *they* please, they say I'm squeamish.

FLAMINIA: What do you expect? They will think what they want to think; it's in their interest for the Prince to be happy.

SILVIA: But why doesn't he go after a girl who will have him? It's so absurd to desire someone who doesn't desire you. No, it's a big mistake, what he's doing—all the music, the plays, the food, the jewels he sends me. It must be costing him a *fortune,* it's appalling, he'll be ruined. And what does he gain by it? Even if he gave me an entire haberdashery shop it wouldn't give me as much pleasure as the little pincushions Harlequin gives me.

FLAMINIA: I understand. I once loved in the same way, and I know exactly what you mean about pincushions.

(A beat.)

SILVIA: Listen, if I had had to trade Harlequin for someone else, it definitely wouldn't have been for someone I'd never *met*. It would have been for a royal guardsman who used to visit me and who is about as fine a figure of a man as I've ever seen. There's not a chance the Prince could match *him*. It's too bad I *couldn't* really love him, but I pity *him* more than I do the Prince.

FLAMINIA: Silvia, I assure you that when you meet the Prince you will pity him as much as you do this guardsman.

SILVIA: Well, whatever, I just wish he'd try to forget me, I wish he'd send me home, I wish he'd pursue other women. There are plenty of them here who already have lovers, just as I have, yet they seem to remain somehow... available. It doesn't seem to bother them at all, but I could never be like that.

FLAMINIA: My dear girl, is nobody here worthy of you? Have we nothing that meets your standard?

SILVIA: Oh but of course you have. Some of the women here are prettier than I am, or maybe they're not, but they certainly know how to make the most of what they have. And they get further with it than I could even if I were utterly ravishing. I've seen ugly women here who decorate their faces so artfully that one is deceived into thinking they're beautiful.

FLAMINIA: Yes, but *your* face needs no such decoration, and that is charming.

SILVIA: Well that's as it may be, I'm not trying to be someone I'm not. I'm very simple compared to them. I just stand here and be, I'm not flouncing back and forth, but *they*—they're always so devil-may-care, their eyes caress everything in sight, their beauty is so...unabashed. So *provocative*. And that's all more pleasing than a little shameface like me, who hardly dares look at people and who is embarrassed when someone says she's beautiful.

FLAMINIA: Yet *that* is exactly what captivates the Prince, that's why he respects you. It's that ingenuousness, that simple, unfussy beauty, that *natural* charm. Believe me, you shouldn't give the women around here so much credit. Because they don't exactly give you any.

SILVIA: What are they saying about me?

FLAMINIA: Oh...rude things. They mock you, they make fun of the Prince, they ask him how his barnyard beauty is doing. I heard them working you over—"Have you ever *seen* anything so common?" "Could her dress *be* any more gauche?" There were even several *men* who didn't find you too pretty. I was in a *state*...

SILVIA: *(Upset.)* I should hope so—it's a miserable excuse for a man who would stoop to saying things like that to please those ninnies!

FLAMINIA: And so offhandedly!

SILVIA: God how I hate them! But since I am, by their reckoning, so unattractive, how is it that the Prince loves me and not them?

FLAMINIA: Oh, they're convinced that he won't love you for long, that it's a freak infatuation, and that he'll be howling about it in no time.

SILVIA: They should be glad I love Harlequin; if I didn't, I would take great pleasure in proving them wrong, the flibbertigibbets.

FLAMINIA: I told them, "You are doing everything you can to get rid of Silvia and to humor the Prince, but one encouraging word from her and he wouldn't deign even to look at you.

SILVIA: You can say that again! *(A beat. Flaminia's words echo in Silvia's ear.)* One simple word from me, and they'd be...*silenced*.
(Flaminia, behind Silvia's back, motions to someone offstage.)

FLAMINIA: It seems we have company.
(Silvia looks offstage to see the Prince, who is dressed as the guardsman.)

SILVIA: *(A gasp.)* Oh no...I think that's the guardsman I told you about. *(She peeks offstage again.)* It *is!* *(A beat.)* He *is* a fine figure of a man, isn't he?

SCENE II

(Enter Lisette, as a lady of the court, escorted by the Prince-as-guardsman. Upon seeing Silvia, the Prince bows deeply to her.)

SILVIA: What, Sir, you here? You knew that I was here?

THE PRINCE: Yes, Mademoiselle, I knew, but when last we met you asked that I not seek you out again. I would not have dared to do so had this prominent lady... *(Indicating Lisette.)* ...not requested that I introduce her to you. She wishes to pay you her respects.
(Lisette looks Silvia up and down. Flaminia signals to Lisette to curtsey, but Lisette doesn't. Silvia glares at Lisette and addresses the Prince.)

SILVIA: *(Meekly, to the Prince.)* I am not angry with you, although I have been quite upset. As for Madame... *(Indicating Lisette.)* ...I thank her for wishing to pay me her respects, though I'm sure I really don't deserve them. But as she wishes to pay them, she may do so. Now.
(Flaminia signals to Lisette to curtsey. Lisette curtseys, tersely.)

SILVIA: I shall pay her mine in return, as best I can. She will forgive me if I offend her by doing it wrong.

LISETTE: I have already forgiven you, dear girl, for I would never expect you to do it right.
(Silvia, infuriated, curtseys to Lisette, muttering under her breath.)

SILVIA: "Never expect you to do it right..."

LISETTE: *(Aside, moved.)* She is beautiful.

SILVIA: *(Aside.)* She is jealous.

LISETTE: *(To Silvia.)* How old are you, dear thing?

SILVIA: Younger than your children, Madame.

FLAMINIA: *(To Silvia.)* Good one!

LISETTE: *(To the Prince.)* She is put out, I take it?

(The Prince turns to Lisette, pretending surprise.)

THE PRINCE: But Madame, whatever can this mean? Is this how you pay her your respects? By insulting her?

LISETTE: That was not my intention. I was curious to see this young thing who is so…loved here at court, who has sparked such passion, and debate. I wanted to know what it is that makes her so loveable. They say it's her simplicity, a sort of pastoral charm, that makes her amusing. *(To Silvia.)* Pray, be so kind as to show us what it's all about. Amuse us. Be…*fresh*.

SILVIA: Oh no Madame, it would be a waste of time: I am nowhere near as amusing as you.

LISETTE: Ah, she is charming. You ask for fresh, and you get it.

THE PRINCE: *(To Lisette.)* I think you should go, Madame.

LISETTE: I can see when I'm not wanted.

SILVIA: She'd *better* go, or I'll lose my temper.

THE PRINCE: *(To Lisette.)* You will pay for this little maneuver.

LISETTE: *(To the Prince.)* That the Prince should not choose me is my loss; that he should choose *her*…is my revenge. *(Lisette leaves.)*

SCENE III

FLAMINIA: Now *that* was brazen.

SILVIA: That was *outrageous!* A lot of good it does me to be kidnapped if people are just going to belittle me. Everybody is worth *something*. Don't you think I'm worth as much as that kind of woman? I certainly wouldn't want to be in *her* shoes. And I wouldn't *consider* letting her get into mine.

FLAMINIA: Silvia, her jealousy *increases* your worth; it is the ultimate compliment.

THE PRINCE: Silvia, beautiful Silvia, that woman misled me…*and* the Prince. I am mortified, please believe me. You know that *I* am filled with respect for you, that *I* know your worth. You know my heart. Yes, I came here to see you again, to dream once again a dream that haunts and beguiles me, to defer again to the future queen…of my heart. But I am being reckless—I ought to take care not to be…exposed, not to let Flaminia hear what I am saying, not to trouble you further.

FLAMINIA: I already know she's irresistible, you're not giving anything away.

SILVIA: *(To Flaminia.)* Well I would prefer that he not love me, because it saddens me that I can't love him in return. You know, if he were like so many other men, I'd tell him a thing or two, but he is too obliging for me to be hard on him. He has always been like this.

THE PRINCE: Ah, you are too kind, Silvia. If I am always obliging, it is because I must always love you.

(Silvia looks at the Prince, amazed. A beat.)

SILVIA: Oh very well, love me, go ahead—it makes me feel good. But promise to suffer your situation patiently, because I cannot in good faith encourage you, Harlequin came first. That's all that stands in your way— if I had known that you would come along after him, I think I might have waited for you. So now we're both miserable—you for want of me, and I for want of…Harlequin.

THE PRINCE: *(Delighted.)* Flaminia, I put it to you, *could* one stop loving Silvia? Do you know a heart more compassionate or more generous than hers? The love, the life's devotion of another woman would touch me less than Silvia's pity and understanding.

SILVIA: *(To Flaminia.)* And I put *this* to you. You have heard him speak. What am I to do with a man who actually *thanks* me when I discourage him?

FLAMINIA: Frankly Silvia, were I in his place, I would feel exactly as he does. He's right, you are delightful.

SILVIA: Now don't *you* encourage him. He doesn't need to be told that I'm delightful, he's already convinced of it. *(To the Prince.)* Try to love me…calmly. And help me get even with that woman who insulted me.

THE PRINCE: I shall. And as for my love, even were you to forget me from this day forward, I should be protected from your cruelty by the memory of your beauty. However you treat me, I have made my decision. *(A beat.)* I shall have the pleasure of loving you for the rest of my life.

SILVIA: Oh I know. *(A beat.)* I know you.

FLAMINIA: Go, Sir. Tell the Prince how that woman behaved. The court must come to understand Silvia's position here.

THE PRINCE: You will soon have news from me. *(The Prince departs.)*

SCENE IV

FLAMINIA: I'm going to look for Harlequin. *Someone* must stop him eating. Go put on the dress they've made for you, I'm longing to see you in it.

SILVIA: Oh Flaminia, the fabric is so beautiful, and I know it will suit me perfectly, but I really don't want it, or any of the rest, because the Prince wants to *buy* me with it all...and that is one purchase he can never make.

FLAMINIA: You happen to be wrong. *(A beat.)* I mean...even if he gave you up, he would never take back what he has given you. You don't know him.

SILVIA: I'll take your word for it then, as long as he doesn't say to me when it's all over, "Then why did you accept my gifts?"

FLAMINIA: All he'll say is, "Why didn't you accept more of them?"

SILVIA: *(With some glee.)* Well then I'll accept as many as he wishes to give me, and he won't be able to reproach me for anything! *(Silvia rushes away delighted.)*

SCENE V

FLAMINIA: *(Thoughtful.)* It seems to me that things are beginning to take shape. *(A beat. She looks offstage.)* There he is. *(She reflects.)* I am not sure yet... *(A beat. She smiles.)* ...but I think if this little man came to love me, I might get...more than I bargained for.

(Harlequin enters, laughing uproariously, with Trivelin.)

HARLEQUIN: *(To Flaminia, between guffaws.)* Greetings, my dear.

FLAMINIA: Tell me what you're laughing about, so I can join in.

HARLEQUIN: Well my valet Trivelin—whose services, you might be interested to know, are free—showed me through all the rooms in the house, and they are *all* huge, my dear, I mean carriages could get through the doors, and there are so many people milling about they're all like public streets, and everyone's gossiping and carrying on like pigs in a market, without so much as a peep to or from the master of the house, who is nowhere to be seen. They just troop into his house and prance around, and he doesn't even offer them a *beer,* but they plop themselves down at his table anyway, and watch *me* eat! Now, in the midst of all this I saw one of those crackpot valets lift the dress of a lady *from the rear!* I thought he was playing a trick on her, so I went up behind him and said, "Stop that, you smutty rogue, would you stoop so low? I am quite aware that people take obscene liberties around here, but the lady is not a wheelbarrow. If you're looking for the servants' entrance, you're on the wrong floor!" And the lady turned around and said to me, "Can't you see that he is carrying my train?" "He's carrying it too far!" I responded, "How can you allow it?!" At which the lady laughed, and her assailant laughed, and Trivelin laughed, and everyone laughed. So to keep them company I also laughed, and now you can too.

(They all three scream with laughter. When the laughter subsides, Harlequin turns to Flaminia.)

HARLEQUIN: Why is that funny?

FLAMINIA: Well, it's just that you didn't realize that…what the lady let the lackey do…is common practice among women of rank.

HARLEQUIN: *(To Trivelin.)* So this is another…honor?

TRIVELIN: Right you are.

HARLEQUIN: Right I am to laugh then, too, because that is no honor. People's dresses are being lifted all the *time!* I assure you, peasant women receive this honor on a daily basis!

(More laughter.)

FLAMINIA: You *are* merry. I love it when you're like this. Did you eat well?

HARLEQUIN: An unforgettable fricassee! And the wine…irresistible! I drank Silvia's health—and yours—so many times that if you get sick, it won't be my fault.

FLAMINIA: You could still remember me after all that wine?

HARLEQUIN: *(Drawing close to Flaminia.)* When I give my friendship to someone, I never forget her, *especially* if wine is involved. *(A little confused by his proximity to Flaminia.)* But Silvia—is she still with her mother?

TRIVELIN: But My Lord Harlequin, you really must stop thinking about Silvia.

HARLEQUIN: You be quiet while I'm talking.

FLAMINIA: You're wrong, Trivelin.

TRIVELIN: What do you mean I'm wrong?

FLAMINIA: I mean you're wrong to keep him from thinking about the woman he loves.

TRIVELIN: You seem too little concerned with the interests of the Prince, *Madame.*

FLAMINIA: *(Feigning fear.)* Harlequin, this man will get me in trouble because of you.

HARLEQUIN: *(Confidential.)* Not a chance, my sweet! *(To Trivelin, with flourish.)* Listen you lout, you tell me I am your master, so you'll do as I say. If you tattletale to the Prince and anyone so much as looks askance at this blameless maid, you will have two ears fewer. I guarantee you!

TRIVELIN: One ear more or less isn't going to keep me from doing my duty to my country.

HARLEQUIN: *(Screaming directly into Trivelin's ear.) GO AWAY!*
(Trivelin is stunned.)

TRIVELIN: I forgive you everything, My Lord Harlequin, because after all I must. But you, Flaminia, you will pay for your meddling. *(Trivelin leaves.)*

SCENE VI

(Harlequin returns.)

HARLEQUIN: This is *terrible!* I find only one person here who listens to reason, and that lummox tries to sabotage my conversations with her. Beloved friend, now we can speak of Silvia at our leisure. The only way I can bear being without her is...being with you.

FLAMINIA: *(With a simple air.)* I do appreciate your saying so. There is nothing I wouldn't do to make you two happy. And besides, you are such an excellent person, Harlequin—when I see that they have made you unhappy, I suffer as much as you do.

HARLEQUIN: *You* are a wonderful person! Every time you pity me it calms me down, and being unhappy becomes quite agreeable.

FLAMINIA: For heaven's sake who *wouldn't* pity you? Who *wouldn't* take an interest in you? You don't know your worth, Harlequin. *(Flaminia is rather close to Harlequin.)*

HARLEQUIN: That could well be. I've never considered it all so...closely.

FLAMINIA: I wish I had the power to... If you knew how difficult it is for me... If you could read my heart...

HARLEQUIN: Alas, I don't know *how* to read, but maybe you could *show* me what you mean. Oh, I don't want to be unhappy anymore, if only to keep from causing *you* anguish. But surely that time will come...

FLAMINIA: *(Seemingly sad.)* Yet I'm afraid I won't be around to see it. Trivelin will talk, they'll separate us and take me away, who knows where... Harlequin, perhaps even now I am talking to you for the last time!

HARLEQUIN: *(Truly sad.)* For the last time! I really have the worst luck. First, all I have is a simple sweetheart, and they snatch her away, and now they're going to cart *you* off? Ah! Where will I find the courage to endure all this? Do they think my heart is made of iron? Are they trying to kill me? Will they come at night and beat me with clubs and disembowel me with rusty bayonets while I scream and scream?! What will they do to me?!

FLAMINIA: Whatever they do, I hope you will never forget me, whose greatest wish was for your happiness.

HARLEQUIN: Oh winsome friend, you've won my heart. Help me in my sorrow, what do *you* think I should do? As you can see I lose my concentration when I'm distraught. I must love Silvia, yet I mustn't lose you. My love oughtn't to suffer on account of our friendship, nor should our friendship suffer on account of my love; and so I'm truly in a cul-de-sac.

FLAMINIA: And I am in one too! Since losing my first love I have found peace only in your company. I have felt alive again, I *breathe* with you. You resemble him in so many ways that I sometimes think I am talking to him.

HARLEQUIN: Well it's too bad I love Silvia, because I am beginning to *enjoy* this resemblance. So, he was…a handsome fellow?

FLAMINIA: Didn't I say he looked just like you?

HARLEQUIN: And you…loved him very much?

FLAMINIA: Think, Harlequin, how much *you* deserve to be loved—and you will know how much I loved him.

HARLEQUIN: No one has ever spoken to me as you do. Your friendship touches every part of me. I never thought I was so attractive as you say, but since you loved the original so much, I guess the copy must be *somewhat* appealing.

FLAMINIA: Perhaps I would have found the copy even more appealing than the original…had I been appealing enough for the copy.

HARLEQUIN: God help me but you're appealing when you say that!

FLAMINIA: You confuse me. I must go. It is so hard to tear myself away from you that if I didn't go, I'm not sure what would happen. Farewell, Harlequin, I will see you again whenever they allow it. *(She tries to leave but cannot.)* I don't know where I am…

HARLEQUIN: Neither do I.

(A beat.)

FLAMINIA: Looking at you gives me so much pleasure, *too* much.

HARLEQUIN: Well who am I to refuse you that pleasure? *(Striking a pose.)* Feast your eyes!

FLAMINIA: *(Hurrying away.)* I dare not… Adieu.

HARLEQUIN: *(Watching her go.)* This place doesn't deserve that woman. *(A beat. Harlequin ponders.)* If something terrible happened, and Silvia were to…drop out of the picture, I think in my grief and desperation I might take comfort in *her* arms.

SCENE VII

(Trivelin enters, followed by a Lord.)

TRIVELIN: My Lord Harlequin, here is a Lord who wishes to speak with you.
(The Lord approaches, doffs his hat, and makes deep bows to Harlequin, who doffs his hat and makes deep bows in return. Trivelin withdraws.)

THE LORD: I come to ask a favor of you, and I hope it will not inconvenience you, Monsieur?

HARLEQUIN: It's all the same to me, *Monsieur.*
(The Lord puts back on his hat.)

HARLEQUIN: Am I supposed to put my hat back on too?

THE LORD: Whatever you choose to do with your hat, you do me honor.

HARLEQUIN: Several things come to mind. *(Putting back on his hat.)* But don't pay me any expensive compliments, because I can't pay them back. I am so often complimented that I am already *deep* in debt.

THE LORD: Shall we then say, they are not compliments at all, rather tokens of my esteem?

HARLEQUIN: Shall we then say that this is all honey-tongued gobbledygook? You're up to something. Everyone here is up to something. Now what do *you* want?

THE LORD: It's like this: Unfortunately for me I spoke…cavalierly, of you, in front of the Prince.

HARLEQUIN: And I suppose that was also a token of your esteem?
(A beat.)

THE LORD: And the Prince is annoyed with me.

HARLEQUIN: What, he doesn't like mudslingers?

THE LORD: Just so.

HARLEQUIN: Well that's the right attitude, maybe he *is* a man of honor after all. Now if he'd just give me back my beloved, I think I could actually like him. And what did he say to you? That you were an ill-bred clod?

THE LORD: Yes.

HARLEQUIN: Well that's very reasonable, what are you complaining about?

THE LORD: That's not the whole of it. "Harlequin," he said to me, "is an honorable fellow, and I want him to be honored. I value him; his candor and lack of guile are qualities I wish you all had. I am devastated that *my* love for Silvia forces me to lay siege to his."

HARLEQUIN: *(Touched.)* For heaven's sake…I am in his debt. And here I thought I was angry at him!

THE LORD: Then he dismissed me, whereupon my friends tried to make him relent.

HARLEQUIN: It would be no great loss to the Prince if he dismissed them too: A man is defined by the company he keeps.

THE LORD: He did dismiss them.

HARLEQUIN: Good riddance to the mischief makers!

THE LORD: And we're not allowed to come back, any of us, unless you plead personally for our reinstatement.

(A beat.)

HARLEQUIN: *(Waving.) Bon voyage!*

THE LORD: But if you refuse to intercede for me, I will be ruined, I will be *nothing* at court. I shall have to retire to my country estates, an exile!

HARLEQUIN: So that's what exile is? Being sent home to spend your own fortune instead of remaining at court to spend the people's?

THE LORD: That's one way of putting it.

HARLEQUIN: *(Incredulous.)* And you'll live there in peace and quiet, eating as much as you like, and so on?

THE LORD: But of course. It *is* my home.

HARLEQUIN: You're not fooling me? They send you home for slander?

THE LORD: They often do, yes.

HARLEQUIN: *(Triumphant.)* Well then that's that, I'll slander someone at the first opportunity, tell Silvia and Flaminia to do the same, and we'll all three get the hell out of this place! From what I see around here, you're much better off being punished than honored.

THE LORD: Be that as it may, spare me *my* punishment, I beg of you. Besides, what I said about you didn't amount to anything.

HARLEQUIN: What *did* you say about me?

(A beat.)

THE LORD: Really, it was nothing.

HARLEQUIN: I'll be the judge of that.

THE LORD: I said that you seemed…well…naive. Simple, even. And very…*frank.*

HARLEQUIN: Well, what harm in that? I *seem* unrefined, and you *seem* refined, but can appearances be trusted? No! Especially at court, where no one's what he seems. Is that all you said?

THE LORD: No. I also said that when you speak to people you make a sort of…ridiculous spectacle of yourself.

HARLEQUIN: Well I look ridiculous to you, but you look ridiculous to me, and I think you're more ridiculous than—oh this is *ridiculous!* You don't *deserve* to get exiled for this!

THE LORD: Well then don't let me be. For you see, I am a true courtier: Certain people envy me my position here, and the only way I can secure the power to prevent them from weakening it, is to curry favor with the Prince and cultivate the friendship of those whose positions *I* envy.

HARLEQUIN: I would rather cultivate a field. There's probably less manure in it.

THE LORD: You are right, in essence. But one doesn't dare resent or defy them; one accommodates them, one is…suggestible, because it is only through them that one can get back at one's enemies.

HARLEQUIN: What a racket. You have to get slapped on one hand in order to have the privilege of slapping with the other. To see you all endlessly humbling yourselves, one would never think you were so proud and petty.

THE LORD: Now listen. You wouldn't have any trouble restoring me to favor, because you know Flaminia quite well, isn't that so?

HARLEQUIN: She is my *bosom* friend!

THE LORD: She is very much in the Prince's favor, she is the daughter of one of his most loyal servants. And it has occurred to me that if I made her fortune by marrying her to a cousin of mine in the country, who is my ward and who has *much* to offer her, it might restore me to the Prince's good graces.

HARLEQUIN: *(Jealous.)* To his, perhaps, but not to mine. Because I become irrational when people marry my friends—I brood, I lose my appetite, I hurl heavy knives at milkmaids. No, the country cousin will play no part in my drama!

THE LORD: But I thought you had Flaminia's best interests at heart.

HARLEQUIN: *(A sudden passionate outburst.)* I *do!* *(A long beat. Then Harlequin moves close to the Lord.)* If you will forget the cousin, I will promise to intercede for you, but *only* if you forget the cousin.

THE LORD: He is quite forgotten.

(Both are very still.)

THE LORD: I eagerly await the outcome. I leave you, Monsieur. *(The Lord takes his leave of Harlequin.)*

HARLEQUIN: *(Alone.)* I have influence. I can make people do what I want. *(He sees Flaminia enter.)* But not a word to Flaminia about the cousin!

SCENE VIII

FLAMINIA: My dear.

HARLEQUIN: Ah, my little cake!

FLAMINIA: Silvia follows close behind me.

HARLEQUIN: You should have come to tell me sooner, so we could have waited for her together, and had a chat.

SILVIA: *(From offstage.)* Harlequin!

SCENE IX

(Silvia enters, excited.)

HARLEQUIN: You came to see me!

SILVIA: I've just been trying on the most beautiful dress. If you saw me in it, you would think I'm very pretty, ask Flaminia. I'm telling you, if I wore clothes like that all the time, I'd really have the people around here in the palm of my hand. And they certainly wouldn't be able to call me gauche. Oh Harlequin, the seamstresses here are very good with their hands.

HARLEQUIN: Ah, m'love, they're not so good with their hands as you are shapely.

SILVIA: And I am not so shapely as you are kind.

FLAMINIA: And I am not so sad as I was, now that I see you both feeling better.

SILVIA: *(Still excited.)* I should say so! Since they're not getting in our way anymore, I'd just as soon be here as anywhere else. *(To Harlequin.)* What difference does it make whether we're here or there? People can be in love anywhere.

FLAMINIA: Indeed.

HARLEQUIN: *(Not pleased with Silvia's outlook.)* What do you mean they're not getting in our way? Ladies confess their love to you, you trip over servants, and they send people to beg your pardon for the least little thing they say about you. I've just had a formal apology from a lord. It took forever.

SILVIA: Really? I came here now to accept one from a lady. I hope it takes forever, too. She was very rude to me. It was thrilling. I'm dying to get back at her.

FLAMINIA: From now on if anyone offends either of you, you have only to tell me.

HARLEQUIN: Thank you! *(To Silvia.)* You see? Flaminia loves us like a brother and sister. And we love her back, don't we? We'll be like three peas in a pod!

(An awkward beat.)

SILVIA: Harlequin, you'll never guess who I saw here. My admirer, who came to see me in the village—the tall, handsome guardsman? He has a kind heart, just like you; I want you to be friends.

(A beat. Harlequin is unsure.)

HARLEQUIN: *(Offhanded.)* Yes! Fine! Why not?

SILVIA: After all, there's nothing wrong in his finding me…to his liking. All things being equal, the people who love us *are* better company than the ones who take no interest in us, isn't that true?

FLAMINIA: *(To Harlequin.)* Isn't it?

HARLEQUIN: *(Gaily.)* Yes! Of course! And Flaminia—is another example. She is loving, she takes an interest in us, and she's the best company imaginable!

FLAMINIA: Thank you Harlequin!

HARLEQUIN: We'll be like *four* peas in a pod!

(Another awkward beat. Silvia is unsure.)

SILVIA: Yes.

HARLEQUIN: *(Grasping at straws.)* So! Let's all go have a bite to eat.

SILVIA: You go, Harlequin. Since we can see each other as much as we like, it's silly not to take advantage of our freedom.

FLAMINIA: *(Moving past Harlequin and offstage.)* But the lady is here, good-bye!

SILVIA: Good-bye!

HARLEQUIN: *(To Silvia.)* Good-bye! *(Harlequin rushes away after Flaminia.)*

SILVIA: *(Perplexed.)* Good-bye.

SCENE X

(Silvia stands looking after them for a moment. The Prince ushers Lisette into the room and remains hidden from Silvia, listening. Lisette curtseys several times.)

SILVIA: *(Curt.)* Pray, don't make me so many curtseys, Madame, or I'll have to return them. And I do them so poorly, as you have been kind enough to point out to me.

LISETTE: *(Contrite.)* But you are more than worthy of my respect. The Prince has given me to understand that you have many admirable qualities. The court considers you extraordinary.

SILVIA: That will pass, people will tire of admiring me. And anyway, I'm not trying to *make* them admire me. It just so happens that I am pretty enough for the Prince, and that you are not.

LISETTE: Alas, this is so difficult for me.

SILVIA: And where is that witty repartee from this morning? Or have you lost your tongue now that you have to say something nice?

LISETTE: I just don't know what to say.

SILVIA: Well then don't say anything, because it's not going to change things. Call it pretty, call it ugly, my face is what it is, and it's staying that way.

Now what do you want? Didn't you already make your point? Or do you want to start all over again?

LISETTE: Spare me, Mademoiselle. The Prince has demanded that I offer you my heartfelt apology, and I beg you to accept it without humbling me any further.

(A beat. Silvia considers.)

SILVIA: Oh very well, let's call it quits. I *won't* humble you anymore. Humility doesn't seem to sit well with the people around here. And since resenting you would just make me mean, I'll pity your discomfort and forgive you.

(She takes Lisette's hand. The Prince exits, satisfied. Lisette sees him go.)

SILVIA: But why did you take it into your head to slight me?

LISETTE: *(Sincere, purposeful.)* I was sure that the Prince harbored certain... feelings for me, as I do for him, and I did not think my appearance unworthy of his interest. But I do understand now that it isn't only to appearances that men surrender.

SILVIA: *(Offended.)* I suppose you mean to say that because they surrender to me men must like only ugly or uncouth women?! You are jealous of me.

LISETTE: I am jealous, it is true.

SILVIA: And here I had forgiven you!

LISETTE: But I didn't mean it that way. I meant that I now realize that it is not only to a woman's superficial charms and skills that men surrender...but also to the beauty within her, to her heart. I am jealous of you because you have understood that, and I have not.

SILVIA: You want something from me.

LISETTE: I do. Since you do not love the Prince, help me to revive the feelings I believe he once had for me. I am sure that I don't *dis*please him, even now, and I might cure him of his feelings for you, if you would help me. You could write him a letter, he is not insensible. And then leave...without ever having to see him.

SILVIA: Leave...

LISETTE: Don't you *want* to leave?

(A long beat. These words echo in Silvia's heart.)

LISETTE: If you *don't* leave, the Prince will marry you, and you neither love him nor want him. Write to him, tell him you could never love him, and I'll help you get away. You'll be free within the hour.

SILVIA: But I can't leave...

LISETTE: But you *can!*

SILVIA: You don't understand.

LISETTE: There's nothing for you here.

SILVIA: *(Cornered.)* But...

LISETTE: You love Harlequin.

SILVIA: Harlequin…

LISETTE: And *I* love the Prince!

SILVIA: But don't you see? The Prince loves *me,* not you, and I have no reason to believe he will *stop* loving me. My advice to you is to forget him; he's dead set on me, and I don't think there's anything you could do to sway his heart.

LISETTE: But I still think I might.

SILVIA: You can't just rearrange people's affections!

LISETTE: Perhaps I am not so inept or so unattractive as you imply.

SILVIA: I thought you had learned that it takes more than beauty spots and subtle maneuvering to win a man!

LISETTE: *(Vulnerable, but defiant.)* I have learned to *love,* and when I see the Prince, he will see my heart, and he will see that it is a good heart.

SILVIA: Be that as it may, it is *my* heart he desires!

LISETTE: *(Pointed.)* Yet he will find in *my* heart what he would not be able to find in yours—a sure knowledge of what it wants, an ability to choose one man over another, and a readiness to give itself honestly!
(Silvia stops dead.)

SILVIA: How dare you! *(A beat.)* I will write to the Prince if you like. *(Defiant.)* But if I go, he will come after me!

LISETTE: *(Touching her heart.)* I shall do everything in my power to keep him here.

SILVIA: *(Distraught.)* Leave me!

LISETTE: I hope you will forget my indiscretion.

SILVIA: *(Bitterly.)* If you will just *leave,* I will forget you entirely.
(Lisette, very distraught, rushes away, passing Flaminia on her way out. Silvia cannot contain her distress.)

SCENE XI

FLAMINIA: Silvia, what is wrong? Are you crying?

SILVIA: I am *furious!* The lady came to beg my pardon for her effrontery, and without even seeming to do so, like a snake in the grass she attacked me again. She said that the Prince didn't like me for my looks, that my heart is not honest, that I don't know what I want! Don't I have good reason to cry?!
(Flaminia gives Silvia a handkerchief. Silvia dabs at her eyes.)

FLAMINIA: Silvia, if you don't do something to stop these women, you'll be sorry for the rest of your life. You could make every man here love you.

SILVIA: It's not that I don't want to, but Harlequin is holding me back!

FLAMINIA: I think I understand what you are saying—that with things as they are just now it is frustrating to be obliged to someone.

(Silvia nods yes.)

FLAMINIA: That it would be simpler to be free.

(Silvia nods yes.)

FLAMINIA: That you sometimes feel that you are mismatched, that your love is…misdirected, even.

SILVIA: Why did I have to meet the right man at the wrong time?

FLAMINIA: And is *Harlequin* going to respect you if you let these women walk all over you?

SILVIA: He won't love me as much, is that what you mean to say?

FLAMINIA: It could easily happen, I suppose.

SILVIA: That reminds me—don't you think he's been rather…negligent, since we've been here? I mean, a little while ago he just left me standing here, alone, to go *eat* something! A fine expression of devotion *that* is!

FLAMINIA: I noticed that too. But listen, since we are speaking frankly, and you mustn't tell him I said this, I must beg your trust and ask you something in earnest. *Do you really love him?*

SILVIA: Well…of course, yes, I love him. I have to.

FLAMINIA: Do you want to know what I think? You just don't seem to *go* together. You have taste, wit, elegance, refinement; and he has…a boorish quality, and *very* coarse manners. These attributes of yours, and those of his, are so much at odds that I cannot understand why you fell in love with him.

SILVIA: *(Gravely.)* Put yourself in my place. He lived in my village, he was my neighbor, he is funny, and I like to laugh. He used to make me laugh so sometimes, he followed me everywhere, he *loved* me. I grew accustomed to seeing him, I enjoyed being with him, and being with him became…a habit, and one habit led to another, and I also grew to love him. For want of something better, perhaps. He was the best man I knew. *(A beat.)* Though I could see clearly enough that he was given to drink and ate like a hog.

FLAMINIA: Not exactly the qualities one looks for in a suitor. But Silvia, what are you going to do about him? What will you decide?

SILVIA: *(Her anxiety returning.)* I don't know what I should do, what I should say. So many yesses and nos are running through my brain, but none can I grasp, none can I act upon. And then there's that *guardsman*…

FLAMINIA: *(Interrupting.)* And?

(A beat.)

SILVIA: I will tell you a secret. I don't know what has happened to me since I saw him again. He said such tender things to me, he spoke of his love so eloquently, so humbly, so gently, that he made me feel...sorry for him. And feeling that way makes me, well, uncertain.

FLAMINIA: Do you love him?

SILVIA: I don't know... *(Remorseful.)* I think of Harlequin.

FLAMINIA: This man is worthy of your love.

SILVIA: But I couldn't *think* of loving him, unless Harlequin fell in love with someone else and left me. Then, fine, I would have the right to tell him, "You leave me, I leave you, tit for tat." But I can't see that happening— he's so cheeky and outlandish, which of those women would have him?

(A beat. Flaminia considers this.)

FLAMINIA: May I tell *you* something?

(Silvia nods yes.)

FLAMINIA: I have always dreamed of living more simply, of living in the country. *(A beat.)* Harlequin *is* boorish, and I don't love him. But I don't hate him either. And given how I feel, and what I really want, and if he consented, perhaps I could...free you of him. And help you to have what *you* really want. *(Flaminia turns to look Silvia in the eye. A long beat.)*

SILVIA: *(Confused and distraught.)* But... *(Another long beat.)* ...what *do* I really want? I don't know. I search and search for the answer.

(The Prince enters, unseen by Silvia.)

FLAMINIA: You have a visitor.

(Silvia turns to see the Prince, who is still dressed as the guardsman. Flaminia whispers urgently in her ear.)

FLAMINIA: Try to make up your mind.

SCENE XII

(Flaminia curtseys to the Prince and leaves the room. Silvia and the Prince look at each other. A long beat.)

SILVIA: You've come back. You're going to tell me you love me again, and make me feel even worse.

THE PRINCE: I came to see if the lady did as she was bidden and offered you her apology.

(Silvia nods yes.)

THE PRINCE: And I came also to say...for my own part...I have been thinking... you gave me permission to love you, Silvia, but if my love bores or offends you, if I should displease you in any way, you have only to order me to quit your presence and never speak to you again, and I shall be silent, I shall leave you, and go as far away as you say. I shall suffer without complaining, for I am resolved to obey you in everything.

SILVIA: There, you see? You did just as I predicted, and I *do* feel worse. Oh, how am I supposed to send you away? How can you expect me to tell you never to speak to me if you speak to me like *this?*

THE PRINCE: You are mistress of my fate. What else can I do but try to please you, even if I *must* leave you forever?

SILVIA: *(Distraught.)* But what good is that going to do? If I tell you to go away, you will think that I hate you; if I tell you never to speak to me again, you will think that I take no interest in you, and if you thought these things you would be wrong. They would just distress you, and would I be any better off for having said them?

THE PRINCE: Then what should I do, Silvia? What do you want?

SILVIA: What do I want?! I'm waiting for someone to tell *me!* I'm no better informed on that subject than you. There is Harlequin, who loves me; there is the Prince, who begs for my heart; there is you, who deserves to have it; and there are those meddlesome women who make me want to show the world what I'm worth. The Prince makes me feel anxious, Harlequin makes me feel guilty, and you make me feel...absolutely *awful. You love me too much!* I wish I'd never met you, I can't think straight, I'm miserable.

THE PRINCE: Your words pierce my heart, Silvia. You are too much affected by my suffering. My love, limitless as it is, is not worth the pain it causes you, when I know you could never love me.

SILVIA: I could too love you—that wouldn't be difficult...*if I wanted to...*

THE PRINCE: *(Falling to his knees.)* But you do not. So allow me at least to lament always that I lost you.

SILVIA: *(At sixes and sevens.)* I am warning you, I won't be able to endure seeing you like this. I almost think you're doing it on purpose, but *why?* Oh Gods! Loving you, surrendering to you, would be easier by far than feeling as I do now! But I must stop, I must leave, because if you insist, I won't have anything to do with you anymore—that's all you gain by pressing your case!

(She rushes away, but the Prince catches her arm.)

THE PRINCE: *(Despairing.)* No! I won't be a burden to you anymore. You *do* want me to go away, I know your true desire. Farewell Silvia!

(He makes to leave; Silvia stops him.)

SILVIA: *(Crying out.)* Farewell? Where are you going? Stay! *That* is my true desire. Don't I know my heart better than you?

(A long beat. They look at each other.)

SILVIA: *(A cry.)* Don't I?!

THE PRINCE: I was trying to do what I thought you wanted!

SILVIA: What a mess this is! The situation is impossible! What about Harlequin? Oh why can't *you* be the Prince!

THE PRINCE: *(Moved.)* And if I *were* the Prince?

SILVIA: Well, I'd tell Harlequin that you were really the Prince, that you claimed your right as my sovereign, and that I couldn't presume to refuse you.

(A beat. The Prince is distraught.)

SILVIA: And that would be my excuse to him. *(Silvia's mind is racing, her heart full.)* But you're not the Prince, and anyway I wouldn't use that excuse for him—only for you.

THE PRINCE: *(Aside.)* God I love her! I must tell her…

SILVIA: What is it? Have I upset you? Oh don't misunderstand—I wish you were the Prince, but not because I desire a kingdom. I like you for *you,* just for you. But if you were the Prince, Harlequin would not have to know that I accepted you out of *love. (A beat.)* That's what I meant.

THE PRINCE: You could love me then?

(A beat.)

SILVIA: But I think it's really better that you're *not* the Prince, because if you were, I might be very tempted. And I could never bring myself to be unfaithful to Harlequin. *(Sadly.)* And that's that.

THE PRINCE: *(Aside.)* It isn't yet time. *(To Silvia.)* Silvia, I hope whatever good feelings you have for me will not change. Tonight the Prince plans a banquet for you; allow me to accompany you there, and to be with you as much as possible. At evening's end you will see the Prince, and he has charged me to tell you that you will be free to go home if by that time your heart does not speak on his behalf.

SILVIA: *(Brightening momentarily.)* Well there's not a chance that it will, so that's as good as a promise that I *can* go home. *(A beat.)* But when I do go home, will you come to visit me there? *(A beat.)* Who knows how things might turn out… *(A beat.)* Well…we'd best be off. Harlequin might come.

(They look at each other.)

(Fade to black.)

ACT III
INTERMEZZO

(Trivelin finds Flaminia alone. She is thinking. He stands with his hands behind his back and watches her for a moment.)

TRIVELIN: I…

FLAMINIA: *(Turning.)* Trivelin.

(A beat. They look at each other.)

TRIVELIN: I…

FLAMINIA: *(Interrupting.)* Trivelin, I have been thinking. I want you to tell Harlequin something for me. I want you to tell him that…you love me.

TRIVELIN: I…

FLAMINIA: *(Interrupting.)* We have known each other a long time, Trivelin, haven't we?

(Trivelin nods yes.)

FLAMINIA: So I can confide in you that I've grown fond of Harlequin. *(Dreamy.)* My sights that were so set on one kind of life now seem to be set on another. *(A beat.)* So rile him up! Leave no doubt in his mind. *(Whispered.)* He must love me.

TRIVELIN: I…

(Enter the Prince.)

FLAMINIA: *(To Trivelin.)* Go.

(Flaminia curtseys to the Prince and confers with him. He talks animatedly. Trivelin watches Flaminia, then turns upstage and walks sadly away. There is a small bouquet of flowers clutched in his hands.)

SCENE I

(The Prince and Flaminia continue their conference.)

FLAMINIA: Yes, My Lord, you were absolutely right not to tell her yet, in spite of whatever tender things she may have said to you. And don't worry, this delay won't spoil anything. If anything it will help, as it will give her time—time in which her feelings for you can take root. You'll soon have what you want.

THE PRINCE: Oh Flaminia, she is so…delicious.

FLAMINIA: She is, infinitely so.

THE PRINCE: I don't know anyone like her. I've never met anyone like her, anywhere. You know, when a woman is moved to say to me the words "I love you," it naturally gives me great pleasure. But Flaminia, that pleasure pales—it seems positively dull and old hat—when compared with the pleasure my conversations with Silvia have given me, even though she has never actually said the words, "I love you!"

FLAMINIA: Dare I ask you, Sire, to tell me some of what she did say?

THE PRINCE: I *can't*, I'm sorry—I am enchanted, I am…ravished, that's all I can tell you. It's like a beautiful dream in which things don't quite follow.

FLAMINIA: This is very promising indeed.

THE PRINCE: *You* heard her say how much it grieves her not to be able to love me. She as much as said to *me*, "If you love me for one moment longer, so help me God I shall have to love you back, so stop, I beg of you!"

FLAMINIA: Well that's even better than a confession.

THE PRINCE: *(Excited.)* I'll say it again and again, but the love of Silvia is truly what love is all about. All the other women I know are women of the world, whose cultivation, and artfulness, whose manners and preoccupation with honor, go against what is natural…get in the way. They've…*thought* about it too much. With Silvia it is the heart in all its purity that speaks; the instant a feeling comes to her, her heart shows it to me. Her *simplicity* is her art; *candor* is *her* standard of honor. All that's holding her back now are…her scruples.

FLAMINIA: She told me she *could* be unfaithful to Harlequin, but only if he were unfaithful to her.

THE PRINCE: So Flaminia, hurry up! Can he be conquered? Can he be wooed? Where does he stand?

FLAMINIA: To tell you the truth, My Lord, I think he's head over heels in love with me, but he doesn't realize it yet. As long as he can call me his beloved *"friend,"* he doesn't have to listen to his conscience, and he gets to enjoy love at the price of friendship. But he will soon be enlightened on the subject of where he stands.

THE PRINCE: Excellent!

FLAMINIA: Trivelin will excite his jealousy, I will tell him that I might lose my heart to him, that Lord will promise him your friendship, you will give it to him—the coup de grâce, and he will cede Silvia to you. Then, I think, this gambit will be over and our fears quelled. And I shall emerge from it all, Sire, both the conqueror and the conquered.

THE PRINCE: And why conquered?

FLAMINIA: Oh it's nothing of importance, just another little affair of the heart. You see, to amuse myself during the course of our intrigue, I've developed a sort of fondness for Harlequin, and now…

(Flaminia trails off. A beat.)

HARLEQUIN: *(Offstage.)* Bring me paper!

FLAMINIA: But here he comes!

HARLEQUIN: *(Still offstage.)* And a quill!

FLAMINIA: And he's not ready for you yet. Go!

(The Prince flees, Flaminia hides.)

SCENE II

(Trivelin and Harlequin enter, both of them brisk and short-tempered. Trivelin carries a writing desk. Flaminia listens from her hiding place.)

TRIVELIN: Well now, you asked for pen and paper. What do you want me to do with them?

HARLEQUIN: Don't rush me. Underling.

TRIVELIN: My time is yours.

(A beat. Harlequin paces.)

HARLEQUIN: Tell me, who is it who is feeding me here?

TRIVELIN: The Prince.

HARLEQUIN: I'm living so well, it makes me wonder…

TRIVELIN: Wonder what?

HARLEQUIN: Well, I'd hate to be running up a bill without knowing it.

(Trivelin laughs.)

HARLEQUIN: What are *you* laughing at?

TRIVELIN: Don't worry, My Lord, you can eat and drink all you want. It's on the house.

HARLEQUIN: Good! I am relieved. And another thing. Who's the person who handles the Prince's affairs?

TRIVELIN: That would be his secretary of state.

HARLEQUIN: I intend to send this person a letter, asking him to inform the Prince that it no longer interests me to dally here, and to find out when he'll be through with us. Whereupon! They should marry me and Silvia and unlock the gates, because I am used to coming and going as I please. Whereupon! We shall take up residence here with our friend Flaminia, who insists that we stay because of her fondness for…us. If the Prince agrees to these conditions and is still of a mind to feed us, then I shall stay, and enjoy what he feeds us even more than I do now.

TRIVELIN: But Sir, is it really necessary to mix Flaminia up in this business?

HARLEQUIN: It suits me to do so.

TRIVELIN: *(Sad.)* Oh God…

HARLEQUIN: What do you mean "Oh God?!" You are presumptuous for a flunky. Now raise your pen, and draw up my epistle!

TRIVELIN: *(Correcting Harlequin's pronunciation.)* Epistle.

HARLEQUIN: *(Pronouncing the word correctly, annoyed.)* Epistle!

TRIVELIN: *(Pen poised.)* Ready.

HARLEQUIN: *(Dictating.)* "Dear Sir…"

TRIVELIN: Stop! That won't quite do. You must say, "Very dear Sir," or "August Sir."

HARLEQUIN: Put them both in, he can choose. New sentence: "I am Harlequin. Your master will know the name…"

TRIVELIN: Wait, you must say, "His *Highness* will know…"

HARLEQUIN: Why, is the Prince unusually tall?

TRIVELIN: No, it is on account of his *eminence* that we call him "Your Highness."

HARLEQUIN: Well as I have never seen him, I think I shall call him, "Your Minus."

TRIVELIN: I shall write what you say.

HARLEQUIN: Good.

TRIVELIN: Onward.

HARLEQUIN: *(Dictating again.)* "He will also know that I have a sweetheart whose name is Silvia, a person from my village, and as honest a girl as could be found; *and* that we have recently made a friend, Flaminia, who can't live without us, nor we without her. Therefore, immediately upon receipt of this letter…"

(Trivelin pushes the writing desk to the floor.)

TRIVELIN: *(Distraught.)* Flaminia can't live without you? Ah! The pen falls from my hand… *(Trivelin collapses.)*

HARLEQUIN: What, sleeping? Have you lost possession of your… Are you *incontinent?!*

TRIVELIN: I cannot say it…

HARLEQUIN: You must!

TRIVELIN: I won't!

HARLEQUIN: You will!

TRIVELIN: I shan't!

HARLEQUIN: You shall!

TRIVELIN: I can't!

HARLEQUIN: *(Drawing forth his bat.)* Then die!

TRIVELIN: For two years, My Lord…for two *years* I have pined for Flaminia!

HARLEQUIN: No!

TRIVELIN: But I haven't ever told her!

HARLEQUIN: *(Raising his bat.)* And I'll thank you *never* to tell her!

TRIVELIN: *(Humiliated and enraged.)* Well I have no use for your thanks!

What's it to you if I love her? You don't care about her as I do, you're only her friend. Friendship shouldn't make you jealous.

HARLEQUIN: *(Threatening Trivelin.)* Well it does! Friendship has the same effect on *me* as love has! And here's the proof!

TRIVELIN: *(A heartfelt cry.)* Then a pox on friendship! A pox on love!

(Trivelin runs away. Harlequin calls after him.)

HARLEQUIN: And don't you dare betray her to the Prince!

SCENE III

(Flaminia secretly emerged from hiding, rushes to Harlequin.)

FLAMINIA: Harlequin, what's going on? What's wrong?

HARLEQUIN: That miscreant says that he has loved you for two years!

FLAMINIA: That could well be.

HARLEQUIN: And what do you have to say to that?

FLAMINIA: Too bad for him.

HARLEQUIN: Seriously?

FLAMINIA: Absolutely. But would you really be bothered if someone loved me?

HARLEQUIN: Alas, dear *friend,* you are your own woman; but if you *had* a lover, you would love the lover perhaps, and that would spoil the lovely affection you feel for me. You would give me a smaller share of your friendship, and I wouldn't want to lose any of what I enjoy now.

FLAMINIA: Harlequin, perhaps you are being careless with my heart.

HARLEQUIN: Me? How? That's the *opposite* of what I meant to do!

FLAMINIA: If you go on forever talking to me in this manner, pretty soon I won't know anymore exactly what my feelings *are* for you. To be honest I don't dare examine them too closely; I might discover more than I want to find!

HARLEQUIN: Then don't! Don't *ever* examine them, Flaminia. Let things just…fall where they may. But don't ever take a lover, either. I have one, and I'm keeping her, but if I didn't have one, I wouldn't go looking for one, because what would I do about *you?* She would be…inconvenient.

FLAMINIA: Ah, how am I supposed to remain your *friend* when you say these things?

HARLEQUIN: What *else* would you be?

FLAMINIA: Don't ask me, I don't want to know! What I *do* know is that I don't love anyone in the world more than you, and *you* can't say that much: Silvia comes first, and that's as it must be…

HARLEQUIN: *(Afraid he has hurt her.)* Oh no, don't say that! You *both* come
first.

FLAMINIA: I was looking for her now. If I find her, shall I send her to you?
Would that make you happy?

HARLEQUIN: *(Grasping at straws.)* Whatever you want...well, no, don't send
her alone, you should come back *with* her!

FLAMINIA: I cannot, because the Prince has sent for me. Good-bye Harlequin, I
shall return! *(Flaminia rushes away.)*

HARLEQUIN: Oh no!

(The Lord enters.)

SCENE IV

THE LORD: Monsieur Harlequin.

HARLEQUIN: *(Agitated, impatient.)* Great heavens, Monsieur Mudslinger! I
never did get your other name. I haven't yet said anything to the Prince
on your behalf, for the simple reason that I have never met him.

THE LORD: I am obliged to you for your kind intentions, Monsieur Harlequin,
but I have restored myself to the Prince's favor by the mere *promise* of
your intercession on my behalf; so I hope you will make good my promise
to him by making good yours to me.

HARLEQUIN: Well, I know I seem naive and ridiculous, but I am a man of my
word.

THE LORD: *Please* forget what went before and be reconciled with me, if only
in consideration of the gift I bring you from the Prince. And of all the
gifts he could make you it is the finest.

HARLEQUIN: *(Brightening.)* Oh, so it's Silvia!

THE LORD: No, the gift in question is in my pocket. *(The Lord produces a sheaf
of papers.)* These documents establish your nobility, which the Prince
bestows on you as a relative of Silvia. Apparently all the people in the
villages are somewhat related?

HARLEQUIN: At the moment I am not in the *least* related to Silvia, though I
will be soon. Take the papers back, I can't accept them on *that* pretext.

THE LORD: But accept them you must. Why not, after all? It will please the
Prince. Would you refuse what is the ambition of every...person
of...character?

HARLEQUIN: Well, I'm a character, but I don't want your papers, and although
I have heard people speak of it, I don't even know what ambition *is*.
What is it?

THE LORD: Ambition?

HARLEQUIN: *(In assent.)* Mmmm.

THE LORD: Ambition is the…noble pride one takes in rising in the world.

HARLEQUIN: I rise every morning, but I wouldn't say it made me *proud*. And since when is it noble to be proud?

THE LORD: You're not understanding me. More simply put: Ambition is the desire…to be thought well of.

HARLEQUIN: That definition is no better than the last one, I can just *tell*.

(The Lord snaps the papers at Harlequin. The conversation grows increasingly heated.)

THE LORD: Take them, I beg of you. Wouldn't you enjoy being a *gentleman*?

HARLEQUIN: Maybe, maybe not.

THE LORD: You would find you have an advantage. You would be respected and feared by your neighbors.

HARLEQUIN: But then they wouldn't *love* me, because when I respect people *and* fear them, there's no time left over to love them. And anyhow I can't do so many things at the same time.

THE LORD: You astound me.

HARLEQUIN: Yes, I am astounding, am I not? I just came out that way. I am a nice person, the nicest person in the world. I wouldn't hurt a flea, and even if I wanted to, I don't have the influence to manage it. But if I *did*, if I were a nobleman like you, I still wouldn't want to *have* to be nice all the time. Because every now and then I'd want to do as the gentlemen in *our* neck of the woods do: just give someone a good smack without worrying about who he is, or if he fears me, or if he's in a position to smack me back.

THE LORD: But *if* someone smacked you, wouldn't you *want* to be in a position to smack him back?

HARLEQUIN: Of course I would!

THE LORD: Well then, since men are sometimes wicked, you should do what you can to be in a position to smack them *conclusively*, so that they won't even *think* of smacking you in the first place. And these papers of nobility will put you in the safest position. *(The Lord thrusts out the papers.)*

HARLEQUIN: *(Snatching them, exasperated.)* Oh all right fine, I'm noble!

THE LORD: *(Turning immediately to go.)* I am delighted that you are now content. Good day to Your Lordship.

HARLEQUIN: Good day to yours.

(The Lord is gone. The Prince has appeared.)

SCENE V

THE PRINCE: Harlequin!

HARLEQUIN: Ah *you!* Our royal guardsman, who goes around telling princes that people's sweethearts are pretty, and who causes mine to be pilfered from me! Informer! Scandalmonger!

(The Prince is surprised by Harlequin's anger.)

THE PRINCE: Harlequin...

HARLEQUIN: I'm going to tell you what you deserve, and you're going to have to smack me, and I'm going to have to smack you back!

THE PRINCE: *Please* calm down Harlequin!

HARLEQUIN: *(Furious.)* No!

THE PRINCE: Please hear me with an open heart. *(A beat.)* You must know sooner or later who I am. Your Prince himself addresses you, and not an officer of the guard, as you, and also Silvia, have believed.

HARLEQUIN: Are you telling the truth?

THE PRINCE: You must believe me.

(A long beat, in which Harlequin understands and takes stock of events.)

HARLEQUIN: *(Suddenly bowing low, with great gravity and humility.)* Pardon me, Sire, I have been a fool to be impertinent to you.

THE PRINCE: *(Warm.)* I pardon you gladly.

HARLEQUIN: *(Sad.)* Since you bear me no ill will, I can hardly bear you any. I am too...simple to presume to be angry with a prince. If you wrong me I shall cry my heart out, but that is all I could do. Perhaps that will merit your royal compassion. *(A beat.)* But...I do not believe that you would want to rule for your peace of mind alone.

THE PRINCE: *(Averting his eyes.)* Do you have reason to complain of me then, Harlequin?

HARLEQUIN: What else *can* I do, My Lord? I have one beloved girl who loves me, you have a palace full of them; yet even so you take mine away from me. Look at it in this way: I am poor, and have but a penny, you are rich in all things; yet you covet my tiny fortune and wrest from me my solitary penny. This is sad, is it not?

THE PRINCE: *(Aside.)* He is right, and I feel his sorrow.

HARLEQUIN: I know you are a good prince, everyone in the country says so. I alone would be deprived of the pleasure of agreeing with them.

THE PRINCE: I am taking Silvia from you, it is true. But ask of me *anything* you want, I offer you the wealth of my kingdom, in exchange for the only penny of it that I care about.

HARLEQUIN: But this is an unfair trade: You gain much more than I do. Let us speak candidly. If someone other than you had taken Silvia from me, wouldn't you make that person give her back? This is the perfect opportunity to show that justice is for everyone.

THE PRINCE: *(Aside.)* How to answer him? What can I say?

HARLEQUIN: Well My Lord, you can say this: "Ought I to withhold happiness from this simple man because I have the power to do so? Isn't it up to me, isn't it my duty as his ruler and protector to protect his rights? Can I let him leave here without justice? Wouldn't I regret it if I did? Who will fulfill the sacred trust of my office if I do not? I have no choice, then, but to sacrifice my own pleasure and order that Silvia be returned to him."

THE PRINCE: *(Upset.)* Do you never change your tune? Notice how I am handling the matter with you. I could have sent you away and kept Silvia without even hearing your side. However, despite the feelings I have for her, despite your tenacity and the little deference you show me, I take an interest in you and am concerned by your anguish. I have tried to assuage it by offering you wealth, privileges, and my protection, and now I am kneeling and begging you to give Silvia to me out of the kindness of your good heart. Everyone encourages you to do so, everyone criticizes and reprimands you for refusing and tries to impress on you that it is important to please me, and what pleasing me can mean to you, yet still you resist. You say that I am your Prince; give evidence of it!

HARLEQUIN: *(With great sadness.)* Ah My Lord, don't put your trust in those people who tell you that you are right to ask this of me, because they are flattering and deluding you. If it weren't for these people, you wouldn't be trying to trick me; you wouldn't be saying that I lack respect for you because I stand up for what is rightfully mine. Yes, you are my prince, and I love you well, but I am your subject, and that is worth something.

THE PRINCE: *(Distraught.)* Go, you're breaking my heart.

HARLEQUIN: Because my situation is truly pitiable.

THE PRINCE: *(Crumbling.)* Must I renounce Silvia? But how can I win her love if you will not help me? Harlequin, I have caused you terrible grief, but what you are causing me is even worse.

HARLEQUIN: *(Concerned for the Prince.)* Take heart, My Lord. Go for a walk, go on a journey. Your grief will pass with time.

THE PRINCE: *(Desperate.)* No, my friend, it will *never* pass! I was hoping you would find it in your heart to pity me. But you have hurt me as no one has hurt me before. Go, it doesn't matter!

HARLEQUIN: *(Teary-eyed.)* Ah! Life is hard!

THE PRINCE: *(Moved to tears.)* It is true that I have wronged you! I reproach myself for what I have done to you! It is unjust, but you are already well avenged for it!

HARLEQUIN: You are so sad to have wronged me that I am sad for *you!* I am afraid I am beginning to see your side of it.

THE PRINCE: *(An outcry.)* No, you should be happy, it *is* your right. You have asked for justice: I *shall* sacrifice my pleasure, all my peace of mind, for your happiness... She is yours!

HARLEQUIN: You have such compassion for me; oughtn't I to have some for you?

THE PRINCE: Don't concern yourself with me.

HARLEQUIN: *(Stricken with remorse.)* How difficult this is! His heart is breaking!

THE PRINCE: *(Embracing Harlequin.)* I am grateful to you for the sensitivity you have shown me. Farewell, friend, I shall respect you despite your refusal.

(They embrace. A beat. The Prince turns to go. Harlequin takes a step or two after him.)

HARLEQUIN: My Lord...

THE PRINCE: *(Turning back.)* Yes?

(A beat. The Prince sees that Harlequin is struggling with himself.)

THE PRINCE: What do you want?

HARLEQUIN: I don't know...how to give you what *you* want.

THE PRINCE: You *do* have the kindest heart.

HARLEQUIN: So do you. How weak good people can be.

THE PRINCE: You speak the truth. I admire you.

HARLEQUIN: I believe you. *(A beat.)* But if I did give Silvia to you, do you really intend to give me your friendship?

THE PRINCE: How could I not?

HARLEQUIN: *(Worried.)* They told me you were accustomed to being flattered by your friends, and I am accustomed to saying what I think. I don't think our ideas of friendship are compatible.

THE PRINCE: We will be friends *only* if you always say what you think. *(A beat.)* Harlequin, remember that I love you, that is all I ask. *(The Prince walks to the door.)*

HARLEQUIN: And would Flaminia be free to do as she chooses?

(The Prince spins around and looks at Harlequin. A beat.)

THE PRINCE: *(Suddenly cold.)* Don't talk to me about Flaminia. If it hadn't been for her meddling, you might not have caused me so much grief.

(Exit the Prince. Harlequin calls after him.)

HARLEQUIN: *(Plaintive.)* But she didn't do anything wrong! You shouldn't wish her ill! She's the best woman in the world!

SCENE VI

HARLEQUIN: Oh *no!* That rascal Trivelin must have betrayed her! I'd better go find her! *(He starts off, then stops short, deep in his thought.)* But...but what should *I* do now? Should I give up Silvia? *Could* I? But how? Upon my faith, no. *(A beat.)* No. *(A beat. Softly.)* I made a bit of a fool of myself with the Prince just now. Because I am so sensitive to the suffering of others. But he is sensitive, too, and he wouldn't tell anyone what passed between us. No one will ever know that I am... *(Whispered.)* ...uncertain.

SCENE VII

(Flaminia rushes in. She appears desperate.)

FLAMINIA: Good-bye, Harlequin!

HARLEQUIN: What do you mean *good-bye?*

FLAMINIA: Trivelin betrayed us. The Prince knows I have helped you and Silvia behind his back. He has ordered me to leave the palace and forbidden me to see you again. But I had to speak to you one last time, then I shall depart, and run and run until I feel his wrath no more!

HARLEQUIN: *(Aggrieved.)* Oh that's wonderful, that's grand.

FLAMINIA: I am disconsolate! To be separated forever from you, from all that I hold dear. There is no time, I must fly, but before I go I must open my heart to you.

(Harlequin gasps for breath.)

HARLEQUIN: What is it, benighted friend? What is in this dear heart of yours?

FLAMINIA: It is not friendship at all that I have felt for you, Harlequin, I was deceiving myself.

HARLEQUIN: *(Breathless.)* Is it...*love?*

FLAMINIA: The very tenderest love. Farewell!

(She moves away. Harlequin trembles in the moment of decision. A beat.)

HARLEQUIN: Wait! Maybe I was deceiving myself, too!

FLAMINIA: What? You too? We love each other, and now we can't see each other anymore?! Harlequin, I can't bear it. I must escape!

(Again she flees, again he catches her. They are breathless.)

HARLEQUIN: Stay!

FLAMINIA: What shall we do?

HARLEQUIN: Discuss it like grown-up people!

FLAMINIA: But what can I *say?!*

HARLEQUIN: That your friendship, like mine, is gone. And that, well, I love you, I guess. There, that's decided, and I don't understand any of it, it's all gone too fast for me.

FLAMINIA: Such *things!* What's to be *done?*

HARLEQUIN: I'm not *married,* for heaven's sake!

FLAMINIA: That's something.

HARLEQUIN: I guess Silvia will probably marry the Prince, and he will be… happy…probably.

FLAMINIA: Probably.

HARLEQUIN: And so, since our hearts were beating…mistakenly, and since we love each other rather…inadvertently, we will have to be patient and, well, adjust to our…predicament…accordingly.

FLAMINIA: *(Thrilled.)* I understand! You mean to say that we will be married.

HARLEQUIN: Yes! *(Aside, cornered.)* Oh, is it really my *fault? (To Flaminia.)* Why didn't you warn me that you would snare me and become my sweetheart?

FLAMINIA: Did you warn me that you would become my lover?

HARLEQUIN: Did *I* know?!

FLAMINIA: You were adorable enough to suspect *something,* weren't you?

HARLEQUIN: Well if it's a matter of being adorable, you're more to blame than I!

FLAMINIA: Marry me. I give you my hand. But there's no time to lose—I'm afraid they'll come any second and throw me out.

HARLEQUIN: I must take this up with the Prince immediately! Don't tell Silvia I love you. She will think that I did something wrong, and it's perfectly obvious that I didn't know I was doing it. I won't let on either: I'll tell her that it's for her great fortune that I'm giving her up.

FLAMINIA: Good! That's just what I was going to suggest.

HARLEQUIN: Give me your hand, that I might kiss it. *(He seizes her hand and kisses it.)* Who would have believed that I would take it in mine with such pleasure? I am so…perplexed.

(They hear the rustle of skirts and freeze.)

FLAMINIA: It is Silvia! Run for your life!

(Harlequin leaps away with a cry.)

SCENE VIII

FLAMINIA: The Prince is right, the way these little people make love is absolutely irresistible.

(Silvia enters, preoccupied.)

FLAMINIA: What are you contemplating so intently, Silvia?

SILVIA: *(Rapt.)* It was a love that just…*happened* to me. And now, it is a love that has…ceased…to happen. *It* came to *me,* not of my will or choosing, but because it was there. And now, it is going away in the same way. But sometimes I am afraid he will be absolutely devastated. *(A beat.)* And I don't think I am to blame, somehow.

FLAMINIA: *(With a compassionate little laugh.)* You are definitely not to blame for what has happened.

SILVIA: You laugh, but I'd like to see *you* in my place!

(A beat. The Prince enters, unseen by Silvia.)

FLAMINIA: He is here. Listen to me, do what you must do with him. And don't worry about…the rest.

(Flaminia leaves. The Prince comes forward. Silvia, confused, avoids his eyes.)

SCENE IX

THE PRINCE: What's this, Silvia? You won't look at me? You grow melancholy every time I come near; and every time I come near I think you'd rather I didn't.

SILVIA: *(At a loss.)* Rather you didn't…yes… *(A beat.)* I've just been thinking about you.

THE PRINCE: And what were you thinking about me, my beautiful Silvia?

SILVIA: Tell me something, you are an honest man, and I'm sure you will tell me the truth. You know where things stand with me and Harlequin; now, if I felt like loving you, and if I satisfied that desire, would I be doing the right thing? Or not?

THE PRINCE: Since we cannot always control the way our feelings…change, I suppose that if you felt like loving me, you would be within your rights…to satisfy that desire. That is my opinion.

SILVIA: And you are speaking as a friend? Sincerely?

THE PRINCE: I am speaking to you in all sincerity, Silvia, as an honest man.

SILVIA: Well that is my opinion, too. I've come to the same conclusion, and I believe we are right. So, *if* I feel like it, I *will* love you, and not let my heart argue against it.

THE PRINCE: But you *don't* feel like it, so what have I gained?

SILVIA: Now don't you start telling me what I'm feeling, because I'm not at all sure I trust you… *(A beat.)* …to see clearly. But now this Prince—since I must deal with him, when is he going to put in an appearance? Not that I'm looking forward to it.

THE PRINCE: Whenever he comes, it will be too soon for my liking.

SILVIA: Now you're afraid. Oh, take heart! Honestly, sometimes I think you've taken a vow to be depressed.

THE PRINCE: I admit that, right now, I am afraid.

SILVIA: What a man! Well I can reassure you: Fear not, whoever and whatever the Prince turns out to be, *I shall never love him.* I solemnly swear not...

THE PRINCE: *(Interrupting her.)* Stop Silvia, don't swear that, I implore you!

SILVIA: Here I swear an oath for you, and you don't want that either! You are impossible! What do you *want?*

THE PRINCE: I don't want you to swear an oath *against* me.

SILVIA: Against you...

(Both are silent for a beat. Silvia realizes. Then she spins to face him.)

SILVIA: Are you the Prince...Sir?

THE PRINCE: Yes, Silvia.

(Silvia drops to the floor in a deep curtsey.)

THE PRINCE: I wanted to win your love with love, and only love. And so my love is all I revealed to you. I could not have enjoyed your love without knowing that it was given freely, without the pleasure that that knowledge gives. Now that you know me, you are free to refuse my hand, and my heart, or to accept both. What do *you* want, Silvia?

SILVIA: My dear Prince, I was going to swear such a *pretty* oath... *(Silvia moves slowly toward the Prince and, at length, reaches out to touch him.)* This is what I want.

THE PRINCE: Then you shall have it.

SCENE X

(Harlequin enters and removes his hat.)

HARLEQUIN: I heard everything, Silvia.

(Silvia turns to see him. A beat.)

SILVIA: Well, Harlequin, then I'll be spared the difficulty of having to tell you what has happened. You'll have to find consolation where you can— perhaps the Prince can help you. My heart is too...full. Oh Harlequin, reconcile yourself to it, there's no reasoning with me about it, it's as simple as that. What would you say to me? That I am leaving you. What would I answer? That I know it. Let's just say that you said it, and that I answered. Put me behind you, and so...it's over.

(A long beat. Harlequin stands alone, his hat in his hands. Flaminia enters.)

THE PRINCE: Flaminia, I deliver Harlequin into your care. I value him, and I mean to honor him accordingly. *(He approaches Harlequin.)* You,

Harlequin, accept Flaminia, as your betrothed. And be forever assured of the gratitude and love of your prince. *(He turns to Silvia.)* My beloved, my beautiful Silvia, our celebration will proclaim my happiness to the people of this land, of whom—as of my heart—you are now sovereign. *(He kisses Silvia's hand.)*

HARLEQUIN: What sport. Friendship played a trick on me. But one of these days I'll be back on top. *(He fights to master his feelings.)* Hold on, heart.
(The Prince and Silvia leave together, and Harlequin watches them go. Flaminia watches Harlequin quietly, then draws him gently to a seat at the window. He eventually sits down next to her, but he is lost in his own world. He rests his head against her shoulder.)
(Fade to black.)

END OF PLAY

PLATE I

The Prince dressed as the guardsman
Robert Sean Leonard in *Changes of Heart*, McCarter Theatre 1994

Photo by T. Charles Erickson

PLATE 2

Trivelin urges Silvia to yield to the Prince's blandishments (I,1)
Natacha Roi and Laurence O'Dwyer in *Changes of Heart,* McCarter Theatre 1994

PLATE 3

Flaminia deconstructs Lisette's coquetry (I,3)
Mary Lou Rosato and Sheryl Taub in *Changes of Heart*, McCarter Theatre 1994

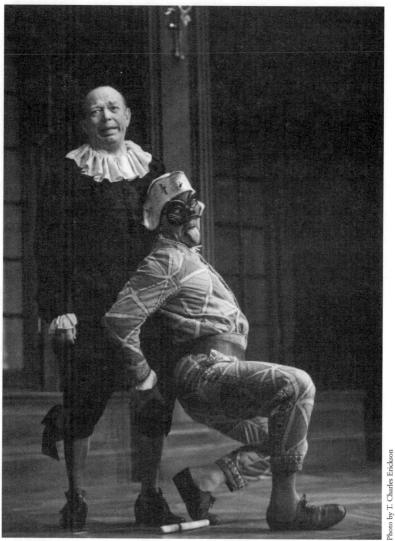

PLATE 4

Trivelin conquers Harlequin with a litany of food (I,4)
O'Dwyer and John Michael Higgins in *Changes of Heart,* McCarter Theatre 1994

PLATE 5

Harlequin sees Lisette for exactly what she is (I,6)
Higgins and Taub in *Changes of Heart,* McCarter Theatre 1994

PLATE 6

Harlequin and Silvia are at first leery of Flaminia (I,11)
Rosato, Higgins, and Roi in *Changes of Heart,* McCarter Theatre 1994

PLATE 7

Harlequin and Silvia are "left alone" by the intriguers (I,12)
Roi, Higgins, Leonard, O'Dwyer, Rosato in *Changes of Heart,* McCarter Theatre 1994

PLATE 8

Harlequin invites Flaminia to dine, to Trivelin's dismay (I,13)
Rosato, Higgins, and O'Dwyer in *Changes of Heart,* McCarter Theatre 1994

PLATE 9

Flaminia, Trivelin, and Harlequin find Harlequin hilarious (II,5)
Rosato, Higgins, and Taub in *Changes of Heart,* Mark Taper Forum, 1996

PLATE 10

Harlequin and Flaminia are alone for the first time (II,6)

Higgins and Rosato in *Changes of Heart,* McCarter Theatre 1994

PLATE 11

Harlequin and Flaminia (II,6)

Higgins and Rosato in *Changes of Heart,* McCarter Theatre 1994

PLATE 12

Harlequin caught between loves (II,9)

Rosato, Higgins, and Roi in *Changes of Heart,* McCarter Theatre 1994

PLATE 13

Flaminia: "Perhaps I could…free you of him,
and help you to have what you really want." (II,11)

Rosato and Roi in *Changes of Heart,* McCarter Theatre 1994

PLATE 14

Silvia: "Oh why can't you be the Prince?" (II,12)
Leonard and Roi in *Changes of Heart,* McCarter Theatre 1994

PLATE 15

Trivelin's confession (III,2)
O'Dwyer and Higgins in *Changes of Heart,* McCarter Theatre 1994

PLATE 16

Flaminia and Harlequin despair of a solution (III,7)
Rosato and Higgins in *Changes of Heart,* McCarter Theatre 1994

Photo by T. Charles Erickson

PLATE 17

Silvia expresses her true desire to the Prince (III,9)
Roi and Leonard in *Changes of Heart*, McCarter Theatre 1994

PLATE 18

Harlequin and the Prince: compassion (III,5)
Higgins and Leonard in *Changes of Heart,* McCarter Theatre 1994

PLATE 19

Flaminia and Harlequin at the end of the day (III,10)
Rosato and Higgins in *Changes of Heart,* McCarter Theatre 1994

Photo by T. Charles Erickson

PLATE 20

Sheryl Taub with Stephen Wadsworth in rehearsal
Changes of Heart, McCarter Theatre 1994

The Game of
Love and Chance

1730

For Brigitta and Paul, who can still feel emotion,
and Tyne, who gets it.

ORIGINAL PRODUCTION

The Game of Love and Chance was played for the first time by the Comédie Italienne in Paris on January 23, 1730, with Marivaux's remarkable *première amoureuse* Silvia in another of the roles he named for her. Tomasso Vicentini was again Harlequin, his wife Violette again Lisette. Dorante was probably played by François Riccoboni (son of the troupe's leaders, who had created the roles of Flaminia and the Prince in *Changes of Heart* and were now on leave in Italy), Mario probably by Antoine Balletti, and Orgon probably by Domenico Biancolelli.

This adaptation was originally commissioned and produced, as *The Game of Love and Chance* by the McCarter Theatre in Princeton, New Jersey, on May 9, 1997, with the following cast and creative contributors:

SILVIA. . . . . Francesca Faridany
LISETTE. . . . . Margaret Welsh
DORANTE . . . . Neil Maffin
HARLEQUIN . . . . John Michael Higgins
ORGON . . . . Laurence O'Dwyer
MARIO. . . . . Jared Reed
ORGON'S VALET . . . . Reid Armbruster

Director . . . . Stephen Wadsworth
Set Designer . . . . Thomas Lynch
Costume Designer . . . . Martin Pakledinaz
Lighting Designer. . . . . Peter Kaczorowski
Production Stage Manager. . . . . Mary Sue Gregson

Artistic Director, McCarter Theatre. . . . . Emily Mann
Staff Producer . . . . Mara Isaacs
Dramaturg. . . . . Janice Paran

This version of *The Game of Love and Chance* was developed further in a 1997 run at the Huntington Theatre Company, Boston, Peter Altman, Artistic Director.

CHARACTERS

SILVIA

LISETTE: Silvia's chambermaid

MONSIEUR ORGON: Silvia's father

MARIO: Silvia's brother

DORANTE: Silvia's intended

HARLEQUIN: Dorante's valet

A VALET: in the employ of Monsieur Orgon

SETTING

The action takes place at Monsieur Orgon's house in or near Paris.

ACT I
SCENE I

(It is morning. Silvia and Lisette are talking animatedly.)

SILVIA: I shall ask you one more time, why are you interfering? What makes you so sure of my feelings that you can answer for them?

LISETTE: Well you see, Madame, I thought that, at least in this case, your feelings would resemble anyone else's. Monsieur your father asks me if you're pleased that he's marrying you off, and I assume you are happy about it, so I tell him yes.

(Silvia is appalled.)

LISETTE: Well *naturally* I assumed. You know, you are possibly the only unmarried girl on this earth for whom that yes would not be valid. *No* simply isn't natural.

SILVIA: Isn't natural, that is so utterly stupid. I take it you think marriage has some sort of magic power?

LISETTE: Well since you ask, uh…yes.

SILVIA: Oh be quiet. Go air your idiotic ideas somewhere else. You should know better than to make assumptions about my heart based on yours.

LISETTE: My heart is just like everyone else's, why must yours take it into its head to be different?

SILVIA: *(To the air.)* I tell you, if she dared, she'd say I was an eccentric.

LISETTE: Were I your equal, I just might.

SILVIA: You are trying to annoy me, Lisette.

LISETTE: That's not at all what I'm trying to do, Madame. Look, what harm have I done, really, telling Monsieur Orgon you'd be glad to get married?

SILVIA: To begin with, it's not the truth. I happen to enjoy being *un*married

LISETTE: Well *that's* an interesting point of view.

SILVIA: And it is hardly necessary for my father to think that by marrying me off he's making me happy. Because he will then set about the thing confidently, and all perhaps to no avail.

LISETTE: You mean you won't marry the person he has chosen for you?

SILVIA: How do I know? Perhaps the person won't suit me. And that worries me.

LISETTE: They say that he's one of the most refined young men imaginable, that he's well-built, good-looking, charming, that he couldn't be more intelligent or have a nobler character. What more do you want? Can you imagine a more perfectly delicious setup?

SILVIA: Delicious! The way you put things is so ridiculous.

LISETTE: Come now Madame, it's lucky that a suitor of his caliber would consent to get married at all. Most of the girls he courts would probably end up marrying him, how shall I say, without a ceremony. Handsome and well put-together—that's what gets love going; clever and companionable—that's what makes it last. For God's sake, *everything's* bound to be good with this man, he's got it all. One could combine business with pleasure.

SILVIA: One could, yes, if he resembles the portrait you paint of him. And they say he does, but that's only what *they* say, and *I* might very well disagree with them. He's a handsome man, *they say,* but that's not necessarily in his favor. In fact it's sort of too bad.

LISETTE: Sort of too bad! But this is really a *highly* irregular way of thinking.

SILVIA: It is a very sensible way of thinking. A handsome man is all too often conceited, I've noticed that.

LISETTE: Well he's wrong to be conceited. But he's right to be handsome.

SILVIA: And, *they say,* he's well put-together. Be that as it may.

LISETTE: Indeed, that we can forgive him.

SILVIA: But I can live without handsome and well put-together. Those are dispensable amenities.

LISETTE: So help me God, if I ever marry, those amenities will be *in*dispensable.

SILVIA: You don't know what you're talking about. In a marriage, it's the *reasonable* part of a man which one deals with most of the time—much more than the attractive part. I require of a man only that he have a good nature, and that is more difficult to find than you might think. *They* always said about Monsieur Ergaste, "Our neighbor has such a sensible, sociable, gallant air about him, the air of a truly reasonable man." "And that is exactly what he is," *they* said back. I said so myself. His face never lies, it's totally open and candid, sweet, and considerate. But don't you believe it, because a quarter of an hour later it changes into a sullen, surly, *vicious* expression that every member of his household dreads. We see the nice face, but his wife sees only the nasty one.

LISETTE: What a bizarre person, with the two faces.

SILVIA: And isn't Léandre charming when we pass him in the street! Well he doesn't laugh at *home;* he is solitary, inaccessible, and ice-cold. His wife doesn't know him at all, she has absolutely no business with him—no intimacy, no communication. Everyone who comes anywhere near him gets depressed and practically dies of frostbite. It must be fun to be married to *him,* don't you think?

LISETTE: You're giving me the shivers.

SILVIA: And then there's Tersandre! When I got *there* the other day he had just blown up at his wife. I arrive, I am announced, and the man comes toward me with his arms flung wide, serene, and relaxed. The cad! And does anyone think for a moment that his wife is very much to be pitied because of him? I found her completely demoralized, ashen, her eyes red from crying. She was the very portrait of what I could so easily become. I pitied her, Lisette. I'd hate to make you feel as sorry for me as I did for her. It's awful, don't you think? Consider what a husband really is.

LISETTE: A husband is a husband. If I could just have one, I wouldn't really care about all the rest of it.

(Enter Orgon.)

SCENE II

ORGON: Ah, good morning, my dear. I wonder if my news will make you happy. Your fiancé will be visiting us today, his father has written to me. *(He holds up a letter. A beat.)* You seem a little sad. And Lisette here is lowering her eyes. What's going on?

(Silvia and Lisette avert their eyes.)

ORGON: *(To Lisette.)* Well say something, you.

LISETTE: Well Sir, there's one man who's surly and vicious, another who freezes you to death, and another who smiles a lot after abusing his wife. And then there's a woman, who is completely demoralized and deadly pale and has puffy eyes from weeping. This, Sir, is what we are pondering with such solemnity.

ORGON: What is this gibberish? Freezing? Abusing? Weeping? Kindly explain.

SILVIA: I was telling Lisette, father, about the unhappiness of wives who are mistreated by their husbands. I was just sharing my thoughts on the subject.

LISETTE: She was saying that some husbands wear a smile with their friends and a scowl with their wives.

ORGON: *(To Silvia.)* I take it that marriage alarms you, my child. And all the more because you don't know the boy at all?

LISETTE: To begin with, he's good-looking, which is sort of too bad.

ORGON: Sort of too bad? Are you mad?

LISETTE: I'm saying what I've been taught. It is Madame's philosophy. I just study with her.

ORGON: Come come, there is no reason for all this. My dear child, you know how much I love you. On my last visit to the country I settled on this marriage with Dorante's father, who is one of my oldest, dearest friends. But we settled on it only on the condition that you two like each other, indeed that you have complete freedom to say and do what you like about it all. Now I forbid you to do anything just to please *me*. If Dorante doesn't suit you, you have only to say so, and off he goes. And if you don't suit *him*, off he goes.

LISETTE: A tender little duet will decide the matter, like at the opera: "You want me," "I want you," "Get a priest!" Or maybe: "Are you in love?" "Neither am I," "Get a horse!"

ORGON: *(To Silvia.)* I myself have never seen Dorante, he was away when I was staying with his father, but from all the wonderful things I've been told about him, I doubt either of you will be calling for a horse.

SILVIA: You are so wonderfully kind, father, and I shall obey you.

ORGON: Good.

SILVIA: I *shan't* do anything just to please you.

ORGON: Good.

SILVIA: But if I dared, I might ask you—something just occurred to me—to grant me one thing that would really set my mind at ease.

ORGON: If the thing is feasible, I'll grant it.

SILVIA: It's very feasible, but I don't want to abuse your kindness.

ORGON: Oh, abuse away! You know, in this world one must be a little too kind, to be kind enough.

LISETTE: Only the kindest of men could say that.

SILVIA: When Dorante comes…if I could see him, study him a little without his knowing who I am… Lisette is clever, she could take my place for a while. And I could take hers.

ORGON: *(Aside.)* How amusing. *(To Silvia.)* Give me a moment to think. *(Silvia and Lisette move away. A beat. Aside.)* If I let her do this, something singular is bound to happen. Something even she couldn't anticipate. *(To Silvia.)* All right, my love, I'll allow you your disguises. Lisette, are you sure you can handle your part? It's one of the great roles.

LISETTE: I, Sir? You know me. *(Grandly, to Orgon.)* I dare you to make love to me. And take care not to show me any disrespect. *(Simple again.)* That is a mere taste of what I have in store for you. What do you think, huh? Aren't I refined? Did you recognize me?

ORGON: My my, I was actually taken in. But there's no time to lose, go dress up, Dorante could surprise us at any moment. Hurry up, and make sure the servants know about it.

SILVIA: All I really need is an apron.

LISETTE: I, on the other hand, must make an elaborate toilette. Come do my hair, Lisette, you'd better start learning how to do your job. And don't dawdle, thank you very much.

SILVIA: I aim to please, Marquise.

LISETTE: March!

(Exit Lisette as Mario enters. He detains Silvia.)

SCENE III

MARIO: Sister, I congratulate you on your news. I hear we're going to meet your lover.

SILVIA: Yes brother, but unfortunately I haven't any time to stop and talk to you about it, I have more important things to do. Good-bye. *(Exit Silvia.)*

SCENE IV

ORGON: Mario, pay attention, and I'll tell you what's afoot.

MARIO: You mean there's more?

ORGON: I shall begin by asking you to be very discreet about this.

MARIO: I shall do as you tell me.

ORGON: We're going to see Dorante today, as you know, but there's a twist.

MARIO: Oooo.

ORGON: Your sister, who is not at all sure what she thinks of marrying this Dorante, would like a chance to study him a little without his knowing who she really is. So Silvia has asked me to allow her to spend the day dressed as Lisette.

MARIO: How amusing.

ORGON: And Lisette will spend the day dressed as Silvia.

MARIO: How *extremely* amusing.

ORGON: Now this morning I received a letter from Dorante's father. *(He skims the letter looking for his place. He then finds it.)* Blah blah blah blah, ah! "I wonder what you will think of an idea that has occurred to my son. It is peculiar, he himself admits as much, but his reason is understandable, indeed it shows a certain sensitivity. He has asked me to allow him to come to your house dressed as his own valet, who meanwhile will come…"

ORGON AND MARIO: …dressed as Dorante!

ORGON: "My son understands the seriousness of this engagement to your daughter, and he hopes, he says, in this short-lived disguise, to perceive her character, and to know her better, the better to judge how she should proceed. In view of what you've told me about your remarkable daughter, I consented to his scheme but am taking the precaution of warning you, in spite of his insistence that I *not* do so. You may make such use of this information as you deem appropriate—tell your daughter even, if that seems right," and so on, etcetera. Mistress and maid are dressing up even as we speak.

MARIO: My God, this is good!

ORGON: What do you think, Mario, should I tell her or not?

MARIO: Well Sir, things seem to be taking a certain direction, I would hate to stand in the way. If I were you, I'd respect the plan. There must be something to it if Silvia and Dorante have each come up with it. There they'll be, dressed up as servants, chatting away. We'll see whether their hearts can gauge each other's true worth. Perhaps Dorante will develop a taste for her, chambermaid though she'll be, and I am sure she'd find that delightful.

ORGON: We'll see whether she manages to find her way out of her own plot.

MARIO: It is a plot that cannot fail to amuse us. Think how we can torment them.

(Enter Silvia, dressed as Lisette.)

SCENE V

SILVIA: *(To Orgon.)* Here I am. Do I look terrible as a maid? *(To Mario.)* Brother, you know about maids. *(Noticing Mario's expression.)* And you seem to know what we're up to. I want your expert opinion.

MARIO: Well I think you'll definitely get Dorante's valet, and you could very possibly steal his master away from your mistress.

SILVIA: Frankly, I wouldn't *mind* attracting Dorante, in my little costume. I wouldn't mind waylaying his reason, making him lose his bearings, getting him good and confused about why he's so drawn to a chambermaid, like me. Besides, it would help me to unravel him, to figure him out, and if my charms can achieve *that* coup, I shall hold them in high regard. As far as this *valet* is concerned, naturally he will sigh *over* me, but he would never dare sigh *to* me. There will be that something in my eyes that will naturally inspire *respect,* in his servant's heart, more than love. I'm sure he's a rascal.

MARIO: Easy does it, sister, don't forget that this person will be your fellow servant...

ORGON: And he will undoubtedly love you.

SILVIA: So be it. The distinction of pleasing this person as well will have its advantages—valets are by nature indiscreet, and Love likes to talk, so he will become his master's biographer, and I shall find out everything I want to know.

(Enter Orgon's Valet.)

ORGON'S VALET: Monsieur Orgon, a servant has just arrived who wants to speak with you. He is accompanied by the porter, who is carrying the luggage.

ORGON: Show him in.

>   *(Exit Orgon's Valet.)*

ORGON: This is probably Dorante's valet. But where is the master, do you suppose? And where is Lisette?

SILVIA: She's still admiring herself in the mirror and thinking we're foolish to entrust Dorante to her. She plans to make short work of him.

>   *(Mario sees someone coming.)*

MARIO: Sshhh!

ORGON: Quiet, they're here.

>   *(Enter Dorante, dressed as a valet. Orgon's Valet and the porter continue on to the guest rooms.)*

SCENE VI

DORANTE: I am looking for Monsieur Orgon. Is it not indeed to him that I have the honor of paying my respects?

ORGON: Indeed it is, my friend.

DORANTE: Sir, I am in the employ of Monsieur Dorante, who follows presently and who has sent me ahead to pay *his* respects as well, until he can do so himself.

ORGON: You certainly do his bidding with distinction. Lisette, what do you think of this fellow?

SILVIA: Well, Sir, I think that he is…welcome, and that he is…well turned out.

DORANTE: *(To Silvia.)* You are most kind. I always try to do my very best.

MARIO: *(To Silvia.)* And he's not bad looking.

ORGON: *(To Dorante.)* This is my son.

MARIO: Your heart had better steel itself, Lisette.

SILVIA: My heart! Let's not jump to conclusions, *Sir*.

DORANTE: Don't be annoyed, Mademoiselle. Just because Monsieur says it doesn't mean it's true.

SILVIA: Your modesty is appealing. Pray continue in the same vein.

MARIO: This is all very good! But it seems to me that his calling you Mademoiselle is unnecessary. Surely among servants, like yourselves, the exchange of compliments needn't be so formal. Come now, let's be more familiar with each other. Your name is Lisette, and you, dear boy, what's yours?

DORANTE: Bourguignon, Sir, at your service.

MARIO: Bourguignon! Well.

SILVIA: Then I shall call you Bourguignon.

DORANTE: And I shall call you Lisette, but I shan't be any less your servant for doing so.

MARIO: *Her* servant, she's a servant herself! And that's surely not how servants talk. You should be more…intimate.

(Orgon laughs.)

SILVIA: *(Aside, to Mario.)* You're trifling with me, brother.

DORANTE: As far as intimacy is concerned, Sir, I shall await Lisette's word on the matter.

(Orgon and Mario are amused.)

SILVIA: *(Cheerfully.)* There now, the ice is broken! However intimate you choose to be with me, Bourguignon, at least we know these gentlemen will be amused. Do as you wish.

DORANTE: You honor me, Lisette. From this moment on I shall endeavor to be more intimate with you.

ORGON: Don't be shy, children, if you fall in love now, you'll be way ahead of the game.

MARIO: *(To Orgon.)* Falling in love! That's something else again. Perhaps you didn't realize that…*I* desire Lisette?

(Orgon laughs. Silvia looks sharply at Mario.)

MARIO: True, her heart is indifferent to mine, but I don't want Bourguignon poaching on my preserves.

SILVIA: And is that how you would win my heart, Sir, by hunting it down? Well I wish Bourguignon *would* love me.

DORANTE: Perhaps you needn't make a wish, beautiful Lisette, to have what you desire.

MARIO: My dear Bourguignon, surely you stole that little gallantry from somewhere.

DORANTE: You are right, Sir. I stole it from her eyes.

MARIO: That one was even worse. I forbid you to be so clever.

SILVIA: He's not being clever at your expense. Besides, he can help himself to whatever he might find in my eyes.

ORGON: I think we should go, Mario. Dorante will be here soon, go tell your sister. Lisette, show this fellow his master's rooms. Good-bye, Bourguignon!

DORANTE: Sir, you are too kind.

(Exeunt Orgon and Mario, delighted.)

SCENE VII

SILVIA: *(Aside.) They're* enjoying the show. Well no matter, I'll make the most of it all. *(Eyeing Dorante.)* Now this boy is no fool, and I don't pity the servant girl who gets him in the end. If he wants to woo me, I say let him, provided he's got something useful to tell me.

DORANTE: *(Aside.)* This girl is astonishing. Her face would grace a woman of any class. Perhaps she can tell me something about her mistress. *(To Silvia.)* Since we have taken a more intimate tone and dispensed with formalities, tell me, Lisette, do your mistress' charm and beauty match yours? She is certainly rash to have a chambermaid like you.

SILVIA: I gather, Bourguignon, that, according to the old custom, you have come here with the intention of whispering sweet nothings in my ear. Am I right?

DORANTE: To be perfectly honest, I had no such intention when I came here. I have never enjoyed any particular intimacy with ladies' maids. Although I am, of course, a servant. I usually don't like the way servants think, but you are different. You disarm me. I feel almost shy. I wouldn't dare whisper in your ear, my instinct is to take my hat off to you. In short, I am inclined to treat you with a respect that you would probably find ridiculous. What kind of lady's maid *are* you, with your air of a princess?

SILVIA: You know, everything you say you feel when you look at me is exactly what all valets say they feel when they look at me.

DORANTE: I really wouldn't be surprised if all their masters felt the same when *they* looked at you.

SILVIA: That's very well said, I'm sure, but it may interest you to know that I do not respond to the amorous attentions of gentlemen in livery.

DORANTE: You mean you don't like my costume?

SILVIA: That's what I mean, Bourguignon. Now let's leave love alone, and just be friends.

DORANTE: You ask me to do only two things for you, Mademoiselle, and alas, I can do neither.

SILVIA: *(Aside.)* What an unusual valet! *(To Dorante.)* Well you have no choice but to do them both, because it was once predicted that I would marry only a well-born man, a man of position, and I have sworn never to listen to any other kind of man.

DORANTE: That's curious. I resolved long ago to love only a well-born girl and never to concern myself with any other kind of woman.

SILVIA: Well then, I hope you won't stray from your resolution.

DORANTE: Perhaps I am not straying from it as much as we think. You have a very refined way about you, and servants can sometimes be well-born without knowing it.

(Silvia laughs.)

SILVIA: I would thank you for the compliment, if it weren't at my mother's expense. I assure you, she and my father were of the same class.

DORANTE: Then please feel free to compliment me at *my* mother's expense—if you think my manner convincingly aristocratic, or my looks sufficiently refined, or if you think for any other reason I am worthy of the compliment.

SILVIA: *(Aside.)* He *is* worthy of the compliment. *(To Dorante.)* But it's not a question of your manner or your looks. Now enough of this banter, a man of position is going to be my husband, that's the prediction, and I won't take anything less.

DORANTE: By God, if I *were* a man of position, that prediction would worry me, because I think I just might make it come true! And wouldn't *that* be a difficult situation. Fortunately I don't believe in astrology. But I do believe in your beauty.

SILVIA: *(Aside.)* He never stops. *(To Dorante.)* Do you ever stop? What interest can the prediction have for you anyway, since it excludes you?

DORANTE: It didn't predict that I would never love you.

SILVIA: *(Firmly, a little glacial.)* No, but it did say that you could gain nothing from it, and I am now confirming that for you.

DORANTE: *(Smiling, charmed by her.)* And you are absolutely right to do so. You know, Lisette, this hauteur suits you perfectly, I almost expected to see it in you when I first saw you, it completes the picture somehow, and even if it weakens my case, I am actually happy to see it in you. It's hard to explain why.

SILVIA: *(Aside.)* He really surprises me, although naturally I'm skeptical. *(To Dorante.)* Tell me, who are *you,* who speaks to me like this?

DORANTE: The son of honorable people…who weren't…rich.

SILVIA: Well, I honestly wish your situation had been different. And that I could help you somehow. Fortune made a mistake with you.

DORANTE: Love made a bigger mistake. *(A beat. Sudden, ardent.)* I would rather be allowed to ask for your heart than to have all the advantages of a man of means.

SILVIA: *(Aside.)* Thank heavens I am in control of this conversation. *(To Dorante.)* Bourguignon, you say such sweet things to me, I could never lose my temper, but please, let's change the subject. Tell me about your master. I think you should stop talking to me about love.

DORANTE: Then I think you should stop making me feel it.

SILVIA: You're trying my patience, perhaps I *shall* lose my temper! Once again: Leave your love out of it.

DORANTE: Once again: Leave your eyes out of it.

SILVIA: *(Aside.)* You know, I think he's up to something. *(To Dorante.)* All right Bourguignon, you won't stop? I guess I'll have to leave. *(Aside.)* I should have done so before.

DORANTE: Wait, Lisette, I was about to change the subject…

(Silvia turns back. They look into each other's eyes.)

DORANTE: …but I can't remember what I was going to say.

SILVIA: And there was something I was going to say to you, but you made me forget what it was.

DORANTE: I do remember having asked if your mistress was a match for you.

SILVIA: You're not changing the subject at all, you're just sneaking back to where you left off. Good-bye. *(She starts to leave again.)*

DORANTE: No, wait, Lisette, listen—my master *ordered* me to ask you about your mistress.

SILVIA: *(Turning back.)* Oh! And I want *you* to tell me about *him.* I want to know if *he's* a match for my *mistress.* Your affection for him makes me think well of him. He must have some merit if *you* serve him.

DORANTE: I hope you will permit me to thank you for what you just said.

SILVIA: If you will not remark further on the impropriety of my having said it.

DORANTE: That's another one of those things you say which *thrill* me.

(Silvia, in confusion, starts to leave again.)

DORANTE: Go if you must, I can't stop myself, you are absolutely enchanting!

(Silvia stops.)

DORANTE: I assure you, I am ashamed, but I have no choice but to acknowledge what I see.

SILVIA: And I have no choice but to wonder how it happens that I am so good as to go on listening to you, because really…the whole situation is…unusual, to say the least.

DORANTE: You're right, our situation is probably unique.

SILVIA: *(Aside.)* In spite of everything he's said to me, I haven't walked away yet, I don't seem to be going anywhere now, and I am still talking to him. It's completely absurd. *(To Dorante.)* Good-bye. *(She starts to leave.)*

DORANTE: But let's at least get said what we've been meaning to say.

SILVIA: *(Turning back.)* I've just said it—good-bye. No more concessions. I'll just have to wait until your master gets here to find out what I wanted to know. *(Pointing.)* Meanwhile, you see that room? That's his.

DORANTE: But here he is!

(Enter Harlequin, dressed as Dorante.)

SCENE VIII

HARLEQUIN: Ah, there you are, Bourguignon! Have you, and the rest of my luggage, been graciously received?

DORANTE: We could only be graciously received here, Sir.

HARLEQUIN: Some servant, back there, told me to come in this way. He said that my father-in-law, and my wife, had been told of my arrival. *(Pointedly.)* Where are they?

SILVIA: You mean Monsieur Orgon and his daughter, Sir, I'm sure.

HARLEQUIN: *(Glancing at Silvia.)* Hello? Yes, quite. His daughter, my wife, it amounts to the same thing. I've come for a wife, and they're waiting to marry me, it's all agreed, so all that remains to be done is to sign our lives away, and that's just a trifle.

(Silvia does not appreciate Harlequin's tone.)

SILVIA: It's a trifle that one would do well to think about seriously.

(Harlequin does not appreciate Silvia's tone.)

HARLEQUIN: Yes, but if one has already thought about it, one isn't thinking about it anymore. Is one?

SILVIA: *(Aside, to Dorante.)* Do people buy titles in the public market where you're from?

HARLEQUIN: What, lady fair, are you saying to my valet?

SILVIA: I was saying that I should go tell Monsieur Orgon that you are here. Sir.

HARLEQUIN: And why not call him my father-in-law, as I do?

SILVIA: Because he isn't yet.

DORANTE: She is right, Sir. The marriage is not yet official.

HARLEQUIN: Well I am here to make it official.

DORANTE: Then wait till you have done so.

HARLEQUIN: *Really!* What's the big difference whether you call him a father-in-law the day before or the day *of?*

SILVIA: *(Taking his tone.)* You're right Sir, and what's the big difference whether you call his daughter your wife the day of or the day *after?*

HARLEQUIN: *(Enjoying this train of thought.)* What's the big difference if she's even pretty!

SILVIA: What's the big difference if you even marry her!

(Harlequin laughs.)

SILVIA: Now I must run and get Monsieur Orgon. *(Silvia starts to leave.)*

HARLEQUIN: Get my wife too, if you don't mind. But before you go, you pretty little thing, tell me—are you not the chambermaid *de la maison?*

SILVIA: You have guessed it.

HARLEQUIN: Splendid! You are delightful. Do you think I am delightful? Do you think I will amuse them?

SILVIA: I think you are…amusing.

HARLEQUIN: Good! Keep on thinking that way, it may come in handy. You and I are going to have more to do with each other than you think. I'm certainly glad that you think I'm amusing.

(Silvia is appalled.)

SILVIA: I'm certainly glad it pleases you that I do. Now if you'll excuse me, I wouldn't want you to wait any longer for Monsieur Orgon.

HARLEQUIN: Oh, not to worry, I'm a very good waiter.

DORANTE: *(In a cautionary tone.)* Monsieur Dorante…

(Silvia starts to leave.)

HARLEQUIN: Tell him I'll be waiting on him with bated breath.

(Silvia groans sharply as she leaves.)

SCENE IX

HARLEQUIN: *(Delighted.)* Well Sir, that was a good start, the maid is already crazy about me.

DORANTE: You are such a…*monstrosity.*

HARLEQUIN: But why? My entrance was perfect. I was so elegant!

DORANTE: You and your stupid, vulgar attempts at politesse! I gave you such clear instructions. I told you to be earnest, sincere, self-effacing, *serious!* Oh, I must have been out of my mind to entrust you with this.

HARLEQUIN: I'll be better in the next scene. I'm not very *good* at being serious. But I could be…melancholy! I'll sigh, I'll weep, I'll *sob* if necessary!

(Harlequin throws himself down with a dark cry.)

DORANTE: *(To the air.)* It's all so confusing, what should I *do?*

HARLEQUIN: Well there's always that chambermaid!

DORANTE: Shut up!

ORGON: *(From offstage.)* Right this way!

DORANTE: Here he comes.

(Enter Orgon.)

SCENE X

ORGON: *(To Harlequin.)* My dear Sir, a thousand apologies for keeping you waiting, but I've only just now heard that you were here.

HARLEQUIN: A thousand pardons, Monsieur! But that's far too many—only one is necessary when one has done only one thing wrong. Besides, my pardon is yours for the begging.

ORGON: I shall endeavor never to trouble you for it.

HARLEQUIN: Oh please, *you* are the master here, I am the servant.

ORGON: It is a great pleasure to have you here, I assure you. We have eagerly awaited your arrival.

HARLEQUIN: I would have come before with Bourguignon, but when one is at the end of a journey, staggering off the coach, you know, one *looks* so impossible—crumbs on one's coat, wrinkled shirt, the hair alone! So I took a moment at the post-house, because I wanted to put my best foot forward, and tried to make myself more...appetizing.

ORGON: Well you have certainly succeeded. You are a veritable pâté. My daughter is busy dressing; while we wait for her to come down, would you like to take some refreshment?

HARLEQUIN: Oh, I never refuse a drink with anyone.

ORGON: Bourguignon my boy, maybe you can find someone in the kitchen to help you.

HARLEQUIN: Oh, he's quite the gourmet, I'm warning you, and he loves good wine. Only the best for Bourguignon!

ORGON: *(To Dorante.)* Well don't hold back then. I think you'll find everything you want.
(Dorante starts off.)

LISETTE: *(From offstage.)* Father! Yoo-hoo!

HARLEQUIN: *(Turning in the direction of the voice.)* Silvia!

ORGON: At last!
(Lisette, dressed as Silvia, explodes onto the stage. Dorante turns back, curious, and eavesdrops.)

SCENE XI

LISETTE: Father you darling, I've been looking everywhere for you. *(Seeing Harlequin.)* Ah! Are you...

HARLEQUIN: *(Grandly.)* I am.

LISETTE: *(Proffering her hand to him.)* Ah!
(Harlequin bows rather elaborately then takes her hand and kisses it. Lisette is immediately amused by him.)

LISETTE: What a lovely bow.

HARLEQUIN: My dear and esteemed lady, I should really prostrate myself.

LISETTE: Oh, that would be lovely, pray do.

(Harlequin prostrates himself.)

ORGON: My dear Dorante, you must forgive my daughter. She is unusually spirited today.

LISETTE: Yes, I am full of surprises.

HARLEQUIN: Ah, so am I. *(Getting up.)* Monsieur Orgon, I shall forgive your daughter her high spirits. How could I not? But there is one thing for which I may never forgive her.

LISETTE: Oh let me guess. Being horrifyingly late?

HARLEQUIN: No! Being horrifyingly ravishing.

(Dorante slips away.)

LISETTE: Ah.

ORGON: *(To Lisette.)* My dear Silvia…

LISETTE: *(Interrupting her father suddenly.)* Oh *Father! (She kisses Monsieur Orgon enthusiastically on the lips.)*

ORGON: Dorante seems every bit as spirited as yourself. Why don't you get to know each other. I have some business to see to and shall come find you again when I am—

LISETTE: *(Interrupting.)* Run along, Father.

(Orgon looks at her, surprised. She motions him away with her fingers. Exit Orgon. Harlequin and Lisette regard each other nervously.)

SCENE XII

LISETTE: My dear Monsieur Dorante, are you exhausted from your journey? You have traveled for three days.

HARLEQUIN: Ah Madame, the roads are poor, but my spirits are excellent. I chose my most comfortable carriage, and although one cannot read in a coach, one can certainly eat in one!

LISETTE: But one cannot eat for three days, surely?

HARLEQUIN: I can! *(Recovering, elegant.)* Madame. I love…to eat!

LISETTE: They told me you were handsome and intelligent, but they didn't tell me you would also be hungry.

(They laugh merrily.)

HARLEQUIN: Well it is true. We stopped several times along the road. There is a post-house a day from here which serves a magnificent chop. I liked it so much I had seconds and thirds. I could hardly tear myself away from the kitchen.

LISETTE: *(Surprised.)* You were in the kitchen?

HARLEQUIN: I'm *always* in the kitchen! *(Realizing his gaffe and recovering.)* To…compliment the chef!

LISETTE: Ah.

HARLEQUIN: And he gave me an entire rack of lamb for the carriage, and I made short work of it, I can tell you.

(Lisette laughs.)

HARLEQUIN: Oh don't think ill of me, Madame. I'm afraid I am talkative, I apologize.

LISETTE: I wasn't thinking ill of you at all, Sir, I was finding you charming.

HARLEQUIN: Good!

LISETTE: I was thinking that I have never met a gentleman as…animated as yourself. Here you are, you have been on a tiring journey, and you don't seem cranky at all. My brother Mario is always very cranky after traveling. But you are different. You disarm me. You look fresh as a daisy. Even your clothes do.

HARLEQUIN: Ah, I shall tell you a secret. *(Conspiratorially.)* I changed at the post-house in the village, I wanted to look my best for you. Bourguignon laid out fresh clothes for me. I can't do anything without the help of my excellent valet.

LISETTE: A man's valet is a reflection of his master.

HARLEQUIN: Well, I am sure Silvia's chambermaid is but a poor reflection of Silvia!

LISETTE: Silvia's chambermaid is the best girl in the world—intelligent, pretty, and loyal. There isn't anything she wouldn't do for her mistress.

HARLEQUIN: And Dorante's valet is incredibly resourceful and devoted, and he is also quite handsome, too, if I do say so. He often performs difficult tasks for his master. *(Conspiratorially.)* Once he even impersonated him for a day.

LISETTE: Heavens! I hope Dorante's reasons for this were honorable.

HARLEQUIN: Ah Madame, Dorante is an honorable man. It is his servant who is the trickster.

LISETTE: Servants are often tricksters.

HARLEQUIN: They often have no choice in the matter.

LISETTE: And perhaps they shouldn't be held responsible for their actions. *(A beat.)* It is unusual for a gentleman, is it not, to take the time to imagine how servants think?

HARLEQUIN: Ah yes, well, I have so many of them, you see. And whenever one of them tries to cheat me—be it a sneaky lackey or a guilty lady's maid—it's never long before I sniff it out.

(Lisette is disturbed.)

HARLEQUIN: Have I offended you with this talk of servants? *(Aside.)* I have certainly offended myself.

LISETTE: Let us change the subject.

HARLEQUIN: Yes, let us talk about me…and you. We hardly know each other, but I feel we are perfectly suited to each other. You are clever and lovely to behold, and so am I.

LISETTE: *(Laughing.)* Ah, you are much more so than I, and amusing into the bargain.

HARLEQUIN: It is true, I am amusing, but of the two of us, you are the lovelier.

LISETTE: You are very kind to say so.

HARLEQUIN: You are very kind to allow me to say so. And I hope you will forgive me for saying that I didn't expect that you would *be* so kind, or so approachable. I thought you would be rather grand, and I am not at all grand.

(Lisette looks sharply at him.)

HARLEQUIN: *(Antically.)* Although of course I constantly eat large amounts of food, spend my money freely, and dress as well as fashion will allow!

LISETTE: *(Laughing.)* Ah, Sir, stop, you make me laugh!

HARLEQUIN: Oh please don't think me ridiculous, Madame. You see, I feel that I can tell you the truth. I wish I could tell you *everything* about myself all in one moment. I want to. It's strange, but I feel that, if you and I were really, actually, to marry, we might be very happy together.

LISETTE: You could love me then?

HARLEQUIN: Madame, I hadn't really considered it possible when I came here, to tell you the truth, but I am sure of it now.

LISETTE: *Are* you telling the truth?

HARLEQUIN: If I am not telling the truth…please know that my heart is.

LISETTE: *You*…could love *me?*

HARLEQUIN: I like you very much at the moment. By this evening I'll love you, and tomorrow? You will be worshipped.

LISETTE: *(Aside, troubled.)* Worshipped… *(A beat.)* I suddenly feel quite tired.

HARLEQUIN: Of me?

LISETTE: No! No, believe me. I think I need a rest. My constitution is more delicate than I realized. *(She turns to go.)*

HARLEQUIN: And will you come back?

LISETTE: *(Turning back.)* I shall find you again.

HARLEQUIN: Really?

LISETTE: Really.

(They look at each other for a moment.)

LISETTE: You're not one of those men who puts on one face for the world and a completely different one at home, are you?

(A beat.)

HARLEQUIN: Me? Why do you ask?

LISETTE: I was wondering about it with my maid this morning.

HARLEQUIN: Ah, I'm afraid one can't know me for long and not see what I really am. *(A beat. He bows.)* Madame.

LISETTE: *(Curtseying.)* Sir.

(Exit Lisette. Harlequin thinks deeply for a moment.)

HARLEQUIN: "Sir." *(A beat.)* Worshipped. *(A beat. He thinks. He laughs suddenly.)*

(Blackout.)

ACT II
SCENE I

(Several hours later. Lisette, still dressed as Silvia, pursues Orgon.)

ORGON: Now then, what do you want? What's the matter?

LISETTE: I have to talk to you.

ORGON: About what?

LISETTE: About where things stand, because it's important that you be very clear about it all, and that you have absolutely no reason to complain of me later.

ORGON: This all sounds rather serious.

LISETTE: It's *very* serious. You consented to Mademoiselle Silvia's idea of the disguises. I confess that at first I thought it was a matter of no consequence one way or the other, but I was very much mistaken.

ORGON: And *is* it a matter of consequence?

LISETTE: Sir. One hardly wants to seem to be praising oneself. Nevertheless, all modesty aside, I must tell you that, if you do not intervene and set things right again, your future son-in-law will not be able to offer Mademoiselle your daughter his heart, because there won't be anything left of it to give. It is time for her to drop her disguise and say who she is, because one day more, and I can't be held responsible.

ORGON: What gives you the impression that he's not going to be interested in Silvia? He just has to get to know her. You're not underestimating her charms?

LISETTE: No, but you are underestimating mine. And I am warning you, they are doing what they do, and I don't advise you to let them continue.

ORGON: *(Laughing.)* I compliment you on your progress, Lisette.

LISETTE: I knew it! You think it's a joke, you're laughing at me, and I am really upset about it, because you'll see that I'm right!

ORGON: Don't you worry about that, Lisette, just do what you have to do.

LISETTE: I'll say it again, Dorante is falling fast. Look, he likes me very much at the moment, he'll love me this evening, by tomorrow he'll worship me. You can say what you like—I'm not really worthy of his love, it's all in very bad taste—but that's what's happening. Tomorrow, I guarantee you, *worshipped.* You'll see.

ORGON: Why all the fuss? If he loves you so much, let him marry you.

LISETTE: What?! You wouldn't prevent it?

ORGON: No, I wouldn't. If you can get him.

LISETTE: Sir, take care what you say! So far I haven't really helped my charms along, whatever they've done they've done on their own. But if *I* get involved in this, I'll turn his head for good, and there will be no turning back.

ORGON: Turn him, burn him, ravage him, and then marry him. If you can do it, I won't stand in your way.

LISETTE: If that's the case, my fortune is made.

ORGON: Now tell me, what does *Silvia* think of her fiancé?

LISETTE: *(Still upset.)* But Sir!

ORGON: *(Firm.)* Enough. Have you talked to her?

LISETTE: I've hardly had a chance to talk to her, because her fiancé never leaves *me* alone, but I don't think she's happy. She's pensive. And I fully expect that she'll ask me to turn him down for her.

ORGON: I forbid you to do so. I want her to have plenty of time to study this boy, and to think about her future.

LISETTE: But Sir…

ORGON: *(Interrupting.)* Tell me about the valet, is he behaving? Is he considering falling for *her?*

LISETTE: He's an odd one. He does play the gentleman with her, I've noticed that. Anyway, he looks the part. He does watch her. And he does sigh.

ORGON: And does that annoy her?

LISETTE: Well…she does blush.

ORGON: Oh no, you're mistaken. Being admired by a valet would never bother her that much.

LISETTE: Sir, she *blushes.*

ORGON: Then she's indignant at his effrontery?

LISETTE: That's a good one. I think she likes him.

ORGON: Well, when you do find your moment, tell her this. Tell her you suspect this boy of trying to prejudice her against his master.

LISETTE: Why?

ORGON: Well if she defends him, we'll find out how *much* she likes him.

LISETTE: But if she gets angry with me…

ORGON: If she gets angry with you, we'll know she likes him very much indeed. Now go find Monsieur Dorante, and work your wiles.
(Exit Orgon.)

LISETTE: But this is terrible! What is going on? My master encouraging me to marry a *gentleman?* A gentleman who is courting me and who seems truly to be opening his heart to me? Ah, what can Monsieur Orgon be thinking?!
(Enter Dorante at a distance, unseen by Lisette.)

LISETTE: I am a servant!

SCENE II

DORANTE: Madame.

(Lisette wheels around in surprise and emits a startled noise.)

DORANTE: I beg your pardon, Madame.

LISETTE: You must be Monsieur Dorante's valet.

DORANTE: Yes, Madame, my name is Bourguignon.

LISETTE: Oh yes, I've heard about you.

DORANTE: About *me?*

LISETTE: Yes, my maid mentioned you to me.

DORANTE: She is a credit to you, Madame.

LISETTE: Oh yes, Lisette is quite the lady. And full of ideas, let me tell you.

DORANTE: I have never met a lady's maid more charming or well-spoken, Madame.

LISETTE: Oh, so you like her.

DORANTE: *(Surprised.)* I? Madame, I…hardly know her.

LISETTE: Well surely there's nothing wrong in liking her. You needn't be ashamed.

DORANTE: Madame, I'm not—

LISETTE: *(Interrupting.)* And do you think she likes *you?*

(A beat.)

DORANTE: She seems more interested in finding out about my master, Madame.

LISETTE: I'm not surprised to hear that. Isn't it *so* like a chambermaid to be thinking always of moving up in the world. Well, I admit the girl is charming and well-spoken, as you put it, but if I were you I wouldn't expect her to feel as warmly toward you as you do toward her. She has her sights set on a gentleman.

DORANTE: So she gave me to understand, Madame.

LISETTE: *(Surprised.)* She did?!

DORANTE: She said it had been predicted that she would marry a man of position, and she seems determined to do so.

LISETTE: Ah. Well, I think if a *valet* courted her she would probably detest him. She has an unwavering disdain for people of her own class which is unique among servants, in my experience. And she is a very single-minded person who always gets her way and has very unusual views on marriage.

DORANTE: She does speak very highly of *you,* Madame.

LISETTE: Well she should, considering what I've done for her. And do you speak very highly of your master?

DORANTE: *(Taken aback for a moment.)* Madame, Monsieur Dorante is…an honorable person.

LISETTE: Is that all he has to recommend him? What else can you tell me about him?

DORANTE: Well for one thing, Madame, he is as interested in knowing about you as you are in knowing about him.

LISETTE: And that is why you came to find me, isn't that so.

DORANTE: *(Again, briefly taken aback.)* I confess it is, Madame.

LISETTE: Well let's hear about him first.

DORANTE: As you wish. *(After a moment of consideration.)* He seems, on the surface, to be a rather simple and very…forthright person.

LISETTE: *(Brightly.)* Yes.

DORANTE: And the man you met this morning is also quite…verbose.

LISETTE: Yes.

DORANTE: But the real Dorante is in fact a very different person.

LISETTE: Do you really think so?

DORANTE: I am quite sure of it, Madame. The real Monsieur Dorante is a quieter and more refined man than the man who has been…entertaining you today.

LISETTE: Go on.

DORANTE: *That* man is understandably nervous—after all, it's not every day that he has to do what he must do today, and moreover he has absolutely no experience of courting a lady. I assure you, Madame, that when Monsieur Dorante shows you his *true* face, you will see the face of a true gentleman.

LISETTE: What else would he show me?

DORANTE: Madame. If you have found him to be less discreet than you had reason to expect, or less modest, or more…down to earth, I feel compelled to reassure you—he is not himself today. You mustn't be disheartened.

LISETTE: Disheartened? I'm not at all disheartened. How dare you speak of your master in this way! I have found him to be much *more* discreet and modest and, blessedly, more down to earth than I expected, and I have no reason whatsoever to complain of him. What is more, although I was at first surprised by his high spirits, and although I have learned today that men present to the world quite a different face from the one they wear in private, I am absolutely convinced that whoever that man is, he is very much himself! Furthermore, I *like* him, and I would consider myself very fortunate if, at the end of the day, he found it in his heart to ask for my hand. You may think he is not a gentleman, but I do, and I will thank you to take your divisive remarks back below stairs where they belong. I know what servants are, and better than you might suppose, but I have never seen one quite like you! I had heard that you had spoken disparagingly of your master, and I see now that it's true.

DORANTE: I have never spoken ill of Monsieur Dorante, quite the contrary!

LISETTE: Ha! It's obvious that you have a low opinion of him!

DORANTE: *(Suppressing his anger.)* Madame, I wrongly sensed that you were concerned, when you asked me to tell you about him. And so I was attempting to do so candidly.

LISETTE: I think you were attempting to do something else entirely. There is something very presumptuous about the way you look at me. I don't trust you, Bourguignon. I don't trust you, and I don't like you.

DORANTE: *(Aside.)* And I don't like *her.*

LISETTE: Now go away, and watch your tongue. You may be sorry for what you've said to me.

DORANTE: *(Barely able to restrain himself.)* You may be sorry for what *you've* said to *me.*

LISETTE: *(Pointing offstage imperiously.)* Go!

DORANTE: *(Bowing.)* Madame.

(Exit Dorante.)

LISETTE: It's people like him who give servants a bad name! I should tell Monsieur Dorante about him. *(After a pause.)* Although of course Monsieur will be much angrier when I tell him about *me.* Monsieur indeed…Oh, how could I have thought, even for a moment, that I might marry him? And I shall *have* to tell him, and then… *(A beat.)* …he will never marry *me.*

(Enter Harlequin, still dressed as Dorante.)

SCENE III

HARLEQUIN: Ah, marvelous lady, I have found you! I've been looking everywhere for you, and impatiently, I might add. Since we last spoke I have thought only of you. I am *yearning* to marry you!

LISETTE: It is hard for me to believe, Monsieur Dorante, that it is really so difficult for you to wait for the wedding. I think you're playing the impatient lover to be gallant. Why, you just got here, your feelings couldn't be that strong yet.

HARLEQUIN: Oh singular marvel, you are alas mistaken, for though my love is a newborn, it is indeed love, and since it is love inspired by you, it is not long for the cradle. Your first glance gave birth to it, your second nourished it, your third made it grow large, and now it's ready to be married, and we must act fast—remember, you are its mother, you must take care of it!

(He reaches for her hand. Lisette turns away.)

LISETTE: Do you think I am mistreating it? Is it really so neglected?

HARLEQUIN: Well at least give it your beautiful white hand, to keep it busy until we are wed.

LISETTE: Take it then! I can see that if I don't keep this little love of yours busy, it won't leave me in peace.

(She offers her hand. Harlequin takes it and kisses it tenderly.)

HARLEQUIN: Beloved plaything of my heart, you revive me! You are like a fine wine. Too bad I get only a teeny sip.

LISETTE: *(Trying to withdraw her hand.)* Enough now, stop. You are too greedy.

HARLEQUIN: *(Gripping her hand tenaciously and kissing it repeatedly.)* No! Just give me enough to survive on until we are *in flagrante delicto!*

LISETTE: Have you lost your reason?

HARLEQUIN: Yes, your pickpocket eyes robbed me of it!

LISETTE: *(Amazed and confused.)* But Sir, how is it possible that you could love me so much? I cannot let myself believe that it is true.

HARLEQUIN: I am hardly the man to explain how it can be so, believe me, but I do love you, and like a lunatic! And if you look in your mirror, you will see that it isn't just possible, it is inevitable.

LISETTE: But my mirror would show me only my *face,* and I cannot believe that *my* face could make all this happen.

HARLEQUIN: Ah, sweet pet, such modesty! You are an actress.

LISETTE: Someone is coming. It's your valet.

(Enter Dorante, still dressed as Bourguignon.)

SCENE IV

DORANTE: Excuse me Sir, I must speak with you for a moment.

HARLEQUIN: No! *(To Lisette.)* Why can't the damned servants leave us alone?

LISETTE: *(To Harlequin.)* See what he wants, Monsieur.

DORANTE: I have only one word to say to you, Sir.

HARLEQUIN: *(To Lisette.)* Madame, if he says *two* words, *I'll* say two words— "You're fired!" *(To Dorante.)* Now then.

(Harlequin moves away with Dorante.)

DORANTE: *(Aside, surreptitiously kicking Harlequin in the rear.)* Listen here, you upstart!

HARLEQUIN: *(Aside, to Dorante.)* You said a word, not a fracture! *(To Lisette, over his shoulder.)* My queen, a moment.

LISETTE: Very well.

DORANTE: *(Aside, to Harlequin.)* Spare me this ludicrous spectacle. Now listen, you have to get me out of this, and you have to do it fast. This girl doesn't suit me at all. So act reserved, and distant, and even discontent, because it is now up to you to tell her that this marriage will not be happening!

HARLEQUIN: We shall have to see about that!

DORANTE: Harlequin!

HARLEQUIN: *(So Lisette can hear.)* You may go!

(Exit Dorante, furious.)

SCENE V

HARLEQUIN: Ah Madame, before we were so rudely interrupted I was going to say some beautiful things, and now I fear I have quite forgotten them and shall say only ordinary things. I mean apart from telling you about my love, which is *extra*ordinary. But apropos of my love, when will yours be keeping it company?

LISETTE: Alas, we can only *hope* that will come.

HARLEQUIN: *(Passionately.)* And do you think it will come soon?

LISETTE: *(Uncertain of how to proceed.)* The question is very forward. Do you realize you are embarrassing me?

(Harlequin pursues her relentlessly.)

HARLEQUIN: But what do you expect? I am burning up, so I cry *Fire!*

LISETTE: Oh, if only I were in a position to reveal my feelings as straightforwardly as you do.

HARLEQUIN: Believe me, you are in a position to do with me exactly as you like.

LISETTE: But the modesty of my sex does not allow it.

HARLEQUIN: Oh, that's old-fashioned. Modesty allows more these days.

LISETTE: *(Confused, crying out.)* But what are you asking of me?

HARLEQUIN: Give me just a little sign that you love me. Listen: I love you! Be my echo, say it with me!

LISETTE: You are insatiable! Very well, Sir, I… *(A beat. Lisette struggles with her feelings.)* I love you.

HARLEQUIN: Oh Madame! I die! Confounded by my own happiness. I may go stark raving mad! You love me! This is wonderful!

LISETTE: Oh, Sir, I am amazed—and with good reason—by the speed of your courtship. Perhaps you will love me less when we know each other better.

HARLEQUIN: Ah, Madame, on that day of reckoning, I fear I shall be the loser, not you. You seem ever nobler to me, and I am bound to diminish in your eyes.

LISETTE: You credit me with more worth than I have.

HARLEQUIN: You don't know how unworthy I am, Madame. Indeed, I should address you only on bended knee. *(Kneeling.)* Fate often chooses a lowly position for us.

LISETTE: But my heart would have chosen you regardless of who you were or where you came from.

HARLEQUIN: I hope it *will* choose me regardless of those things.

LISETTE: Dare I flatter myself to think that your heart feels the same way about me?

HARLEQUIN: Alas, were you but the gardener's daughter, or a scullery maid, and had I seen you, candlestick in hand, going down to the root cellar, you would have been my princess regardless.

LISETTE: I hope these sentiments will last.

HARLEQUIN: You may be sure that they will last in *my* heart, but can I be sure that they will last in yours? Let us swear an oath to love each other forever, and we'll be covered for all possible mistakes and false assumptions.

LISETTE: Such an oath might mean even more to me than to you. And I swear it with all my heart.
(They look into each other's eyes. A beat.)

HARLEQUIN: *(Kneeling and kissing her hand.)* Your goodness dazzles me, and I kneel before it.

LISETTE: *(Ravished.)* Stop, I can't bear it. *(Trying to pull him up.)* It would be presumptuous of me to allow it. Get up, please. Someone is coming.
(Enter Silvia, still dressed as Lisette. Harlequin is still kneeling.)

SCENE VI

LISETTE: What do you want, Lisette?

SILVIA: To speak with you, Madame.

HARLEQUIN: Well I never! *(To Silvia.)* Listen, sweetheart, come back in a quarter of an hour. *(Waving Silvia away.)* Go on! Where I come from chambermaids never make an entrance until they've been cued.

SILVIA: Sir, I must speak with Madame.

HARLEQUIN: We have strict orders to love each other before we marry, and we can't be constantly interrupted in the performance of our duties! *(To Lisette.)* Queen of my world, send her away.

LISETTE: Couldn't you come back in a few minutes, Lisette?

SILVIA: But Madame—

HARLEQUIN: *But?!* I get very angry when servants don't do as they're told.

SILVIA: *(Aside.)* Oh this *dreadful* man!

HARLEQUIN: *Go away!*

SILVIA: *(To Lisette.)* Madame, I assure you this is urgent.

LISETTE: Monsieur Dorante, allow me, please, a moment. I'll get rid of her.

HARLEQUIN: Patience, Dorante, patience!

LISETTE: *(To Harlequin.)* Please?

HARLEQUIN: *(To Lisette.)* Well, since the maids and valets seem to be in charge today...I shall take a short walk. *(Pointedly, in Silvia's direction.)* It seems we both have stupid servants!

(Exit Harlequin. Silvia is beside herself and grows more and more agitated during the next scene.)

SCENE VII

SILVIA: You astonish me! How dare you not send him away immediately, how dare you force me to endure the indignities of that *animal!*

LISETTE: For heaven's sake, Madame, I can't play two roles at the same time! I have to be either mistress, or maid—either I command, or obey!

SILVIA: Fine, but now that he is gone, I am telling you, you will *obey!* You can see perfectly clearly that this man does not suit me in the least.

LISETTE: You haven't had the time to examine him very closely.

SILVIA: Are you mad? Do you really think a close examination is necessary? You think I need to take more than one quick look to judge his suitability? *I simply will not have him!* And since my father is nowhere to be found—apparently he is not going to allow me complete freedom in this matter after all—it is now up to you to get me out of this impossible situation by telling this young man, nice and neat, that you're not of a mind to marry him.

LISETTE: I couldn't do that, Madame.

SILVIA: You couldn't do that? And who is preventing you?

LISETTE: I...

SILVIA: Who.

LISETTE: Monsieur Orgon told me not to.

SILVIA: He told you not to!

LISETTE: Not under any circumstances.

SILVIA: This is so unlike him. Well I am telling *you* to communicate to *him* my total aversion to this obnoxious man, and to assure him that nothing will change my mind. I cannot imagine when he hears *that* he will push things any further.

LISETTE: But Madame, what is it about this gentleman that you find so obnoxious?

SILVIA: I'm telling you, I do not *like* him, any more than I like you arguing for him.

LISETTE: Take the time to see what he's really like. That's all you are being asked to do.

SILVIA: I hate him. I couldn't hate him more. Except maybe if I were married to him!

LISETTE: I don't suppose his valet has influenced your opinion of his master's character? *He's* rather presumptuous, I've noticed.

SILVIA: Oh you *idiot!* As if a servant could affect me in that way.

LISETTE: Well I don't trust him, he has a line for everything.

SILVIA: I have no use for your thumbnail sketches. I take care that this person doesn't say much to me, but the little he has said to me has been very sensible, I assure you.

LISETTE: I think he might tell you unlikely stories to make himself seem cleverer. I know the type, believe me.

SILVIA: Because I am dressed as a maid, do I have to stand here and listen to this? Why are you suddenly blaming this boy for my aversion to his master? He has no part in it. Why are you obliging me to take his side? Who are you for, and who are you against? You're supposed to be *helping* me today!

LISETTE: Oh Madame, since you take that tone when you stand up for him, and since standing up for him seems to make you so touchy, I shall say no more.

SILVIA: Since I take that tone when I stand up for him! And what exactly is the tone *you're* taking when you say *that?* What are you implying? What is going on in your head?

LISETTE: It's just that I've never seen you like this, Madame, and I don't understand why you're so worked up. If this valet hasn't said anything, fine, stand up for him, you don't need to get in a rage about it. I believe you, end of story. *I* don't object to your having a high opinion of him!

SILVIA: *(Terribly distraught.)* How can you stoop so low?! You're turning everything around! I am outraged! I am so angry I feel like...crying!

LISETTE: Over what, Madame? What innuendo are you hearing in what I'm saying?

SILVIA: I hear innuendo, that's what I hear! Standing up for him makes me *touchy?!* I have a high opinion of him?! Have you such a low opinion of me? High opinion, my God! High opinion! What am I supposed to say to that? What is it supposed to mean? Who do you think you are talking to?

LISETTE: I have no answers for you.

SILVIA: If I'm not safe from all this, who is? What is going on here?!

LISETTE: I don't know, but it'll be a long time before I get over seeing you like this.

SILVIA: Go away, you are insufferable! Leave me alone. I shall have to resort to other measures.

(Exit Lisette.)

SCENE VIII

(A beat. Silvia's mind is racing.)

SILVIA: I can't believe what she said, it's absolutely *frightening,* I'm trembling. The way servants must think of us, they're so impudent, they bring us right down to their level! I just can't get over it, I don't even want to *think* of the things she said, they frighten me somehow. And it's all about some *valet.* The idea! It's too bizarre. But I must put it out of my mind, I will not allow it to blacken my thoughts. *(She sees Dorante coming.)* It's Bourguignon! *(Dismissively.)* Worked up about *him!* Well, it's not his fault, the poor boy, and I mustn't take it out on him.

(Enter Dorante, still dressed as Bourguignon.)

SCENE IX

DORANTE: I think you are avoiding me, so I am forced to come to you. I believe I have reason to complain of you, dear Lisette.

SILVIA: Dear Bourguignon, we must stop speaking so intimately with each other, please.

DORANTE: As you wish, dear Lisette.

SILVIA: But, dear Bourguignon, you said "dear Lisette."

DORANTE: And you, dear Lisette, said "dear Bourguignon."

SILVIA: Well it just slipped out.

DORANTE: Let us speak openly. It isn't worth standing on ceremony when we have so little time left together.

SILVIA: So your master is leaving?

DORANTE: He has decided he must.

SILVIA: That's no great loss.

DORANTE: It would be no great loss if I left too, would it? I am completing your thought.

SILVIA: I could perfectly well complete it myself if I wanted to. But I am not thinking about you.

DORANTE: Well I am thinking about you—always.

SILVIA: Look Bourguignon, once and for all: Whether you stay, go away, or come back, it's all the same to me, it *has* to be, and it is. I have no particular feelings for or against you. I don't hate you, I don't love you, nor *shall* I love you, unless I go out of my mind. That's how I feel, my reason won't allow me to feel any other way, and I shouldn't even have to say this to you.

DORANTE: I am so unhappy! Ah, why has this happened? You don't realize it, but you have the power to destroy my peace of mind, everything I—

SILVIA: *(Interrupting.)* What ideas you have! Come to your senses. You talk to me, and I respond—that's a lot already, it's too much really. You can take my word for it, if you really knew me and who I really am, you'd be very happy with how I treat you. You would think me singularly kind, kind to a fault as far as I'm concerned, it's more than I think is proper, and it won't last—it mustn't! In any case I can't be forever convincing myself that my intentions are innocent. I mean, when you really think about it, what would that look like? I can't be forever examining my heart, and anyway I am destined to marry a well-born man, we can't forget *that!* So let's stop it right here and now, Bourguignon, it's over. What was it all about anyway? Nothing. It was a bagatelle, it was ridiculous. There now, let it not be spoken of again.

DORANTE: Ah, beloved Lisette, how I suffer!

SILVIA: Now what did you come to say to me? You said you had reason to complain of me? What was that about?

DORANTE: I thought perhaps you had spoken ill of me to your mistress.

SILVIA: She thinks you have spoken ill of your master to *me!*

DORANTE: She did seem to accuse me of having done so.

SILVIA: Well, she's just imagining it, and if she speaks to you about it again, you can deny it to her face. Leave the rest to me.

DORANTE: *(Trying to approach the truth.)* And yet...that's not what is really concerning me.

SILVIA: If you go on changing the subject, we shall have nothing further to do with each other. *(She starts to leave.)*

DORANTE: Then I'll say nothing more, but at least allow me to be near you.

SILVIA: *(Turning back.)* Is that a reason for me to stay? So I can indulge the lovelorn Bourguignon? The memory of all this will make me laugh some day.

DORANTE: You are mocking me, and you are right to do so. I don't know what I'm saying, nor really what I am asking of you. I'd better go...
(Silvia is alarmed.)

DORANTE: ...back to the kitchen. Good-bye.

SILVIA: You are doing the right thing. Good-bye.
(A beat. Dorante starts to leave.)

SILVIA: But speaking of good-byes, there is still one thing I'd like to know.
(Dorante turns back to her.)

SILVIA: You said you were leaving us. Is that really true?

DORANTE: I know that if I *don't* leave, I shall go out of my mind.

SILVIA: That's not the answer I was asking for.

DORANTE: In fact I made a big mistake not leaving the moment I laid eyes on you.

SILVIA: *(Aside.)* I simply shall *not* listen to him!

DORANTE: If you knew, Lisette, my... *(Touching his heart.)* ...position...in all this, I think you would be surprised.

SILVIA: Oh, it's not so surprising as my position, I assure you.

DORANTE: You have been reproaching me, but I am not trying to make you love me, believe me.

SILVIA: *(Aside.)* I wish I could.

DORANTE: And why would I try to make you love me, what could I hope? For you see, alas, even if I did claim your heart—

SILVIA: *(Interrupting.)* God, save me from that! If you claimed my heart, you wouldn't know it, and I would definitely arrange things so that I wouldn't know it either. The very idea is mad.

DORANTE: Is it really true then that you neither hate me nor love me, and that you'll never love me?

SILVIA: Absolutely.

DORANTE: Absolutely! What is it that's so horrible about me?

SILVIA: Nothing. That's not what stands in your way.

DORANTE: Well then dear Lisette, tell me again that you will never love me. You must say it a hundred times for me to accept it, and I *must* accept it!

SILVIA: I think I've said it enough. Try to believe me.

DORANTE: I should believe you, I know, but *help* me! Disabuse me of this mad, impossible love, I am afraid of its unthinkable consequences. Tell me again, crush my heart with absolute *certainty,* put me out of this inexplicable misery! I am speaking in good faith, not because I want you to love me, I *don't*—but because *I* don't want to love *you!* You must save me from *myself,* it is essential! Ah!

(He throws himself down before Silvia. At the same moment Orgon and Mario enter unseen and watch.)

DORANTE: I must believe that you will never love me! Tell me that you won't, I am *begging* you!

SILVIA: *(Aside.)* It is because I played along with him that this has happened. I am so unhappy! *(To Dorante.)* Oh Bourguignon, get up, please, I implore you. Someone might come. I shall say whatever you want to hear. Ah, what are you asking of me? I do not hate you. Get up! I don't dislike you. Get up! I would love you if I could. Get up! That will have to do for now.

DORANTE: You mean, Lisette, if I were not what I am, if I were rich, if I were a gentleman, and if I loved you as much as I love you now, your heart would not shut me out?

SILVIA: Certainly not.

DORANTE: You wouldn't hate me? You would tolerate me?

SILVIA: With pleasure. Now get up.

DORANTE: You seem to be telling the truth, and if you are, I shall *truly* go out of my mind!

SILVIA: I said what you wanted to hear, but you're not getting up, that's not *fair!*

(Orgon steps out into the open.)

SCENE X

ORGON: It seems to be going quite well, children.

(Silvia and Dorante are horrified.)

ORGON: It's a pity to have to interrupt you. Bravo!

SILVIA: I could not prevent this boy from kneeling here, Sir. I have hardly encouraged such a tribute, nor do I think it is suitable.

ORGON: Nonsense, the two of you suit each other perfectly. But I must have a word with you, Lisette, and then you can pick up where you left off. Do you mind, Bourguignon?

DORANTE: I shall withdraw, Sir. *(He bows and turns to go.)*

ORGON: Oh, and try to speak of your master a little more discreetly from now on.

DORANTE: *(Turning back, surprised.)* I, Sir?

ORGON: Yes, you, Bourguignon. They tell me that respect for your master is not your strong suit.

DORANTE: I fear I have been misunderstood, Sir.

ORGON: Go on now, good-bye. You can justify your actions another time.
(*Exit Dorante.*)

SCENE XI

ORGON: Silvia, you're not looking at me. You seem quite embarrassed.

SILVIA: I, father? And why would I be embarrassed? I am, thank heaven, very much myself. I'm sorry to have to tell you that you're imagining things.

MARIO: (*Studying her closely.*) There is *something,* sister, there is something.

SILVIA: Something in your head, brother, to be sure. But as for what's in mine? Merely surprise at what you're saying.

ORGON: So it is this boy, then, who has just left, who is prompting your extreme distaste for Dorante?

SILVIA: Who, his valet?

MARIO: The gallant Bourguignon.

SILVIA: The gallant Bourguignon—I didn't know he had that sobriquet—doesn't talk to me about Dorante.

ORGON: Nevertheless I am told that it is he who is prejudicing you against Dorante, and that is what I wanted to talk to you about.

SILVIA: There's nothing to talk about, father. No one has prejudiced me against Dorante except Dorante himself, and it shouldn't surprise anyone that I don't like him!

MARIO: But no matter how many times you say it, dear sister, your dislike for him still seems unnaturally strong. Someone must have been helping it along.

SILVIA: (*Heatedly.*) How mysterious you are, dear brother. Who is this someone? Out with it.

MARIO: Are you in a bad mood, sister? Your dander is up!

SILVIA: Well the truth is, I am sick and tired of acting in this play, and I would gladly give up my part in it if I weren't afraid of irritating Father.

ORGON: Take good care that you don't do that, my dear, take good care. Now since I was willing to allow you your charade, you really ought to be willing to suspend judgment on Dorante, and to see if the bad impression this someone has given you of him is legitimate.

SILVIA: Did you not hear what I just said, Father? The only person who has given me a bad impression of Dorante is Dorante.

MARIO: Oh come come! Are you trying to tell us that this blabbermouth who just left us really didn't do *anything* to encourage your...disgust?

SILVIA: (*Catching fire.*) How can you be so unkind? Encourage my disgust?

Disgust?! The choice of words in this conversation is rather pointed. I "look quite embarrassed," "my dander is up," "the gallant Bourguignon" has "encouraged my disgust"? It's all what you want to think, but I don't understand any of it. It is absolutely unheard of!

MARIO: Your *reaction* is unheard of. What evil plot do you suspect us of? Why are you so jumpy?

SILVIA: Excuse me brother, but why is every word out of your mouth offensive? *(Enraged.)* What evil plot do you *want* me to suspect you of?

ORGON: *(To Silvia.)* Mario is right, you are so angry that I hardly recognize you. I see now that it is this pandemonium in your heart that prompted Lisette to speak to us. She was suspicious of the valet and accused him of trying to discredit Dorante in your eyes. She said, "In defending him to me Madame flew into such a rage that I am *still* suspicious."

SILVIA: How dare she!

MARIO: We reprimanded her for using that word *suspicious,* but people like her don't understand the implications of such words.

SILVIA: How could anyone be so hateful? I admit that I was indignant, but only because her accusation of this boy was so unfair!

MARIO: *(Sarcastic.)* Well I see nothing suspicious in *that.* It's perfectly normal to champion a servant you met this *morning!*

SILVIA: *(Lighting into Mario.)* Yes it is, pure and simple! What, because I am fair-minded, because I don't think people should be accused unjustly, because I want to protect a servant from being discredited in his master's eyes, you say that you hardly recognize me, that my defending him is *suspicious?* And that petty, meddling girl starting rumors! Think of the possible consequences of what she said about him! You were right to reprimand her, you *should* shut her up and take my side. Yes, *my* side! I need somebody to defend *me,* to protect *my* interests. It's all very easy to misconstrue what I was doing when I tried to protect *his.* But what did I *do?* What *am* I being accused of? Enlighten me, I implore you, this is a serious business! Are you making fun of me? Amusing yourselves at my expense? Because I am not happy about it! *(She hurls herself at Mario.)*

ORGON: Calm down, my dear!

SILVIA: No, Father, calm is out of the question. There are suspicions here! And consequences! *(Going at Mario again.)* So please explain! What are you insinuating? You accuse this valet, and you're wrong, you're all wrong! Lisette is a stupid fool, the boy is innocent, and that's the end of it! Why are we still talking about this? I am *seething!*

ORGON: Your restraint is admirable, my dear. Now listen, I have a solution:

The only person under suspicion is the valet, Dorante should simply dismiss him. Doesn't that seem fair?

SILVIA: *(Clutching at her apron.)* How miserably this charade has turned out! Don't let Lisette anywhere near me, I hate her even more than I hate Dorante.

ORGON: But you should be glad the boy is going away, because he *loves* you, and that must be annoying for you.

SILVIA: He has done nothing to annoy me. He takes me for a chambermaid and speaks to me in the appropriate tone. In fact, he wants to tell me more than I let him, but *I* am in control of the situation.

MARIO: You're not as much in control of the situation as you say.

ORGON: Didn't he throw himself down on the ground before you despite your protests?

MARIO: And wasn't the only way you could make him get up to tell him that you would love him *if you could?*

SILVIA: *(Aside, furious that she's been overheard.)* I am suffocating!

MARIO: *(Kneeling before her.)* And wouldn't he still be there on his knees if we hadn't come to save you?

SILVIA: Very observant, brother, but your reenactment is just as distasteful as his kneeling in the first place.

ORGON: Silvia, I require of you that you not decide to refuse Dorante until you have a full understanding of the situation. Wait it out a bit longer.

(Silvia turns to him in frustration.)

ORGON: You will thank me, you have my word on it.

MARIO: You will marry Dorante, and you will even marry him for love, I predict it. But father, please don't make the valet leave.

SILVIA: He can go to the farthest corner of the earth, as far as I'm concerned.

ORGON: Come along now, Mario.

MARIO: Adieu, sister dear. No hard feelings!

(Exeunt Orgon and Mario.)

SCENE XII

SILVIA: What anguish! I don't understand what is making things so complicated. This day is a torment, I trust no one, everyone upsets me, I upset *myself.*

(Enter Dorante.)

DORANTE: Lisette! I had to come back!

SILVIA: Well it wasn't worth coming back, because now I really *am* avoiding you.

(She starts to leave, but Dorante catches her and keeps her from going.)

DORANTE: No, stop, Lisette! This will be the last time I speak to you!

SILVIA: *(Struggling to get free.)* Leave me alone, every time I see you, you torment me!

DORANTE: And I could say the same about you! But listen, things are going to change completely, because of what I am about to tell you.

SILVIA: Well tell me then, the sooner they change, the better! *(Pulling herself free.)* I'm listening, since it seems to be decided that I'll always do what you want.

DORANTE: Will you promise to keep it a secret?

SILVIA: I am absolutely trustworthy.

DORANTE: I am going to tell you…what I am going to tell you…because I esteem you highly.

SILVIA: I believe you, but try to esteem me without telling me about it, because whenever you tell me about it I suspect that you're up to something.

DORANTE: *(Sharply.)* Well I am no longer up to something, Lisette, and that's the point. *(A beat. He steels himself.)* You have seen that I have been in a very…emotional state. That I cannot keep from loving you.

SILVIA: Well I can certainly keep from listening to any more of this.

(She starts to leave. Dorante catches her again.)

DORANTE: *(Commanding.)* Stay!

(Silvia stops at the change in his voice.)

DORANTE: It is no longer Bourguignon who is speaking to you.

SILVIA: What? *(A beat.)* Who are you then?

DORANTE: Ah, Lisette, now you will know what my heart has suffered.

SILVIA: I am not talking to your heart, I am talking to you.

DORANTE: *(Looking around nervously.)* Someone might come.

SILVIA: No, *speak!*

DORANTE: The situation, as it has developed, requires that I tell you. I am…an honorable man, at least honorable enough not to let it go any further.

SILVIA: Fine. *So?*

DORANTE: You should know that the person with your mistress is not who you think he is.

SILVIA: *(Impatient.)* Who is he?

DORANTE: A valet.

SILVIA: *(Impatient.)* And…?

DORANTE: I am Dorante.

(Silvia turns sharply away from him. A beat.)

SILVIA: *(Aside.)* Ah, now I understand my heart.

DORANTE: I wanted to know something about what your mistress was really like, before I married her, so I came here dressed as someone else. But it has all turned into something...out of a dream. I cannot endure the mistress, whom I was supposed to marry, and I am in love with her maid, who was supposed to think of me as a new master. So what should I do now? I blush to say it, for her, but your mistress has such poor judgment that she has fallen for my valet, and I think she would actually marry him if no one told her the truth. How should I proceed?

(He turns away, ashamed and perplexed. Silvia considers the situation. A beat.)

SILVIA: First of all I must beg your pardon for anything I said to you in our conversations which might have been inappropriate.

DORANTE: *(Interrupting.)* No no, don't apologize. It just reminds me of the fact that separates us, and makes it all the more painful.

SILVIA: Your situation is indeed unusual, but not as unusual as you think.

DORANTE: Gentlemen may sometimes pursue maids, but I think they do not really love them.

SILVIA: Do you mean that you really love Lisette? You love her enough to—

DORANTE: *(Interrupting.)* I love her enough never to marry anyone else. But of course it will never be possible for me to marry *her*. Under the circumstances, the only consolation I could hope to enjoy would be...to know that she didn't despise me.

SILVIA: *(Aside.)* I am not going to tell him. *(To Dorante.)* A gentleman who would offer his heart to me, a lady's maid with no prospects, is surely worthy of more than that. I should offer my heart in return, and I would, gladly, but I fear you are right, it is not possible—such an arrangement could only compromise you.

DORANTE: Were you not already bewitching enough, Lisette? Now this nobility, and grace?

MARIO: *(From offstage.)* Lisette!

SILVIA: I hear someone coming. Listen, about your valet and my mistress— they are not so far along as you think, certain things have yet to be said. So we have some time, and we will see each other again. We must look for ways to...solve your problem.

DORANTE: I shall do what you think best.

SILVIA: Good.

MARIO: *(Calling from offstage.)* Where is Lisette?

(Exit Dorante. A beat.)

SILVIA: Well. I really needed that man to be Dorante.

SCENE XIII

(Enter Mario.)

MARIO: Silvia. I had to come back. I was sorry to leave you so distraught. I want to help you, listen—

SILVIA: *(Interrupting, elated.)* Oh my dear Mario!

MARIO: There is something I have to tell you.

SILVIA: There is something I have to tell *you.*

MARIO: What?

SILVIA: *(Increasingly excited.)* Mario, it's Dorante!

MARIO: What about him?

SILVIA: He was just here, he told me himself!

MARIO: What did he tell you?

SILVIA: He loves me!

MARIO: I thought he loved Lisette.

SILVIA: Oh, he *does!*

MARIO: But *which* Lisette?

SILVIA: Do you really not understand?

MARIO: I don't think so.

SILVIA: *Bourguignon's* Lisette.

MARIO: You mean you?

SILVIA: Come on, let's go find Father, I'm getting new ideas every second. I'm going to need you, brother. You must pretend to love me—remember this morning when you hinted that you did? And you have to keep this a secret.

MARIO: How could I not? I'm not sure I know what it is.

SILVIA: Oh this is priceless, this is a first!

MARIO: Are you out of your mind?

(Silvia pulls Mario to her side.)

SILVIA: I will make him do it!

MARIO: Do what?

(A servant enters. Silvia whispers into Mario's ear.)

MARIO: *(Amazed.)* No!

SILVIA: I will make an honest man of him. Come on!

(Blackout.)

ACT III
SCENE I

(It is afternoon. Harlequin and Dorante, still in their disguises, are deep in conversation.)

HARLEQUIN: Have compassion, master!

DORANTE: Go away!

HARLEQUIN: I beg of you!

DORANTE: Leave me alone!

HARLEQUIN: But I have a real chance here, don't put a hex on my happiness just when everything's going along so well, and so *quickly*. Most deeply revered master, don't slam the gates on me!

DORANTE: I think you're making fun of me, and I think you deserve fifty lashes.

HARLEQUIN: If I deserve them for what I've done, I'll submit to them, but when the thrashing's over, I'll do it again, because I can't help myself. So *you'll* have to do it again. And I'll have to do it again, and you'll have to do it again, and I'll have to do it again, and you'll have to do it again, and I'll have to do it again…

DORANTE: *(Interrupting.)* Shut up!

HARLEQUIN: Shall I go get the lash?

DORANTE: You are such a scoundrel!

HARLEQUIN: I'm a scoundrel, fine. Many scoundrels have made a fortune.

DORANTE: Typical! You *sneak!*

HARLEQUIN: Sneak is fine, too. It certainly suits me, and many sneaks have married well.

DORANTE: You are so presumptuous! You want me to lead an honorable man like Monsieur Orgon into a trap, and let you marry his daughter using my name?

HARLEQUIN: I didn't say that!

DORANTE: Listen, if you speak to me one more time about this gross impertinence, I am going to tell him exactly who and what you are, and I am going to dismiss you, too. Now go away.

HARLEQUIN: I'll make you a deal: This young lady adores me, she *idolizes* me. If I tell her that I am only a valet, and if, notwithstanding, her tender heart still elects to marry me, will you let the violins play?

DORANTE: When she sees you for what you really are, marriage isn't even going to be an issue anymore.

HARLEQUIN: Well, I am going to go right now and tell this generous woman exactly what it is I usually wear. I hope that a pair of scuffed shoes won't keep us apart, and I hope that her love will allow me to sit at the table, despite the fact that destiny stuck me in the pantry!

(Exit Harlequin.)

SCENE II

DORANTE: Everything that is happening, everything that is happening inside me…is past believing. I know nothing of Lisette, only that she is something I am not, and that to love her—ah, to love her—I would have to surrender everything. But one cannot live without position, one cannot betray one's family, one's *honor*. Besides, one cannot *marry* such a person, at best one arranges a sort of…liaison. One is…a gentleman. *(A beat.)* And yet still I want to see Lisette. She said we must look for ways. What could she mean? What solution is there to a problem such as ours? *(Setting off.)* If I could just find her alone…

(Enter Mario.)

MARIO: Wait, Bourguignon. A word with you.

DORANTE: *(Turning back.)* What can I do for you, Sir?

MARIO: You are courting Lisette, I think?

DORANTE: She is so charming, Sir, it would be difficult *not* to do so.

MARIO: And how does she respond?

DORANTE: She…toys with me, Sir.

MARIO: You do have a way with words. Are you hiding something?

DORANTE: But, Sir, why does it matter to you? Supposing Lisette…took a fancy to me?

MARIO: "Took a fancy!" Where does a person like you get an expression like that? Such refined language for a boy of your class.

DORANTE: Sir, that is the only language I know.

MARIO: It is evidently with these little verbal bonbons that you are making your appeal to Lisette? You mean to impersonate a man of position, I take it?

DORANTE: I assure you, Sir, I am impersonating no one. But undoubtedly your purpose in coming here wasn't to subject me to ridicule, and you have something else to say to me. We were speaking of Lisette, of my interest in her, and of the interest you are taking in the matter.

MARIO: Do I detect a touch of jealousy in your response? Curb your passion, boy. Now then, you were saying, supposing Lisette took a fancy to you. What then?

DORANTE: Why, Sir, is it necessary for you to know?

MARIO: Aha, well, there you have it. You see, the fact is, despite the light tone of this conversation, I would be very put out if Lisette loved you. Indeed, without saying too much more about it, I forbid you to make any further appeals to her. Not, mind you, because I am really afraid that she loves you—it seems to me she has too proud a heart for that. But because I would not be…happy to have Bourguignon as a rival.

DORANTE: Well I can understand that, because Bourguignon, for all that he is only Bourguignon, wouldn't be happy to have you as a rival, either.

MARIO: Well then Bourguignon is going to have to suffer in silence.

DORANTE: Bourguignon won't have any other choice.

(They look at each other. A beat.)

DORANTE: Do you really love her?

MARIO: Enough to arrange a permanent liaison with her, as soon as the appropriate measures can be taken. Of course, I would never marry the girl, so…*arrangements* must be made. Do you understand what I mean by that?

DORANTE: I think I know exactly what you mean. I take it you are loved by her, then, in return?

MARIO: What do you think? Don't you think I deserve to be?

DORANTE: Surely you don't expect to be congratulated by your rival.

MARIO: A very sensible answer, I forgive you for it. I am embarrassed that I cannot say she *does* love me in return. And I don't say this because I owe *you* an explanation, because of course you realize that I do not, but simply because it is the truth.

DORANTE: Is Lisette aware of your intentions?

MARIO: Lisette is aware of my *feelings,* and she seems unmoved by them. But I trust that she will have enough sense to give me her heart. Her indifference to me, in spite of all that I have to offer her, should console you for the sacrifice you must make for me.

DORANTE: You astound me, Sir.

MARIO: Your apron is hardly going to tip the scales in your favor, and you are not exactly in a position to compete with me. You may go.

(Enter Silvia, still dressed as Lisette.)

SCENE III

MARIO: Lisette! Have you been listening?

SILVIA: Sir, you seem upset, is anything the matter?

MARIO: Nothing. I was just having a word with Bourguignon.

SILVIA: *(Looking at Dorante.)* He looks sad. Are you scolding him?

DORANTE: Monsieur was telling me that he loves you, Lisette.

SILVIA: I can't help that.

DORANTE: And I have been forbidden to love you.

SILVIA: *(To Mario.)* And I suppose I have been forbidden to be lovable?

MARIO: I couldn't possibly forbid him to love you, my beautiful Lisette, but I can forbid him to tell you that he does.

SILVIA: He's already told me that he does—now he's just repeating it.

MARIO: Well then I forbid him to repeat it. Go away, Bourguignon.

DORANTE: *(A challenge.)* I shall leave when *Lisette* tells me to leave. *(To Lisette.)* I await your word.

MARIO: *(Furious.)* I don't believe this!

SILVIA: *(To Mario.)* Now be patient, Sir.

DORANTE: *(To Silvia.)* Do you have any romantic interest in Monsieur?

SILVIA: Do you mean do I *love* him? Listen, you don't have to warn me away from him.

DORANTE: Are you leading me on? What do you mean?

MARIO: I might as well not be here at all, no one even listens to me. *(To Dorante.)* You will now make your exit.

DORANTE: *(To Silvia.)* What do you *mean?*

MARIO: *(Bellowing.)* Who do you think you are?!

DORANTE: *(Aside, beside himself.)* This is unbearable!

SILVIA: *(To Dorante.)* He's angry, you'd better do as he tells you.

DORANTE: *(Aside, to Silvia.)* You want me to leave, too!

MARIO: That will be all!

DORANTE: You hadn't told me, Lisette, that you cared for…someone else. *(Exit Dorante.)*

SILVIA: If I didn't love that man, let's face it, this would be rather cruel. *(Mario laughs. Enter Orgon.)*

SCENE IV

ORGON: What are you laughing at, Mario?

MARIO: At Dorante, and how angry he was. He was just here, and I ordered him to give up all hope of Lisette.

SILVIA: *(To Mario.)* What did he say to you when it was just the two of you?

MARIO: I have never seen a man in more of a state, or in a worse mood.

ORGON: He's been hoist with his own petard, and I quite approve. And furthermore, if you look at it in a certain way, Silvia, what you have done for him up to this point couldn't be more flattering, or kinder. But I think it's enough now.

MARIO: Where exactly do things stand, "Lisette?"

SILVIA: I confess I have good reason to be happy. Ah, dearest brother!

MARIO: *(Imitating her.)* "Ah, dearest brother!" *(To Orgon.)* Father, have you noticed the sudden sweetness creeping into the way she talks to us?

ORGON: *(To Silvia.)* But my dear, you're not by any chance hoping that Dorante will go so far as to offer you his hand while you are still dressed as a *maid,* are you?

SILVIA: *(Radiant.)* Yes, my dear father, I am.

MARIO: "Yes, my dear father, I am. Yes, my dear father, I am not snapping at you any more, because now *I* am pulling the strings." *(To Silvia.)* You *minx!*

SILVIA: *(To Mario.)* You just can't let me win, can you?

MARIO: *(Laughing.)* I'm taking my revenge, that's all. You were certainly taking issue with *my* way of putting things a while ago. Your happiness is at least as entertaining as your misery was.

ORGON: *(To Silvia.)* I won't give you any trouble, my dear. I will play along.

SILVIA: Oh Father, by letting me have my way today you have laid the foundation of my happiness and ensured that it will last! Dorante and I! We are destined for each other. He *has* to marry me. You know now what he will have to do to win me. If only you knew how much I admire him for it, how dearly my heart will cherish the memory of his *suffering,* and the tender feelings that prompted it! If you knew how much happier that suffering is going to make our marriage! Never did a woman have such an advantage! Whenever he remembers our courtship he will remember his ordeal, and he will love me even more, and whenever *I* think of it I shall love *him* even more. Ours will be a unique marriage. What an unexpected, improbable stroke of luck—the most propitious, the happiest, the most…

MARIO: *(Interrupting.)* Your heart is quite the chatterbox! What eloquence!

ORGON: I have to admit that the play you have put on is charming, especially if you can get the ending to work.

SILVIA: That's as good as done. Dorante is in chains. Now I am just waiting for him to come to me.

MARIO: He doesn't know those chains are made of gold though. He must be suffering terribly, I pity him.

SILVIA: But that suffering—what it costs him to make the right decision—is for me the very measure of his worth. He thinks if he marries me, or the serving girl he believes me to be, he will aggrieve his father. He thinks that he will be betraying family, fortune, and rank. These things are worthy of serious consideration, are they not? So it is surely right that he should suffer over them. Oh, it will give me great pleasure to win, make no mistake, but I must wrest my victory from him, he mustn't just hand it to me. I want a real contest between reason…and love.

MARIO: And may reason perish in the fray!

ORGON: So you're forcing him to reckon fully with the consequences of this mad, reckless thing he thinks he's doing, even before he does it.

SILVIA: Correct.

ORGON: What insatiable vanity! You think very highly of yourself, my dear.

MARIO: Women often do, Father, and that's just how it is.

(Enter Lisette.)

SCENE V

LISETTE: *(Curtsying.)* Monsieur Orgon.

ORGON: Ah, Lisette.

LISETTE: You said earlier that you were turning Dorante over to me, that you would give me his head on a silver platter. Well, I took you at your word. I have acted in my own interests, and I have achieved my objective: He has lost his head. What do you want me to do with it now? Will Madame relinquish it to me?

ORGON: Silvia, for the last time, do you want Dorante's head?

SILVIA: No, it's all yours, Lisette. All my claims to it, and any further involvement with it, hereby pass to you. I have no use for a head that I haven't cut off myself.

LISETTE: You mean you will, in fact, let me marry him, Sir?

ORGON: If *he* can make his peace with it, after all is said and done, yes.

MARIO: I also say yes.

SILVIA: So do I.

LISETTE: I am very grateful to all of you.

ORGON: But I must add one little condition to our agreement. You'll have to tell him a little of who you really are—otherwise his father might hold us responsible.

LISETTE: But if I tell him a little, he'll know everything.

ORGON: Well, if he has lost his head, how can he change his mind? I don't think this particular fellow is the type of person to be put off by what you have to tell him.

(Harlequin is heard offstage.)

LISETTE: I see him, he's looking for me. Be so good as to leave the field to me. I must fight this battle alone.

ORGON: *(To Silvia and Mario.)* Shall we withdraw?

(Enter Harlequin, still dressed as Dorante.)

SILVIA: *(With a conspiratorial curtsey to Lisette.)* You have all my best wishes, Madame.

MARIO: *(To Silvia.)* Come along, Lisette.

(Exeunt Orgon, Silvia, and Mario.)

SCENE VI

HARLEQUIN: At last, oh queen, I have found you. And I shall never again leave your side, for it has too much afflicted me to long for your company, especially when it seemed you were avoiding mine.

LISETTE: I must confess, Monsieur, that there is some truth in what you say.

HARLEQUIN: There is?! Elixir of my heart, my very soul, have you undertaken to end my life?

LISETTE: No, my love, it is too precious to me.

HARLEQUIN: Ah! That's encouraging.

LISETTE: And you must never question my fondness for you.

HARLEQUIN: Would that I could gather those words from your lips, with mine.

LISETTE: My father has just told me…that you may ask him for my hand…but only if I tell you that…

HARLEQUIN: *(Interrupting.)* Before I ask it of him, allow me to ask it of *you.* For should it choose to remain in mine, which is truly not worthy of it, I must offer it in advance my humblest thanks.

LISETTE: I shan't refuse to leave my hand in yours for the moment, if you agree never, under any circumstances, to let go of it.

HARLEQUIN: Dear plump little dumpling of a hand, you needn't set conditions, you will always be welcome in mine. I am so pleased with the honor you show me. I am afraid you might not be so pleased when I show you my honor.

LISETTE: You will show me more than I deserve to see, I am sure, however much you show me.

HARLEQUIN: No no no no no no no, you don't understand the arithmetic of the situation so well as I.

LISETTE: Nevertheless, I think of your advantages as being very numerous, and I regard your love as a gift from heaven.

HARLEQUIN: Heaven can certainly afford it, it's actually quite cheap.

LISETTE: I consider it quite lavish.

HARLEQUIN: All that glitters is not gold.

LISETTE: You are modest, and you wouldn't believe how much your modesty embarrasses me.

HARLEQUIN: Oh, don't waste any time being embarrassed, I would be really shameless if I *weren't* so modest. I am extremely privileged to steal these few tender moments from you.

LISETTE: *(Steeling herself.)* Oh Monsieur, is it really necessary to tell you that, of the two of us, it is definitely *I* who am privileged to steal them from *you?*

HARLEQUIN: *(Aside, full of dread.)* Get me out of here.

LISETTE: *(Determinedly.)* To put it more clearly, Sir, I know who I am.

HARLEQUIN: *(Flustered.)* Well I know who *I* am, too, and I'm not such a great person to know, as you'll realize when you get to know me better. In fact, knowing me is not unproblematic, and I know you're not expecting to know what I know you don't know now...

LISETTE: Exactly what are you trying to tell me?

HARLEQUIN: Ah, the hounds have picked up my scent!

LISETTE: What is going on?

HARLEQUIN: *(Aside.)* Let's work up to it slowly. *(To Lisette.)* Madame. Your love for me. Does it have a robust constitution? Will it be able to withstand the blow which I am bound to deal it? Would it be put off by a house with...fewer rooms? Say, *one?*

LISETTE: Oh, put me out of my misery! What is your name?

HARLEQUIN: My name? *(Aside.)* Should I tell her my name is just Harlequin? No, it sounds too much like Charlatan.

LISETTE: Well?

HARLEQUIN: *(Aside, whispered.)* This is very difficult. *(He considers how to proceed. To Lisette.)* Do you detest...soldiers?

LISETTE: What do you mean, soldiers?

HARLEQUIN: I mean, as a profession.

LISETTE: *Are* you a soldier?

HARLEQUIN: Yes, well, say, a soldier who...fights...in the...kitchen.

LISETTE: *The kitchen?*

HARLEQUIN: The kitchen.

LISETTE: The kitchen.

HARLEQUIN: The kitchen.

LISETTE: The *kitchen!* So you are not Dorante at all.

HARLEQUIN: No, he's my commanding officer. I am his servant.

LISETTE: *(Appalled.)* Charlatan!

HARLEQUIN: *(Correcting her.)* Harlequin. The two words are very much alike.

LISETTE: I cannot believe that I have spent the last hour groveling and humiliating myself for this...*lint-picker!*

HARLEQUIN: Alas, Madame, I could satisfy you as much as any Seigneur, if you could put love before pride.

LISETTE: *(Laughing.)* Pride! That's a laugh! Pride!

(Lisette is convulsed, Harlequin humiliated.)

LISETTE: Well, I might as well resign myself to the inevitable. Don't worry, my pride forgives you for your deception.

HARLEQUIN: You mean it?

LISETTE: My pride is pretty easygoing, as it happens.

HARLEQUIN: Ah, most charitable lady, my love promises to make it up to you.

LISETTE: All right, Harlequin, you duped me, but the kitchen soldier of Monsieur is no worse than the hairdresser of Madame.

HARLEQUIN: The hairdresser of Madame?

LISETTE: The hairdresser of Madame.

HARLEQUIN: The hairdresser of Ma— I cannot believe I've spent the last hour going through the agonies of the damned excusing my existence to this… *washerwoman!*

LISETTE: All right, let's get to the heart of the matter. Do you love me?

HARLEQUIN: Do I love you?! *Yes.* You may have changed your name, but your eyes are the same, and you'll remember that we swore an oath to love each other forever, so we'd be covered for any possible mistakes and false assumptions.

LISETTE: Well, we didn't do each other much harm. Let's be comforted by what we do have, and forget about what we're not going to become.

HARLEQUIN: *(Seeing Dorante in the distance.)* My master's coming!

LISETTE: Wait, Harlequin, we don't want them laughing at us, so let's not tell anyone—*especially* your master, I don't think he knows about my mistress yet.

HARLEQUIN: Here he is.

(Enter Dorante, still dressed as Bourguignon. Harlequin and Lisette laugh ostentatiously, for Dorante's benefit.)

LISETTE: *(To Harlequin, so Dorante can hear.)* Monsieur, I shall serve you like a chambermaid.

HARLEQUIN: *(To Lisette, so Dorante can hear.)* And I, Madame, shall serve you like a valet.

(Lisette kisses Harlequin, for Dorante's benefit. Exit Lisette.)

SCENE VII

DORANTE: You didn't tell her who you are!

HARLEQUIN: Oh yes I did. And that grand lady has the heart of a lamb. When I told her my name was just Harlequin, and that I usually wear an apron, she said, "Never mind, my dear, every man to his place in this world, and to each his own taste in clothes. You may not have paid for yours, but that doesn't make them any less flattering." *(He laughs.)*

DORANTE: What a preposterous story.

HARLEQUIN: And here's the preposterous ending: I am going to ask for her hand in marriage.

DORANTE: She wouldn't marry you!

HARLEQUIN: Oh yes she would! And she'd be none the worse for it either. Why not let that be a lesson to *you!*

DORANTE: You're lying. She doesn't know who you are. She *couldn't.*

HARLEQUIN: Oh for God's sake! If you go on provoking me, I'll marry her in my clogs, or dressed up as a smithie. I want you to understand something— the kind of love I feel, and inspire, can't just be gotten rid of, or broken. And I don't need your fancy clothes to press my advantage. I'll go put my *own* clothes back on, and you'll see that I'm not lying.

DORANTE: You're lying all right, the whole thing is appalling. And if you won't tell this girl who you are, I will tell her father!

HARLEQUIN: You mean *my* father. We've got him in the palm of our hand. And what a lovely little fellow he is, the nicest, most generous person I know. He's going to surprise you.

DORANTE: You're raving. Where's Lisette?

HARLEQUIN: I don't know. She may have passed before my eyes, but a true gentleman doesn't really actually *see* servants. I leave that job to you.

DORANTE: This is all going to your head. Get out of here.

HARLEQUIN: Your tone is amusing but a little too cozy. I know, it's hard to break a lifelong habit of condescension. But we shall soon be equals. Adieu.

(Enter Silvia.)

HARLEQUIN: Ah, here's your little soubrette. Good afternoon, Lisette. I highly recommend Bourguignon to you. The boy has…promise. *(Exit Harlequin.)*

SCENE VIII

DORANTE: *(Aside.)* How beautiful she is. And how worthy of my love. Ah, that Mario should win her!

SILVIA: Where have you been, Sir?

DORANTE: *(Reserved.)* I have never been far from you.

SILVIA: *(Aside.)* So cold.

DORANTE: *(Aside.)* I must close my heart.

SILVIA: After I left Monsieur Mario, I couldn't find you.

DORANTE: *(Jealous.)* Why would you look for *me?*

SILVIA: Listen, I tried to make them see that your valet is unworthy of my mistress, I tried to make a case for postponing the wedding, but all in vain. They are talking about marrying immediately, this evening. I'm warning you, it's time now to declare yourself…and your intentions.

DORANTE: You are right. *(Producing a letter.)* I have written a letter to Monsieur Orgon which will explain everything. I am going to leave here immediately, alone.

SILVIA: *(Aside.)* Leave! That's not going to help me!

DORANTE: Do you not approve of my plan?

SILVIA: Well…hardly.

DORANTE: But I don't see a better solution, given our situation, unless I stay and tell him everything, and I cannot bring myself to do that. Besides, there is now something else—something that gives me no choice but to leave.

SILVIA: As I do not know what that something is, I can neither approve nor disapprove your decision nor argue against it. And it is not my place to ask you what it might be.

DORANTE: You know perfectly well what it is, Lisette.

SILVIA: Well, Sir, I realize that you have taken a dislike to my mistress.

DORANTE: *(Sarcastic.)* And I suppose you think that's the whole of it.

SILVIA: There are indeed other things that I could imagine, but it would be sheer vanity to speak of them here.

DORANTE: You don't have the courage to speak of them, because you have nothing reassuring to say to me. Good-bye, Lisette. *(He starts to leave.)*

SILVIA: Take care what you suppose.

(Dorante turns back.)

SILVIA: I will say that I think you have misunderstood me.

DORANTE: *(Bitterly.)* Better to keep your explanations from me until I am gone.

SILVIA: Are you really going to leave?

DORANTE: You seem afraid that I'll change my mind.

SILVIA: How charming of you to know so much about me.

DORANTE: I think you have not been honest with me. Farewell. *(He goes.)*

SILVIA: *(Furious.)* If he leaves, I shall stop loving him right here and now, and I shall never marry him. *(She watches Dorante go, surreptitiously.)* Aha, he's stopping. He's thinking. He's looking back at me, to see if I'm looking back at him. But I shan't call him back, no… It would be very surprising if he did leave, after all I have done. *(She sneaks a look off after Dorante. She is troubled.)* Ah! He did leave. I don't have as much power over him as I thought. I thought being jealous would make him *stay!* My brother is a clumsy fool, he must have handled it badly. Insensitive people spoil everything. And now where does this leave me? So now it all unravels, what a sad ending. *(She looks into the distance, after Dorante. A beat.)* I think he's coming back! He *is!* I take it all back, I still love him. But what do I do now?! I'll walk away, so he'll stop me again. The reconciliation must cost him something.

(She walks away. Dorante enters running and stops her.)

DORANTE: Stay, I beg of you. I have something else to say to you.

SILVIA: To me, Sir?

DORANTE: It is difficult for me to leave without convincing you that I am right to do so.

SILVIA: But Sir, why should you have to justify yourself to *me?* It isn't worth it, I am only a servant girl, and you are certainly making me feel like one.

DORANTE: *(Snapping at her.)* You complain to me? You who see me agonize over the decision I must make and yet refuse to help me make it?!

SILVIA: *(Her dander up.)* Oh, if I cared to answer that charge, I could answer it well!

DORANTE: Answer it then, I could ask for nothing better than to be mistaken about your true feelings!

SILVIA: And why should I tell *you,* Sir, about my true feelings?

DORANTE: Because I love you! But what am I saying? Mario also loves you!

SILVIA: That is true.

DORANTE: And you are receptive, I saw that earlier—

SILVIA: *(Interrupting.)* Receptive! Who says?

DORANTE: You couldn't wait for me to leave you alone with him. I realize that you could never love me.

SILVIA: I could never love you? What do you know about that? You certainly jump to conclusions.

DORANTE: For God's sake, Lisette, by all that you hold most dear in this world, tell me where things truly stand, I beseech you!

SILVIA: Tell a man who is leaving?

DORANTE: Then I shan't leave. But give me a reason to stay!

SILVIA: You are the master, Sir, you can go or stay as you wish. But if you love me, don't torture me with interrogation. You want nothing more than for me to confess my feelings for you, but you are lucky that I remain silent. Anyway, what can my feelings really mean to you, Sir?

DORANTE: Lisette, can you *doubt* that I adore you?

SILVIA: You repeat it so often that I believe you, but why are you trying to convince me of it? What do you expect *me* to do about it, Sir? I am going to speak freely to you. You love me, but your love isn't really a serious thing for you. Think of all the reasons you have to shake it off when you have had enough of it—the distance between us, the fact of who I am and what I can never be, the thousand women who will fall into your arms on your way through life, all the amusements of a man of your station, all these things will erase this love that you now go on about so relentlessly and so cruelly. You will laugh about it when you leave here, and forget me, and with good reason. But I, Sir, when I look back on it, as I fear I shall, if love has undone me, who will I turn to with all the sorrow in my heart? And what could ever make up for the loss of you, who could ever replace you in my heart? Imagine the position I'd be left in. Do you not realize that, if I loved you, no other man, no matter how wealthy or grand, could turn my head or sway my heart? No, be as noble as your name, and kindly keep your feelings hidden away. As for me, I could never simply tell you that I love you, not with you in your current state. A confession could endanger your reason, and so you see that I, *too,* must keep my feelings hidden away.

DORANTE: Oh my darling Lisette, what am I hearing? I must be dreaming. Your words burn into me like a fire. Nothing could be as true as your spirit, and nothing could be worth more. Everything else pales and slips away—birthright, bloodlines, position, possessions. You have my love, and you have my respect. I would be ashamed if my pride argued against you for one second longer. My heart belongs to you alone.

SILVIA: *(Pleased.)* Ah, Sir, wouldn't you just deserve it if this chambermaid accepted you? And wouldn't she have to be subtler and more poised than a chambermaid could ever be to conceal her pleasure from you? And how much longer do you think she'll be able to do so?

DORANTE: You love me then?

SILVIA: I didn't say that. But if you ask me one more time, there's no telling what I might answer, and what might happen to you.

DORANTE: Your threats don't frighten me at all.

SILVIA: And what of Mario?

DORANTE: Mario doesn't concern me anymore. You don't love him, Lisette, you can't fool me now. Your heart speaks for you, and the rapture in mine is unmistakable—you love me! There is no doubt in my mind, I am certain of it, and nothing you say could convince me otherwise.

SILVIA: *(With rapture.)* Oh, I wouldn't want to convince you otherwise. *(After a pause.)* But we have yet to see what you're going to do about it. *(They look at each other, wondering what will happen. A beat.)*

DORANTE: Will you marry me, Lisette?

SILVIA: You mean you'd marry me in spite of everything—your father, your inheritance, your position?

DORANTE: The moment he lays eyes on you my father will forgive me, and the value of an honest heart is worth a thousand fortunes. I see now that true merit is worth more than position. There's your answer. And nothing you say could make me change my mind. I shall never change it.

SILVIA: Never?

DORANTE: Never.

SILVIA: You are beguiling me, Dorante. Do you know that?

DORANTE: Then do as your heart pleases. *(A beat. Silvia kisses Dorante.)*

SILVIA: It has turned out as I desired. You... *Nothing* could make you change your mind?

DORANTE: No, Lisette, nothing. *(Silvia touches his face gently.)*

SILVIA: So much love. *(Enter Orgon, Mario, Harlequin, Lisette, and other servants.)*

SCENE IX

SILVIA: Father! You wanted me to marry Dorante.

DORANTE: *(Appalled.)* Father?! *(All except Silvia and Dorante laugh.)*

SILVIA: Come look, your daughter obeys you, and with more joy than she ever imagined could fit in one heart.

DORANTE: You, Monsieur, are her father?

ORGON: *(Handing to Dorante the letter from his father.)* Do you recognize this handwriting? I learned of your disguise this morning from your father, but Silvia learned only from you. *(Dorante throws the letter down angrily and turns on Silvia.)*

SILVIA: Yes, Dorante! You and I both had the same idea—to find out exactly who the other was. And now we have. And that's all I can say. You love me, I could never doubt it. But now it is up to you. Judge the case. Here is the evidence: your love, my love. Here is my defense: It may seem that I have played with your heart, but it was with the greatest respect and the tenderest consideration that I have endeavored to win it.

(Dorante remains motionless. Everyone awaits his response.)

DORANTE: *(At length. To Silvia.)* I am inexpressibly...*happy,* Madame, that you played with my heart, and amazed and gratified that my heart defied my reason, and carried the day.

MARIO: Dorante, will you forgive me for making Bourguignon furious?

DORANTE: For that I shall not forgive you, I shall thank you.

HARLEQUIN: *(To Lisette.)* Rejoice, Madame! You have lost your fortune, but you can't very well complain, since you get me in the end.

LISETTE: And what a comfort that is. Though I still think you get more out of it than I do.

HARLEQUIN: I won't argue with that, I definitely won. When I first met you your dowry was worth more than you, but now you're worth more than your dowry. *(To everyone.)* Such happiness. A dance!

(They all dance.)

(Fade to black.)

END OF PLAY

PLATE 21

Harlequin, dressed as his master, meets Monsieur Orgon (I,10)
John Michael Higgins and Laurence O'Dwyer in *The Game of Love and Chance,*
McCarter Theatre 1997

Photo by T. Charles Erickson

PLATE 22

Silvia is appalled by Harlequin; her brother and father eavesdrop (I,8)
Jared Reed (Harlequin), Francesca Faridany, Michael Medico, Nicholas Kepros
in *The Game of Love and Chance,* Huntington Theatre 1997

PLATE 23

Lisette is delighted by Harlequin (I,12)
Reed and Margaret Welsh in *The Game of Love and Chance,* Huntington Theatre 1997

PLATE 24

Lisette's dilemma begins in earnest (II,5)
Reed and Welsh in *The Game of Love and Chance*, Huntington Theatre 1997

PLATE 25

Silvia is perplexed by Lisette's revelations (II,7)
Faridany in *The Game of Love and Chance*, Huntington Theatre 1997

PLATE 26

Silvia to Dorante: "We must look for ways to…
solve your problem." (II,12)
Faridany and Paul Anthony Stewart in *The Game of Love and Chance,*
Huntington Theatre 1997

Photo by T. Charles Erickson

Photo by T. Charles Erickson

PLATE 27

Mario and Silvia torment Dorante (III,3)
Jared Reed (Mario) and Faridany in *The Game of Love and Chance,*
McCarter Theatre 1997

PLATE 28

Harlequin to his master: "We shall soon be equals." (III,7)
Neil Maffin (Dorante) and Higgins in *The Game of Love and Chance,*
McCarter Theatre 1997

PLATE 29

The household notes Dorante's approach (III,7)

Ed Mahler, Reed, Reid Armbruster, Higgins, Welsh, and O'Dwyer
in *The Game of Love and Chance,* McCarter Theatre 1997

PLATE 30

The dance (III,9)

Higgins, Reed, O'Dwyer, Kathleen Heenan, Armbruster, Maffin, Mahler, Welsh
in *The Game of Love and Chance,* McCarter Theatre 1997

Photo by T. Charles Erickson

PLATE 31

Harlequin and Lisette at the end of the day
Higgins and Welsh in *The Game of Love and Chance*, McCarter Theatre 1997

PLATE 32

Léonide makes love to Léontine (I,6)
Katherine Borowitz and Mary Lou Rosato in *The Triumph of Love,*
McCarter Theatre 1992

PLATE 33

Léonide makes love to Hermocrate (I,8)
J. Michael Flynn and Lise Bruneau in *The Triumph of Love,*
Berkeley Repertory Theatre 1994

PLATE 34

Léonide and Agis part hurriedly (II,11)

Borowitz and Mark Deakins in *The Triumph of Love*, McCarter Theatre 1992

PLATE 35

Harlequin notes Léonide's rapture as Corine notes Léontine's approach (II,4)

Borowitz, John Michael Higgins, and Brooke Smith in *The Triumph of Love*,
McCarter Theatre 1992

PLATE 36

Harlequin reads Léontine's heart: "Cat got your tongue, Madame?" (II,6)
Higgins and Rosato in *The Triumph of Love,* McCarter Theatre 1992

PLATE 37

Hermocrate: "I can't believe what I'm seeing.
Or what is happening to me." (II,14)
Borowitz and Chadwick in *The Triumph of Love*, McCarter Theatre 1992

Photo by T. Charles Erickson

PLATE 38

Hermocrate asks Léonide if Agis might live with them (III,3)
Borowitz and Chadwick in *The Triumph of Love*, McCarter Theatre 1992

Photo by T. Charles Erickson

PLATE 39

Léonide's confession (III,9)
Borowitz and Deakins in *The Triumph of Love,* McCarter Theatre 1992

PLATE 40

Léontine, Harlequin, and Hermocrate at the end of the day
Rosato, Higgins, and Chadwick in *The Triumph of Love,* McCarter Theatre 1992

The Triumph of Love

1732

☙

For Anne Roy

**This adaptation is based on a translation
by Nadia Benabid and Stephen Wadsworth.**

The Triumph of Love was played for the first time by the Comédie Italienne in Paris, March 12, 1732. The cast was led by Silvia as Léonide. I imagine that Luigi Riccoboni, now 58, was Hermocrate, and his wife, Elena Balletti Riccoboni, was Léontine. It is likely that their son François Riccoboni played Agis, and that Violette and Dominique (Domenico Biancolelli) played Corine and Dimas. Tomasso Vicentini was, as ever, Harlequin.

This adaptation was originally commissioned and produced by the McCarter Theatre in Princeton, N.J., March 27, 1992, with the following cast and creative contributors:

LÉONIDE. . . . . Katherine Borowitz
CORINE . . . . Brooke Smith
HARLEQUIN. . . . . John Michael Higgins
DIMAS . . . . Tom Brennan
AGIS . . . . Mark Deakins
LÉONTINE . . . . Mary Lou Rosato
HERMOCRATE . . . . Robin Chadwick

Director. . . . . Stephen Wadsworth
Set Designer. . . . . Thomas Lynch
Costume Designer . . . . Martin Pakledinaz
Lighting Designer. . . . . Christopher Akerlind
Production Stage Manager . . . . Susie Cordon

Artistic Director, McCarter Theatre . . . . Emily Mann
Assistant to Artistic Director . . . . Loretta Greco
Dramaturg. . . . . Janice Paran

This version of *The Triumph of Love* was developed further in a 1994 run at Berkeley Repertory Theatre, Sharon Ott, Artistic Director.

CHARACTERS

LÉONIDE: a princess (in disguise as Phocion, also uses the name Aspasie)
CORINE: her maid (in disguise as Hermidas)
HERMOCRATE: a philosopher
LÉONTINE: Hermocrate's sister
AGIS: a prince and Hermocrate's ward
HARLEQUIN: Hermocrate's valet
DIMAS: Hermocrate's gardener

SETTING

The action takes place in the gardens of Hermocrate's country retreat.

ACT I
SCENE I

(Enter Léonide and Corine.)

LÉONIDE: These are the gardens of the philosopher, Hermocrate. I think.

CORINE: But Madame, won't we be thought rude for having entered unannounced? We don't know a soul here.

LÉONIDE: No, the gate was open, and furthermore we have come to speak to the master of the house.

(They look around.)

LÉONIDE: Let's stay here a moment. It's time for you to know more.

CORINE: Finally! I've been dying of curiosity. But Princess Léonide, would you be so kind as to let me ask the questions?

LÉONIDE: As you wish.

CORINE: First you leave the court and the city, and you come here practically unattended to one of your country homes, where you require that I follow you...

LÉONIDE: Exactly.

CORINE: Now, I have learned to paint—and you know that—and soon after we arrive in the country you knock on my door, lock yourself in my room, and show me two portraits, which you ask me to reproduce in miniature—one is of a man of fifty, the other of a woman of shall we say forty, and both are reasonably handsome.

LÉONIDE: That is true—

CORINE: Let me speak. Once the copies are finished you start a rumor that you are feeling unwell and do not wish to be seen. You dress me up as a man, I dress *you* up as a man, and then we set out together in this...getup—incognito, you with the name of Phocion and I with that of Hermidas. And after a fifteen-minute walk, here we are in the gardens of Hermocrate—a philosopher in whose philosophy I believe you have little interest.

LÉONIDE: More interest than you may think.

CORINE: So what does it all mean—the copied portraits, the feigned indisposition, the seclusion in the country, the change of sexes? Who are this man and this woman I painted? Why a philosopher? What do you have in store for him? What do you have in store for *me?* Where are we headed, and how will it all come out? *(A beat.)* These are some of my questions.

LÉONIDE: Listen. Let's start at the beginning. You know that, in a sense, I am not the true princess. My uncle, who was a great general, usurped the throne. King Cleomones had stolen away the woman he loved, so my uncle locked them both up and seized the kingdom. The old king died eventually in the dungeon. But what you don't know, Corine, is that that woman died in childbirth, producing a *prince!* Who mysteriously disappeared without a trace. My uncle had no children, so my father succeeded him, and I succeeded my father.

CORINE: Yes, but you haven't yet said one thing about our disguise or the portraits I painted, and that's all I want to know.

LÉONIDE: Be patient. Now, that *prince!* That prince, born in prison and taken away at birth by an unknown hand—that prince is the true heir to the throne I sit on. And I have just found out where he is.

CORINE: Well thank heavens for that. And will you soon have him in your power?

LÉONIDE: On the contrary, he will have me in his.

CORINE: You, Princess? *No one* will have power over you! The throne is yours—I won't let him take it from you.

LÉONIDE: Ssshhhhh! Some years after disappearing from the prison, this prince was handed over by a relative of the king to the wise Hermocrate and his spinster sister, who for the last ten years have raised him, in secret and very strictly, as my enemy. I heard this whole tale from a servant who worked until recently on this very estate.

CORINE: Servants can lie, we need better sources.

LÉONIDE: But I am not here to disprove the story. A sense of...what is right...of fairness...and some other sense...I'm not sure what...brings me here. First of all I wanted to see Agis—that's the prince's name. The servant promised to point him out to me. He said that Agis and Hermocrate take a daily walk in the wood near my chateau. So I left the city as you know, I came here, I dismissed my escort, entered that wood...and saw Agis. He was sitting under a tree, reading a book. Before that moment I had often heard talk of love, but I knew it only as a word. Imagine, Corine, if the Graces endowed one man with all their gifts—nobility, elegance, charm, and beauty, and you can barely begin to imagine the charms of the face, and of the form...of Agis.

CORINE: What I am beginning to imagine very clearly is that the figure he cuts may explain the figures we're cutting, out here in the pastures.

LÉONIDE: I forgot to tell you that as I withdrew Hermocrate appeared and stopped me! He asked me whether the princess—meaning *me!*—ever walked in these woods. I was startled by his question, but I realized that he did not know me by sight, and I told him that I had heard she was about. And then I went back to the chateau.

CORINE: Well now this, Madame, is quite an unusual tale.

LÉONIDE: The goal I have set for myself is even more unusual. And I feigned illness, and secluded and disguised myself, so that I would be free to pursue it. I'll introduce myself to Hermocrate as Phocion, a young traveler drawn here by the reputation of his wisdom. I will ask him to let me spend time with him, to learn at his knee. I will meanwhile make every effort to speak with Agis and prepare him to feel differently about me. I am born to blood he has been taught to hate, so I dare not tell him my name. Now, Love, make some use of those charms for which I am so often complimented, and protect me from the hate I know he feels for me.

CORINE: But Madame, if Hermocrate were to recognize, under your disguise, the woman he spoke to in the wood, you'd never set foot in his house.

LÉONIDE: I have thought of that, Corine. If he recognizes me, so much the worse for him, because I have set him a snare from which all his rational thinking could not possibly protect him. Mind you, I will not be happy if he forces me to use it, because my *goal* is honorable, even if the snare is…well…less so. I am in love. And there is justice to be done. I need two or three encounters with Agis; I don't expect more than a few, but they are essential, and if I can have them only at Hermocrate's expense, well, then, so be it.

CORINE: But isn't the spinster sister also liable to be inflexible—even with a stranger as young and handsome as yourself?

LÉONIDE: If she stands in my way, so much the worse for *her*. I would no sooner spare her than I would her brother.

CORINE: But Madame, if I understand what you're saying, you would have to deceive them both. This duplicity…doesn't it go against the grain?

LÉONIDE: Despite the worthy purposes that prompt it, yes. I find it distasteful. I would be loath to resort to it. But it will get me even with Hermocrate and his sister, who deserve it. Since Agis has been with them, they have done all they can to inspire him to hate me. They paint the most odious portrait of me, and all without knowing me, without knowing my nature, or any of the virtues with which heaven might have blessed it. They have stirred up all my enemies, and they continue to raise new ones against me. Why do they want to hurt me? Is it because I usurped a throne? But I'm not the one who usurped it! Besides, how could I have returned it when its legitimate heir has never come forward and is thought to have died? No, Corine, I needn't be worried by scruples where they are concerned.

CORINE: Are the portraits of them?

LÉONIDE: Yes. The portraits…I may use them, I may not. Guard them well, and play along, Corine, whatever happens. I'll keep you apprised of things as we go. *(Harlequin enters unseen.)*

SCENE II

HARLEQUIN: *(Aside.)* Now who have we here?

CORINE: This will all have to be quite a performance, Madame, considering your sex.

HARLEQUIN: *(Surprising them.)* Yes indeed, *Madame!* Considering your *sex!* Speak up, men! Are you women?!

LÉONIDE: God in Heaven, I'm done for.

(The women start to leave.)

HARLEQUIN: Uh uh uh, my beauties! Before you go, please—we ought to settle this together. At first I took you for two fellows on the loose, but I must apologize, for now I see you are just two loose women!

LÉONIDE: All is lost, Corine.

CORINE: *(To Léonide, aside.)* No, Madame, let me take care of this, and don't give it a thought. He doesn't fool me for a minute—look at his face. He can be…handled.

HARLEQUIN: And he is, moreover, an honest man who has never let smuggled goods get by him! *(Grabbing the tails of their coats.)* I therefore seize this merchandise. I shall have them close the gates!

CORINE: And I shall certainly stop you from doing that, because you would very much regret it.

HARLEQUIN: Prove that I'd regret it, and I'll let you go.

LÉONIDE: *(Offering him several gold coins.)* Is this proof enough?

(Harlequin takes them.)

LÉONIDE: Now wouldn't it have been foolish to pass that up?

HARLEQUIN: Yes…well…so it would seem, because I feel very good about having it.

CORINE: Do you still feel like making a stink?

HARLEQUIN: I am *beginning* to not feel like it.

CORINE: More proof, Madame.

LÉONIDE: *(Giving him more.)* Here, take this too. Happier?

HARLEQUIN: *(Pointing at the gold in his hand.)* That is the exact extent of my stubbornness! But munificent ladies! What are you doing?

CORINE: Oh it's nothing. My lady saw Agis in the forest, and she lost her heart to him.

HARLEQUIN: Well *that's* honest, anyway.

CORINE: Now Madame, who is independent…and rich…and who would readily marry him, would like a chance to attract his interest.

HARLEQUIN: That's even more honest…

CORINE: But Madame could not do this without engaging him in conversation, without perhaps even living in the same house for a while.

HARLEQUIN: To enjoy all of its...conveniences...

CORINE: And this would not be possible if she presented herself dressed as the woman she is, because Hermocrate would not allow it, and Agis himself would shun her, because of what he's been taught by the great philosopher.

HARLEQUIN: God forbid there should be love in that house! The philosophy of Hermocrate is about as hostile to love as any philosophy could be—and Agis and Léontine are faithful followers. You know, I'm the only one around here with any know-how in affairs of the heart.

LÉONIDE: We saw that immediately.

CORINE: So all this is why Madame decided to come in disguise, and you can see there's nothing wrong in it.

HARLEQUIN: By God, nothing could be more reasonable. My Lady happened to take a fancy to Agis, so what of it? We all take what we can get; that only makes sense. Onward, obliging gentlemen! Good luck to you. I am at your service. *(To Léonide.)* You have lost your heart, concentrate on finding someone else's... *(To Corine.)* I'd happily lose *mine*...if someone else would care to find it.

LÉONIDE: Well in this matter *my* loss will be your gain. You are a lucky man.

CORINE: Don't forget that Madame is called Phocion, and I am Hermidas.

LÉONIDE: And above all, Agis must never know who we are.

HARLEQUIN: Fear not, Lord Phocion. *(To Corine.)* Don't worry, chum. See, I know how to handle myself.

CORINE: Quiet, someone's coming.

(Dimas enters.)

SCENE III

DIMAS: And just who are *you* talking to, friend?

HARLEQUIN: I am talking to people.

DIMAS: For God's sake, I can see that. But what people? And who do they want?

LÉONIDE: Lord Hermocrate.

DIMAS: Well this isn't the way in. The master told me not to let any... antelopers wander around in his garden, so you better go back the way you came and knock at the front gate.

LÉONIDE: We found the garden doors open. Aren't strangers allowed to make mistakes?

DIMAS: No! And they're not allowed to sneak around either, and don't give me this about slipping through open drawers. You have the decency to call out to the gardener, you ask for his permission, you show him certain...considerations, and *then* the drawers are slipped open!

HARLEQUIN: Easy does it, friend, you are speaking to a very important person.

DIMAS: Easy to see that the person is rich, since this person has a lot to guard, and I guard only my garden. But this person should take another road.
(Agis enters.)

SCENE IV

AGIS: What on earth is all this noise about? Dimas, at whom are you shouting?

DIMAS: At this pretty young thing that jumps over the wall to pick the fruit off our trees.

LÉONIDE: You arrive just in time, Sir, to rid me of this man. I came to pay my respects to Lord Hermocrate, I found the garden open, and he wants me out.

AGIS: Enough Dimas, you've made a mistake. Run off and tell Léontine a worthy stranger wishes to speak to Hermocrate.
(Dimas leaves.)

AGIS: I must apologize, Sir, for the rustic greeting he gave you; Hermocrate himself will apologize. Your appearance alone suggests that you be shown every consideration.

HARLEQUIN: For that matter, *both* of them have pretty faces.

LÉONIDE: The gardener was indeed brusque, but your compliments redress the wrong. And if as you say my appearance inspires you to...consider me...favorably, why that would be one of the kindest services it could do me. But mine is only *one* of the fortuitous appearances in this garden today.

AGIS: *(A bit abashed.)* Well let's not make too much of it, Sir, but your appearance does do you credit. And though we met but a moment ago, I assure you that one could not be more...favorably inclined...toward someone than I am toward you.

HARLEQUIN: That makes four of us.

CORINE: *(To Harlequin.)* Let's take a walk and discuss these...inclinations.
(Corine leads Harlequin off. Léonide and Agis are left facing each other.)

AGIS: May I ask who it is, for whom I feel such...affection?

LÉONIDE: Someone who feels it in return, and would…forever.

AGIS: Tell me more; I sense I've made a friend I might soon lose.

LÉONIDE: Our separation would never be *my* doing, Sir.

(A beat.)

AGIS: *(Changing tack.)* What do you want from Hermocrate? Do you want to study with him? He has educated me, you know, and I am proud to say he loves me.

LÉONIDE: His reputation drew me here. I intended only to spend some time at his side, but since meeting you that intention has given way to another, more pressing one, which is…to see you for as long as I possibly can.

AGIS: And then what?

LÉONIDE: I don't know. *(A beat.)* You will decide that. I'll take only your advice in this matter.

AGIS: Then I advise you never to lose sight of me.

LÉONIDE: Then we will always be together.

AGIS: I would like that. *(A beat.)* With all my heart. But look—here comes Léontine.

HARLEQUIN: *(Returning with Corine.)* The mistress approaches. I don't like that pious look of hers at all.

(Dimas returns with Léontine.)

SCENE V

DIMAS: *(Presenting Léonide and Corine.)* Look Madame, here is the squire I told you about. And this pest is in his…retina.

LÉONTINE: *(To Léonide.)* I was told, Sir, that you wish to speak to my brother, but he's not here just now. While we await his return, might you confide in me what it is you want with him?

LÉONIDE: I have no secret business with him, Madame. I have come to ask him a favor, but perhaps you will grant it in his stead.

LÉONTINE: Explain yourself.

LÉONIDE: My name is Phocion, Madame, a name that might be known to you. Perhaps you have heard of my father…

LÉONTINE: *(Interrupting.)* Of course.

LÉONIDE: I have been traveling for some time, alone, and with only my wits to rely on—to educate my heart and my mind.

DIMAS: And to pick the fruit off our trees.

LÉONTINE: Leave us, Dimas.

LÉONIDE: I have met many scholars whose virtue and learning set them apart from other men. Some even allowed me to stay with them and study for a while; and I was hoping that the august Hermocrate would not refuse me, for a few days...the same privilege.

LÉONTINE: By your appearance, Sir, you seem to be entirely worthy of the hospitality you have found elsewhere; but it will not be possible for Hermocrate to offer it to you here. Important reasons, which Agis knows well, make that impossible. I am terribly sorry that your appeal must be denied.

AGIS: We're not lacking in *beds.*

HARLEQUIN: One of them could certainly stay in *my* room!

LÉONTINE: No, but you know better than anyone, Agis, that this cannot be— that we have made ourselves a rule not to share our retreat with anyone.

AGIS: But I have promised Lord Phocion to urge you to consider an exception, for a virtuous person, a friend—surely that would not violate the rule.

LÉONTINE: I could never change my feelings.

HARLEQUIN: *(Aside.)* Pigheaded cow!

LÉONIDE: But Madame, can you be impervious to such good intentions?

LÉONTINE: In spite of myself, yes, I must be.

AGIS: Hermocrate will persuade you, Madame.

LÉONTINE: I am sure he will think as I do.

LÉONIDE: *(Aside.)* The time has come... *(Aloud.)* I will not press you further, Madame, but may I make so bold as to ask for a moment alone with you?

LÉONTINE: Frankly, Sir, your tenacity is off-putting, and will not help your cause, but if you insist...

LÉONIDE: *(To Agis.)* Will you leave us for a moment?
(Agis leaves. Exeunt Harlequin and Corine.)

SCENE VI

LÉONIDE: *(Aside, as Harlequin and Corine leave.)* May love bless this lie. *(Aloud, at first hesitant, as she tests the waters.)* Since you cannot grant what I ask, Madame, it would be unthinkable to press you further, but will you consider doing me another kindness—that is...to advise me in a matter that will...entirely determine my peace of mind...for the rest of my life?

LÉONTINE: I would advise you to wait for Hermocrate, Sir; better to consult him than me.

LÉONIDE: No, Madame, in this...matter, you can help me far more than he can. For I need someone who is not severe...but rather...well, forbearing; whose judgment is...tempered...by compassion. I have found that sweet mixture more often in your sex than in ours. Listen to me, please, Madame. I appeal to all that is good in you.

LÉONTINE: I am not sure exactly what you're getting at, but a stranger deserves certain considerations; so speak. I am listening.

LÉONIDE: A few days ago, as I was passing through these parts, I saw a woman...who did not see me. I will describe her to you; perhaps you know her. *(A beat. She begins her lovemaking cautiously.)* She is small*... but not too small, yet...still she is...really quite...majestic. I have never seen such nobility of bearing. I have never seen a union of such tender features with an air so imposing, so controlled...so stern, even. One could not help loving her...but with a love that is timid...even frightened, of the awe she inspires... *(Gaining confidence.)* She is young... but not with that youthful flightiness that I have always deplored—all unfulfilled promise, knowing how to amuse the eye but not yet deserving to touch the heart. No, she is young in a different way—at an age when her charms, at the height of their powers, are richly and eloquently blended, when she can take pleasure in knowing exactly who she is, when her well-tempered soul has lit up her beauty with its unmistakable, subtle radiance.

LÉONTINE: *(Ill at ease.)* I do not know her, Sir; this woman is unknown to me; and the picture you paint of her is surely too flattering.

LÉONIDE: This woman, whom I adore, Madame, is so many times more wonderful than the picture I have painted of her. I tell you, I had no intention of stopping here, but I was transfixed by her beauty, and I watched her...closely...for a long time. She was conversing with someone; she smiled from time to time; and I saw in her gestures a certain sweetness, a generosity...a *kindness*. And I also saw it shining, with piercing clarity, from her solemn, quiet eyes.

LÉONTINE: *(Aside.)* Who can he be speaking of?

LÉONIDE: After a while she left. When I asked who she was I learned that she is the sister of a distinguished and respectable man.

LÉONTINE: *(Aside.)* Am I dreaming?

LÉONIDE: She has never married, but lives with her brother in a retreat whose stoical pleasures she prefers to the confusion of a world inhospitable to the truly virtuous. In short, I heard only good things about her, and so my reason, as much as my heart, finally determined that I must love her.

LÉONTINE: *(Moved.)* Spare me the rest, Sir. I do not know what love is, and I would advise you poorly on something of which I have no understanding.

LÉONIDE: Please, let me finish—and don't let this word Love shock you; the

---

* The word *tall* can be substituted for *small*, as best befits the person playing Léontine.

love I am speaking of is not at all profane, it is pure, ennobling, virtuous. In fact my love of virtue *kindles* my love for this woman; these two loves are inextricably mingled—they are the same love. For if I love *her,* if I see her form as something perfectly beautiful, it is because my soul sees in everything, everywhere, the image of her perfectly virtuous heart.

LÉONTINE: Please let me go, Sir. I am expected at the house, and we have been speaking a long time.

LÉONIDE: I'm nearly through, Madame. Transported and changed forever by these feelings, I vowed to love her forever, and in so doing to consecrate my days to the service of virtue itself. I resolved to speak to her brother and, under the pretext of improving myself, to get his permission to stay in his house. And once there, close to her, submissive...attentive... tender...I would make her a gift of my love, my respect, my reverence, and my passion, for the gods have willed it so.

LÉONTINE: *(Aside.)* I am trapped. Can I free myself?

LÉONIDE: I did as I had resolved. I came here to speak to her brother but found her instead. I implored her, in vain, to grant my request, but she denied me, and drove me to my present state. Imagine, Madame, my heart—trembling and confused before her...surely she might see its gentleness, its pain; surely she might feel some pity, if nothing more than that. But she has refused me even pity, so I have come to you, Madame, despondent, and here at your feet I confide in you all my sorrow. *(She falls to her knees.)*

LÉONTINE: What are you doing, Sir?

LÉONIDE: I desperately need your help and advice with her.

LÉONTINE: After what I have just heard, I myself need advice from the gods.

LÉONIDE: But your heart, Madame, is blessed with the wisdom of the gods— *follow your heart!*

LÉONTINE: My heart?! But the heart is an enemy to peace, to serenity...

LÉONIDE: Would you be less peaceful or serene for having been generous?

LÉONTINE: Ah Phocion, you say you love virtue; can you love it if you corrupt it?

LÉONIDE: To love—is it to corrupt?

LÉONTINE: But what is your *purpose?*

LÉONIDE: I have given you my life. I want it to be yours. Will you suffer my presence here for just a few days? For now that is my only wish, and if you grant it, I know that Hermocrate will allow it.

LÉONTINE: But *you're* the one who'll suffer—*you,* who love me.

LÉONIDE: What good is love that does not cost?

LÉONTINE: But can a virtuous love inspire feelings that are not virtuous? I don't understand! What have you come here to do, Phocion? What is happening to me? It is inconceivable! Would you have me lose my heart? Would you have me lose my *reason?* Must I now give my life over to my feelings? Am I to love you—I who have never loved? When in the end your flattery is meaningless, for you are young, you are handsome...while I am neither.

LÉONIDE: But how can you say that?

LÉONTINE: Very well Sir, I admit that I had my small share of beauty—or so it was said. Nature did endow me with certain charms, but I have always held them in contempt. Perhaps you will make me come to regret that I disdained them. It shames me to say it, but they are gone...or what little is left of them soon will be.

LÉONIDE: What good does it do you to say this, Léontine? You can't convince me that I do not see what I see. Perhaps you hope to sway me with these very charms you speak of... Ah, could you *ever* have been more enchanting?!

LÉONTINE: I am no longer what I was.

LÉONIDE: Let us not argue, Madame. Yes, I concede it—enchanting as you are, your youth will soon pass, and I am still young; but souls have no age. So I ask you again to let me stay. And I am going to ask Hermocrate, too. I will die of grief if the two of you cannot find it in your hearts to indulge me.

LÉONTINE: I don't know...what I should do...yet. Hermocrate is coming. I will speak on your behalf, until I can decide.

(Agis returns with Hermocrate, Harlequin reappears.)

SCENE VII

HERMOCRATE: *(To Agis.)* Is this the young man of whom you spoke?

AGIS: Yes Sir, the very one.

HARLEQUIN: It is I who had the honor of speaking to him first, Sir, and I took *very* good care of him while we waited for you.

LÉONTINE: This, Hermocrate, is the son of Phocion. His esteem for you brought him here to us. He is a student of reason, and is traveling to improve his mind. Several of your peers welcomed him in their houses. He hopes for the same welcome from you and asks for it with an ardor that commands attention. I promised to intercede for him. Now I leave you together.

(Léontine sighs audibly as she leaves.)

AGIS: And if my vote counts, I add it to Léontine's, Sir.

(Agis exits.)

HARLEQUIN: And I add mine into the bargain.

HERMOCRATE: *(Recognizing Léonide.)* But you…

LÉONIDE: I am very grateful for their kind words on my behalf, Sir. I am even more grateful that you might recognize…in me…a worthy follower.

HERMOCRATE: And I thank you, Sir, for your kind words. But someone who follows as well as you does not seem to need me…to lead him. Perhaps it would be wise to ask you a few questions in private. *(To Harlequin.)* Go. *(Harlequin departs.)*

SCENE VIII

HERMOCRATE: Either I am mistaken, Sir, or you are not unknown to me.

LÉONIDE: I, Sir?

HERMOCRATE: I have my reasons for wanting to speak to you in private; I thought I could spare you some embarrassment. I don't need lightning to confirm my suspicions.

LÉONIDE: And what suspicions are those?

HERMOCRATE: Your name is not Phocion at all.

LÉONIDE: *(Aside.)* He remembers our meeting.

HERMOCRATE: The boy whose name you have borrowed is in Athens at present; I happen to know this from his tutor.

LÉONIDE: There must be someone else with the same name.

HERMOCRATE: And that's not all; this assumed name is not your only disguise. Admit it, Madame, I have seen you before, walking in the wood.

LÉONIDE: *(Pretending to be surprised.)* You speak the truth, Sir.

HERMOCRATE: So you see all of your character witnesses here did you no good. At least they won't have to see you blush.

LÉONIDE: If I *blush* it does me no good, Sir—it's a reflex I regret, and it has misled you. My disguise does not conceal anything of which I should be ashamed.

HERMOCRATE: I am beginning to see your design, and I see nothing in it at all becoming to the innocent virtues of your sex—and certainly nothing of which you should be *proud.* The idea of coming here to take away my student, Agis, of working your dangerous feminine charms on him, of stirring up in his heart a turmoil that is almost always disastrous—this idea, it seems to me, would naturally make you blush.

LÉONIDE: Agis? Who, that young man who was just here? Are *those* your suspicions? What do you see in me to justify them? Or do you suspect me simply because I am a woman? Ah, that it should be you who does me this injury! And that intentions such as mine should inspire it! No, Sir, I have not come here to stir up Agis' heart—far from it. He was raised by your hand, and he is strong through the wisdom of your teaching, but to assume this disguise for *his* sake would not have been necessary. If I loved him, I would hope to conquer him with less effort—I would let him see me as I am; I would let my eyes speak. His inexperience and my "dangerous feminine charms" would have given me the edge. But it is not to his heart that mine inclines. The heart I seek is a more difficult one to entrap—oblivious to the power in my eyes, indifferent to beauty. And as I cannot resort to my feminine charms, I have made a point of not putting them on display. I have hidden them under this disguise because they are useless to me.

HERMOCRATE: But why do you want to stay in my house, Madame, if your scheme has nothing to do with Agis?

LÉONIDE: Why is it always Agis?! *(A beat.)* Don't hold my appearance against me—my "scheme" might be not only innocent, but actually honorable. You will see, I shall stick to it with a determination that will dissolve your suspicions, and when you know its purpose I daresay you may even respect me for it. Don't talk to me any more about Agis, I am not thinking of him at all. Do you want irrefutable proof? *That* would hardly be "becoming to the innocent virtues of my sex." I do not come here with a woman's cunning, or vanity, or pride. I come with something finer and stronger. We were speaking of your suspicions; a few words might dispel them…Will the one I love agree to give me his hand? *(A beat. Extending her hand.)* Here is mine. And Agis is not here to accept my offer.

HERMOCRATE: *(Embarrassed.)* I no longer know to whom this is addressed.

LÉONIDE: You do know, Sir, for I have just told you. I could not have said it more clearly by saying your name. Hermocrate.

HERMOCRATE: I, Madame!

LÉONIDE: You are enlightened, My Lord.

HERMOCRATE: *(Disconcerted.)* I am, I suppose, though your words trouble me deeply. That a heart such as yours could be moved by me…

LÉONIDE: Listen to me, My Lord. I must explain myself after burdening you with this.

HERMOCRATE: No, Madame, I'll hear no more. You needn't justify what you have said to me, I won't judge you for it, but for goodness' sake leave me alone. Was I made to be loved? No. You lay siege to a solitary heart, to which love must remain a stranger. My severity, my self-denial, must combat your youth and your beauty.

LÉONIDE: But I am not asking you to share my feelings. I have no hope of that—or if I do, I disavow it. But allow me to finish. I have told you that I love you; now I must explain myself.

HERMOCRATE: But reason cautions me against hearing any more.

LÉONIDE: But my virtue, and my honor, which I have just compromised, demand that I continue. Please, My Lord, I aspire only to be worthy in your eyes, my heart desires only that reward. Why should you not hear me out? What have you to fear from me—a handful of charms rendered ineffectual by my confession? And a frailty that you disdain and that is powerless in combat against you?

HERMOCRATE: I wish I were not even aware of that frailty.

LÉONIDE: Yes, My Lord, I love you, but do not mistake my love for something it is not. This is no rash infatuation, and my confession is not irrational, nor has it slipped from me in an emotional moment. I am in full possession of my faculties. I don't owe my confession to love—love could never have gotten it out of me—but to…a sense of what is right. I am telling you that I love you so that I will feel confusion—mortification, chagrin. Faced with the grim prospect of feeling such things, maybe I could be cured of my love for you! If I could feel shame at my weakness, I might conquer it; if I could regain my honor, I could use it to fight you off. I am telling you that I love you not so that you should love *me,* but so that you should teach me how *not* to love *you.* You hate love, you reject it. I am all for that, but help me to reject love as you do! Teach me how to get my heart back from you, protect me from my attraction to you. I am not asking to be loved, I swear it, but I *desire* to be loved. Extinguish this desire! I beg you, save me from yourself!

HERMOCRATE: Madame, I can help you in this way only: I absolutely do not wish to love you; let my indifference be your cure, and put an end to this scene. Your words are poison.

LÉONIDE: Great Gods, I expected your indifference, but do you deny me utterly? I have poured out my heart, I have been as brave as I know how to be, I have denied *myself*—and this is your response? Does the wise man serve only himself?

HERMOCRATE: I am not at all wise, Madame.

LÉONIDE: You may be right, but I need time to discover your faults for myself. *Please!* My name is Aspasie, and like you I have lived in seclusion, mistress of myself, and of a sizable fortune, ignorant of love and contemptuous of any effort to arouse it in me.

HERMOCRATE: *(Aside.)* Why am I standing here?

LÉONIDE: Then I met you, walking alone as I have so often. I did not know who you were, but looking at you, I was moved. It seems my heart found you out, Hermocrate.

HERMOCRATE: No! Stop! I cannot endure any more of this. If as you say you are motivated by a sense of what is right, Aspasie, we must end this conversation.

LÉONIDE: I suppose all this must seem frivolous, but I assure you, the importance of recovering my reason is not.

HERMOCRATE: And the importance of safeguarding my own is becoming more and more urgent. As unversed in love as I may be, I have eyes: You have charms…and you love me.

LÉONIDE: I have charms, you say. What, My Lord, you can see them? *(A beat.)* Do you fear them?

HERMOCRATE: Fear is an emotion I avoid.

LÉONIDE: But your avoidance of it proves that you *are* afraid! You do not love me yet, but you are afraid you might. I can't help hoping that it will be so.

HERMOCRATE: You confuse me; I'm not answering you well; I will say no more.

LÉONIDE: Well, My Lord, let us go then. Let us walk. Let us find Léontine. *(Turning back to him.)* Let me stay on here a while. And when you are ready, you can give me your decision.

HERMOCRATE: Go, Aspasie. I will follow….

(Exit Léonide.)

SCENE IX

HERMOCRATE: I almost lost my way there. *(A beat.)* What should I decide?
(Dimas is passing.)

HERMOCRATE: Dimas, come here. Do you see that young man who just left me? I want you to keep your eye on him, follow him as closely as you can, and see if he tries to engage Agis in conversation. Do you hear? I have always appreciated your loyalty, and you could find no better way to show it than by doing exactly as I have told you.

DIMAS: In two shakes of a lamb's tail.

HERMOCRATE: I want to know what he is thinking.

DIMAS: I will bring you his brain in a basket.
(Blackout.)

ACT II
INTERMEZZO

(Harlequin is discovered in a pose of despair, crying noisily. He plays the scene with many changes of voice, gesturing wildly and moving suddenly from one part of the stage to another.)

HARLEQUIN: Ah, unhappy me! Will I ever be able to marry Corine? The situation is rich with misery. First of all, does she even love me? I would think that…to look at me is to love me, and when she *is* looking at me I am sure that she does love me; it's only when she stops looking at me that I'm not sure she does anymore, or ever did really. And even if she did, or does, or always will, she can't just *have* me, as she is a lady's maid, a servant, one of her mistress' belongings, who has as many rights as her petticoat. But I err! For her petticoat can do precisely what she cannot — rise! *(He laughs.)* And though I am but a servant and have no rights, I have only to think of her, and I can do what she cannot—rise! *(More laughter.)* And I cannot just have *her,* either, because not only do I *serve,* but I serve Hermocrate, and the chances of his allowing me to leave his service to pursue *love…*grow slimmer with every panting breast…uh, *passing breath!* Ah, how shall I be able to live without Corine? I would rather die first. *(A beat.) Die?!* Die! That's it. Let me see…some unusual sort of death. An heroic death, a *horrible* death…a *hanging* death! *That's* it! *(Racing frantically about, miming the actions he describes.)* I shall go to my room, tie a chair to a crossbeam, climb upon a rope, place the chair around my neck, kick away the room, and… No. I shall go to my room, tie a rope to a crossbeam, kick away the chair… *(Cheerfully.)* …and I'm hanged! I'll hang now, then elope, and then when I'm arrested for the crime of escaping my master I'll not have to hang again, because who would hang a man who's already been hanged?! It's perfect! *(He notices that he's hanged himself and responds with frantic jerks and terrible noises of death. Eventually he manages to cut himself down, landing with a thud.)* Ha, idiotic servant fool! Poor passionate put-upon Corine! Ah, blasted Mistress Phocion, why have you come here?! *(He muses, pensive and still.)* Perhaps if I were just to be hilarious for a while I could amuse myself to death.

(Dimas enters.)

SCENE I

DIMAS: For God's sake get over here. I tell you, ever since these poachers got here, it's impossible to get a word with you. You're always off in some corner whispering with that whippersnapper valet.

HARLEQUIN: My very old friend, I'm just being civil. If I don't pay constant attention to you, it doesn't mean I love you any less.

DIMAS: But being civil doesn't mean hiding things from very old friends. You know, friendship is like wine, by God—the older the better. That's how it is.

HARLEQUIN: What a tasteful observation. We'll drink to that whenever you say, and it will be my treat.

DIMAS: Aren't you lordly! You say that as if it rained wine *and* money. Think you could scare up enough of either to make it worth my while?

HARLEQUIN: Don't you worry about a thing.

DIMAS: Bless my heart but you're quite the magpie. But then, I'm a magpie too.

HARLEQUIN: *(Suspicious.)* And since when are we scavenger birds?

DIMAS: Ha ha, don't think I don't know you've already picked our visitors clean. You see, I saw you counting your stash.

HARLEQUIN: Ah! It's truly a day of reckoning!

DIMAS: *(Aside.)* I think I've got him. *(Aloud.)* Listen friend, the master is very upset—he doesn't know what to make of it all.

HARLEQUIN: I suppose he also saw me counting my stash?

DIMAS: Oh it's much worse than that. *(Continuing with utmost confidentiality.)* He thinks there's something going on around here. He wants me to play the fox and sniff it out. He wants me to plow those two tresspastures and...gather in their harvest. He wants to know why they cropped up, and what's growing in them. Understand?

HARLEQUIN: Not exactly. Is this how foxes talk?

DIMAS: Uh uh uh! You won't get anything out of me! I only want to find out what *you* know. To begin at the beginning, you're not supposed to tell the master who these vagabonds really are, right?

HARLEQUIN: He'll never get it out of *me!*

DIMAS: Well you don't *have* to tell him! He only listens to me anyway, because I see *everything.*

HARLEQUIN: So you know who they are then?

DIMAS: For God's sake! I know them root and branch.

HARLEQUIN: Oh, I thought I was the only one who knew about them.

DIMAS: You? Ha! Maybe you don't know the first thing about them.

HARLEQUIN: Oh but I do.

DIMAS: I bet you don't, I don't think so. You could never figure it out.

HARLEQUIN: I could too! And anyway, they told me themselves!

DIMAS: What?

HARLEQUIN: That they're women!

DIMAS: *(Astounded.)* They're *women?!*

    (A beat.)

HARLEQUIN: What? You mean you didn't know? You *sneak!*

DIMAS: No I didn't, but by God I do now! I'm a fox.

HARLEQUIN: You're a *fiend!*

DIMAS: I'm a fiend!

HARLEQUIN: And I'm a fool.

DIMAS: I'm going to make the most of this! I'll tell everyone! What a tale! They're *women!*

HARLEQUIN: Dimas, you have cut my throat.

DIMAS: What do I care about *your* throat? Ha! Women in my garden, making payments to the valet behind my back! Let the blood flow! They are *dresspassers!* They must be called to accounts!

HARLEQUIN: So, my friend, you want money, do you?

DIMAS: I would be a damned fool if I didn't. And I bet I can guess where it's going to come from.

HARLEQUIN: I will prevail upon the lady to buy back my blunder, I promise you.

DIMAS: This blunder will not be cheap, I can tell you.

HARLEQUIN: I realize it's going to be overpriced.

DIMAS: And payments begin now: First you tell me every little thing about this swindle. Like how much money did she give you? How many gold pieces? How much loose change? Tell the truth.

HARLEQUIN: She gave me twenty gold pieces.

DIMAS: Twenty gold pieces? That's a new *life!* You could buy a small farm for that. *(A beat.)* What does she want here?

HARLEQUIN: Well, Agis stole her heart while she was out on a walk. And she got herself up like a man so she could steal it back.

DIMAS: Sounds like easy money for me! And that pretty little valet, I suppose we have to cut her in? Does *she* steal hearts too?

HARLEQUIN: I wouldn't mind stealing *hers.*

DIMAS: If you steal like you keep secrets, I don't think you could manage it.

    (Léonide and Corine appear in the distance.)

DIMAS: But look, by God. Here they come. *(Extending his open palm to Harlequin.)* Cash down, skirts up!

    (Harlequin grudgingly tosses Dimas a coin.)

SCENE II

CORINE: *(To Léonide.)* We can't possibly talk to him when he's with that gardener.

DIMAS: *(To Harlequin.)* They seem a little shy. Tell them I already know everything there is to know about their bodies.

HARLEQUIN: *(To Léonide.)* No need for circumspection, Madame. I...am a blabbermouth.

LÉONIDE: *(Still playing Phocion.)* Who are you calling Madame, Harlequin?

HARLEQUIN: *You.* I'm telling you, I let the cat out of the bag. He tricked me into it.

LÉONIDE: You *fool!* You told him who I was?

HARLEQUIN: Lock stock and bosom.

LÉONIDE: Good God!

DIMAS: I know you want to steal a heart, and I know whose heart you want to steal. And I know about Harlequin's money. The only thing I *don't* know is where is my share, because he promised me one.

LÉONIDE: Corine, that does it. My plans are completely ruined.

CORINE: Now Madame, don't be discouraged. To get what *you're* after, we're going to need all the help we can get. There's nothing to do but bribe the gardener as well. Am I right, Dimas?

DIMAS: Absolutely right, Mademoiselle.

CORINE: And your price?

DIMAS: I guess you'll have to pay me what I'm worth.

HARLEQUIN: He's a chiseler, and he isn't worth a sou.

LÉONIDE: That suits me fine, Dimas. *(Tossing Dimas a coin.)* There's something in advance, and if you hold your tongue you will thank your lucky stars for having been associated with this little adventure.

DIMAS: Your servant, Madame. I'm bought and sold.

HARLEQUIN: And I'm ruined! If it weren't for my damnéd tongue all that money would have made its way into *my* pocket. Do you realize that you're buying the confidence of this cutup with *my* savings?

LÉONIDE: Don't be sad, Harlequin, I'll make you *both* rich. Now listen to me, I have a problem. A little while ago Hermocrate promised to let me stay on here, but I'm afraid he may have changed his mind. He is at this very moment deep in conversation about it with his sister and Agis, who want me to stay. *(Aside.)* Tell me the truth Harlequin, you didn't let anything slip to him apropos of my designs on Agis, did you?

HARLEQUIN: Certainly not, My Lady Bountiful. I told only this mercenary dog.

DIMAS: Yes you did, but you'll shut up now if you know what's good for you!

(Harlequin glares at Dimas.)

LÉONIDE: If you haven't said anything, we have nothing to worry about. Corine, let them in on my plans for Hermocrate and the sister. You and Harlequin will handle the portraits, Dimas and I will handle the philosopher. If we don't make *very* careful arrangements…

CORINE: Don't you worry, we'll get it right.

LÉONIDE: I see Agis. Off with you, and for God's sake don't let Hermocrate catch you together!

(The servants hurry off together.)

SCENE III

AGIS: *(Entering, a little out of breath.)* Ah Phocion, I've been looking for you. As you can see, I'm very anxious. You see, Hermocrate seems less inclined to let you stay, but he offers no reasonable arguments, and I still haven't spoken even a *word* on your behalf. I just happened to be present when his sister spoke for you. She was utterly convincing, but I'm not sure what will come of it, because something urgent called Hermocrate away in the middle of their conversation. *(A beat.)* I've never been…displeased…with him, until today. But, my dear Phocion, don't let what I've said discourage you. You have a friend in this conspiracy. I'll speak to him, and we'll convince him yet.

LÉONIDE: Are you really my friend, Agis? Do you still find it nice to have me here?

AGIS: If you left, I expect I'd find it terribly dreary.

LÉONIDE: You are the only thing keeping me here.

AGIS: Do you really feel that way? I do, too.

LÉONIDE: A thousand times more than I can say.

AGIS: Will you give me proof? You see, this is the first time that I have tasted the excitement of…friendship.

(Léonide offers Agis her hand. He clasps it.)

AGIS: You have initiated me. Teach me what friendship is. But please don't teach me the pain of losing a friend.

LÉONIDE: I couldn't teach you that without suffering it myself.

AGIS: That's a very good answer, I am touched by it! Listen—remember when you said to me that only I could decide if we would always be together?

(Léonide nods yes.)

AGIS: Well here's how I see it.

LÉONIDE: Tell me.

AGIS: I won't be able to leave here in the foreseeable future. Important matters prevent that—you'll know them some day. But Phocion, you who are master of your fate, I'm telling you, I shall one day be master of mine. *(A beat.)* You simply *must* stay with us for a while. It's true that life is lonely here, but we will be together, and what sweeter thing can the world offer than the companionship of two honest, loving…hearts.

LÉONIDE: Oh Agis, I will stay, I promise. Hearing you say this, I don't even care about the outside world. My world will be only where you are.

AGIS: I am happy. You know, the gods cursed the hour of my birth, and brought me into a world of misfortune. But if you really do stay, they'll be kinder, I'm sure. This is a sign of good things to come!

LÉONIDE: I am glad to see you so happy, but at the same time I am… apprehensive. *(A beat.)* Love can change these tender feelings so suddenly. A friend can't compete with a lover.

AGIS: Love? You speak to me of *love?* Phocion, may heaven make your heart impervious to love, as it did mine! You don't know me. My education, my sensibility, my *reason*—everything closes my heart to love. It was love that cursed my birth, that tainted the blood I came from. I *hate* love, and I hate even the thought of the female sex, who would urge us to it.

LÉONIDE: *(With gravity.)* You mean…you hate women?

AGIS: I will avoid women all my life.

LÉONIDE: This changes everything between us, Sir. I promised you I'd stay here, but now I can't—not in good faith. It is no longer possible. I must leave. Under the circumstances you would only reproach me for staying, and as I absolutely do not wish to deceive you, I must give you back the friendship you have given me.

AGIS: What are you saying, Phocion? Why this sudden change? What did I say that could have offended you?

LÉONIDE: Don't worry Agis, you will not regret my leaving. You are afraid to know the pain of losing a friend? *I* will soon feel it, but you will not.

AGIS: I…am no longer your friend?

LÉONIDE: No, you shall always be my friend; it is *I* who am no longer yours. For I am nothing more than one of those hated…objects…that you were speaking of a moment ago…

AGIS: Then…you…are not Phocion?

LÉONIDE: No, Sir. My clothes mislead you; they hide from you an unfortunate girl. My name is Aspasie, I am the last of a noble and wealthy family, and I am escaping the persecution of Princess Léonide, who wants me to give my fortune *and* my hand in marriage to a relative of hers who loves me and whom I can't abide. I was informed that on hearing of my refusal the

Princess decided to have me kidnapped, and the only way I could think to save myself was to take refuge in this disguise. I had heard that Hermocrate hated the Princess, and that he lived in seclusion, and I came here, without being recognized, to seek a safe haven. And then I met you. You offered me your friendship, and I could see you were completely worthy of mine. That I trust you with this secret should be proof that I have given you my friendship; and I will never withdraw it, even though yours will soon give way to hatred.

AGIS: I am dumbfounded, I can't unravel my thoughts.

LÉONIDE: I will unravel them for you: Hermocrate wants me gone, and now you do as well. Good-bye Sir. *(She starts to leave.)*

AGIS: No Madame, wait! Your sex is not to be trusted, it is true, but...we must be considerate of those less fortunate than ourselves.

LÉONIDE: You hate me, Sir. *(She makes to leave again.)*

AGIS: No, I'm telling you—Aspasie, stop! I feel sorry for your...situation. I am ashamed of my insensitivity. I'll plead with Hermocrate myself, if necessary, to allow you to stay. Your predicament is...undeniable.

LÉONIDE: So. Pity is all that's left of what you felt for me. *(Indicating her clothes.)* This...*travesty* is so discouraging. This young prince they want me to marry is probably very nice; wouldn't it just be better to give myself up, rather than prolong this dreadful masquerade?

AGIS: I advise against it Madame. It's important that when you give your hand, you also give your heart. I have always heard it said that to be married to someone one doesn't love is the saddest of all fates; that one's life becomes a web of loneliness and melancholy; that the very virtuousness that might have inspired such a decision, and in which one might seek refuge from it, in the end breaks one's spirit. *(A beat.)* But perhaps you could love this...prince they have chosen for you...

LÉONIDE: No Sir, I couldn't. Isn't my running away proof of that?

AGIS: Then be wary of going back. Especially if you harbor any feelings of...feelings for any other...person. Because if you loved someone else, it would be even worse.

LÉONIDE: No, I tell you, I am like you. This is the first time that I have tasted—how did you say it? The excitement of friendship? You have initiated *me*. And if you decide...not to withdraw your friendship, well, that's all I could wish for.

AGIS: *(Embarrassed.)* Well if you feel that way, do not chance another encounter with Princess Léonide. Because I feel now as I did...before.

LÉONIDE: You still love me then?

AGIS: Always Madame. All the more because there's nothing to fear; there's nothing between us, except friendship, which is the only sentiment I could encourage, and undoubtedly...also the only one you are likely to feel.

LÉONIDE AND AGIS: *(Together, variously, nodding.)* Right, yes, absolutely.

LÉONIDE: Sir, no one could be worthier than you to be called Friend. Or to be called Lover, I daresay...though it won't be I who will call you that.

AGIS: That's something I'd never wish to be called.

LÉONIDE: Let's change the subject; it's dangerous even to speak of love.

AGIS: *(A little abashed.)* It seems the valet is looking for you. Perhaps that means Hermocrate is finished with his business. If you'll excuse me...I think I'll go find him.

(Agis backs off and leaves. Harlequin and Corine enter.)

SCENE IV

HARLEQUIN: So, Mistress Phocion, your little interview was well guarded by two hungry watchdogs.

CORINE: The philosopher has not appeared, but the sister is looking for you. She looks a little sad. Apparently Hermocrate won't give in to her demands.

LÉONIDE: He will try to resist, but he will submit. Or all the art of my sex is useless.

HARLEQUIN: And does the Lord Agis show any promise? When you heat him up, does he melt?

LÉONIDE: Another little interview or two and I'll sweep him off his feet.

CORINE: Not seriously, Madame?

LÉONIDE: Yes, Corine. You know the situation, and what I hope to achieve. It seems the gods approve of my love.

HARLEQUIN: And they can't help but approve of mine, because it couldn't be more innocent. *(He throws his arms around Corine.)*

CORINE: Yes...well...here comes Léontine. Let's go.

LÉONIDE: Are you ready for your next scene?

CORINE: Yes, Madame.

HARLEQUIN: You will be *ravished* by my performance!

(Léontine appears; Corine and Harlequin bow and withdraw.)

SCENE V

LÉONIDE: I was just asking after you. They told me that Hermocrate wants to go back on the promise he made me. I am in a terrible state.

LÉONTINE: It's true, Phocion. He also refuses to keep the promise he made *me*—and with an obstinacy that seems positively irrational. I know you'll ask me to press him further, but I've come to tell you that I will do nothing more about it.

LÉONIDE: Léontine, you…

LÉONTINE: No. His refusal has brought me to my senses again.

LÉONIDE: And you call this coming to your senses? So! My love for you blinds me, I can think only of offering myself to you, I *do* offer myself to you, I abandon myself utterly to you, I yearn to touch you yet patiently refrain from doing so—and you want me to leave you? No, Léontine, that is not possible, that is the one sacrifice I could not make for you. Where do you suggest I find the strength to *do* this? What strength have you left me? Consider my situation! I appeal again to your virtue. Let virtue stand between us and judge our case! I am in your garden; you have suffered my presence here. You know that I love you with a passion, infinitely hot, that cuts to the core of my being, a passion awakened by you. And you want me to leave?! Ah Léontine, ask of me my life, tear out my heart— but do not expect the impossible!

LÉONTINE: Such demonstrative behavior! Such *emotion!* No Phocion, now I am *certain* that you must leave; I will not be involved in this anymore. Good heavens! What would become of my heart, were it as…*emotional* as yours? I would have always to struggle, and resist, yet never win? It is love you wish to arouse in me, isn't it? Love, and not the anguish of *feeling* love? Because that is all I *would* feel. So go! Please go away, and leave me *as I am.*

LÉONIDE: For pity's sake, be patient with me, Léontine. If I left this place I would wander blindly, lost to myself. I wouldn't know how to live without you. My grief would paralyze me. I hardly know who I *am* anymore!

LÉONTINE: And because you are devastated, I must love you? What tyranny is this?

LÉONIDE: Do you hate me?

LÉONTINE: I should!

LÉONIDE: But your heart—isn't it disposed to forgive me?

LÉONTINE: I am not listening to my heart.

LÉONIDE: Perhaps, but I am.

LÉONTINE: *(Distraught.)* Stop! Stop!

(Léonide surreptitiously beckons Harlequin.)

LÉONTINE: I hear someone.

(Harlequin enters.)

SCENE VI

(Without saying a word Harlequin stands between Léonide and Léontine, and looks very closely at Léonide.)

LÉONIDE: What is the valet doing here, Madame?

HARLEQUIN: The master, Hermocrate, ordered me to study your behavior very closely, because he doesn't know you from Adam.

LÉONIDE: But since I am with Madame, my behavior needn't be studied quite so closely. Pray tell him to go, Madame.

LÉONTINE: I had better go myself.

LÉONIDE: *(Softly, to Léontine.)* If you run away without promising to intercede for me, I'm not answerable for my actions.

LÉONTINE: *(Upset.)* Run along, Harlequin, it's not necessary for you to stay.

HARLEQUIN: More necessary than you think, Madame. You do not know who you're dealing with. This *gentleman* here is not so much interested in virtue as in women of virtue! And I'm warning you that he intends to corrupt yours…Madame!

LÉONTINE: What are you up to, Harlequin? I've had no indication that what you say is true. This must be one of your jokes.

HARLEQUIN: Ah, Madame, would that it were! But listen to this: Just now his valet, another rapscallion if ever I saw one, comes to me and says, "So! What say you? Let's be friends—*best* of friends! You should be glad to serve here. Honorable types, your employers. *Admirable!* Your mistress is especially obliging. A *divine* woman! Tell me, has she had many suitors?" "As many as she's wanted," I said. "Does she have any at the moment?" "As many as she wants." "Will she have more?" "As many as she may choose to have." "Does she desire…marriage?" "She doesn't tell me her desires." *(Very pointedly.)* "Is she a confirmed spinster?!" *(He pauses for effect.)* "I cannot vouch for her in this matter." "Who sees her and who doesn't? Does anyone come around? Does *no one* come around?" And on and on in this manner. "You won't get a thing out of me," I said. "Why, is your master in love with her?" "Out of his *mind* in love with her," came the answer. "We're only sticking around here to capture her heart, so that she'll marry us; for we have enough money, and enough lust, for *ten* marriages!"

LÉONIDE: Haven't you said enough?

HARLEQUIN: Look how I've upset him! Perhaps *he'll* tell you the rest—if you want to hear it…

LÉONTINE: Your valet, Lord Phocion, wasn't he just amusing himself saying all that? *(She turns to Léonide.)*

(Total silence.)

LÉONTINE: *(Suddenly, passionately.) Answer* me, Phocion!

(A long beat.)

HARLEQUIN: *(To Léontine.)* Cat got your tongue, Madame? You're losing your heart; it is being kidnapped even as we speak. And I am going to call Lord Hermocrate to the rescue. When love has once gangrened the soul, reason flees as though her tail were on fire! *(He turns to go.)*

LÉONTINE: Stop Harlequin, where are you going?! He mustn't know that someone has spoken to me...of love.

HARLEQUIN: *(A feigned revelation.)* Aha! Now that the kidnapper is a *friend* of hers, there's no need to call for help! I guess virtue is *not* its own reward after all...Well well well. Prude goeth before a fall.

(Léontine cringes.)

HARLEQUIN: So elope then! There'll always be *virtuous* women—being honest has *some* advantages!

(Léonide throws Harlequin some coins, then, behind Léontine's back, motions him away.)

HARLEQUIN: *(Looking at the coins in his hand.)* Cat's got *my* tongue now. *(To Léontine.)* I congratulate you, Madame. Good-bye. And rest assured, discretion is the better part...of a valet.

(Harlequin beckons Corine as he leaves.)

LÉONTINE: Where am I? It all seems like a dream. Look what you've exposed me to!

(Corine makes noises in the background.)

LÉONTINE: Ah, *now* who's coming?!

(Enter Corine.)

SCENE VII

CORINE: *(Presenting a small portrait to Léonide.)* Here's what you asked for, Sir. See if you're happy with it. I daresay it would be even better if the subject had actually been present while I painted.

LÉONIDE: *(Sharply.)* Why bring me this in the lady's presence? *(Glaring at Corine.)* Well, let's have a look. Yes, the face is just right; there's that refinement, the selflessness—and all the fire of her eyes. And yet, I think her actual eyes are even a little more fiery than these.

LÉONTINE: Apparently that is a portrait, Sir?

LÉONIDE: *(Handing the portrait back to Corine.)* Yes, Madame.

CORINE: *(Taking the portrait.)* Thank you Sir, I'll work on the eyes.

(Corine and Léonide look at Léontine's eyes.)

LÉONTINE: Might one see it before it's whisked away?

LÉONIDE: It's not finished, Madame.

LÉONTINE: Well, as you have your reasons for not wanting to show it, I won't insist—

LÉONIDE: *(Overlapping her.)* Since you insist, Madame. *(Taking the portrait from Corine.)* But you must promise to give it back to me. *(She gives the portrait to Léontine.)*

LÉONTINE: But…it's of me!

LÉONIDE: I want to have you with me always. The slightest separation—even if it lasts only a moment—makes me suffer. And this portrait will alleviate my suffering. Please give it back now.

LÉONTINE: I shouldn't, but so much love makes me weak.

(She gives the portrait back. Léonide catches her hand.)

LÉONIDE: Doesn't this love tempt you, even a little?

LÉONTINE: God knows I didn't want it to, but I may no longer have any choice in the matter. *(She weeps.)*

LÉONIDE: You don't know what joy you give me.

LÉONTINE: *(Through her tears.)* Is it decided then, that I am to love you?

LÉONIDE: Don't promise me your heart, Léontine, tell me it's mine already.

LÉONTINE: *(Very moved.)* If I did, it would be all too true. Phocion…

LÉONIDE: I will stay then, and you will speak again to Hermocrate.

LÉONTINE: Yes. It must be so. It will give me time to reconcile myself to our… being together.

CORINE: This meeting is now over—I see Dimas.

LÉONTINE: I don't want to be seen like this. I'm so overcome with…feelings… My heart… Phocion.

(Léonide and Léontine look at each other.)

LÉONTINE: I will change his mind. *(Léontine leaves.)*

SCENE VIII

DIMAS: *(Entering.)* The philosopher is here, all dreamy-eyed. Leave the field to me: To plant ideas, one must have the right conditions. When I get through with him, he will be *really* cultivated.

LÉONIDE: Into the breach, Dimas!

(She runs off. Corine follows her. Hermocrate enters.)

SCENE IX

HERMOCRATE: Have you been watching Phocion?

DIMAS: Yes, and I can bring you up to date.

HERMOCRATE: Very well then, have you found anything out? Is he often with Agis? Does he seek him out?

DIMAS: Oh no, hardly. He has other things on his mind. His brain is in a stew.

HERMOCRATE: *(Aside.)* I may not want to hear the rest of this. *(Aloud.)* What things?

DIMAS: Well God in Heaven, you are a wonderful man! One can only marvel at your knowledge, your morals…your good looks.

HERMOCRATE: What has inspired this sudden enthusiasm for me?

DIMAS: Well it's just that all these goings-on make me see you in a new light. And I must tell you, astonishing things are going on—changes!—that show you to be a singular man, a very unusual man, a man so rare you're…practically extinct! People are sighing, people are dying, people are crying out, "How I love this precious man! This *generous* man!" *(He throws himself on Hermocrate and hugs him fondly.)*

HERMOCRATE: Dimas! What *are* you talking about?

DIMAS: I'm talking about *you*. And of course I'm also talking about a boy who's really a girl.

HERMOCRATE: I do not know any persons of that description.

DIMAS: You know Phocion, don't you? Well, there's a woman in his pants.

HERMOCRATE: What are you saying?

DIMAS: And by God she's a charmer.

(Hermocrate turns sharply away.)

DIMAS: What's this face? You should be happy! Guess who she really wants to give all those charms to? I heard them talking about it. *(Proceeding slowly and carefully.)* "I'm saving myself for the most tedious of men!" No no, I've got it wrong, I made a mistake—"…saving myself for the most *fastidious*," no "*hideous* of men," yes. No! "…for the *prettiest*," no! "For the *wittiest* of men!" That's it! *"Hermocrate!"*

HERMOCRATE: Who, me?

DIMAS: I was following her, like you said, and she was wandering around in the bushes with her valet, Hermidas, who's about as much of a man as she is. I crept up on the other side of the bushes, and I heard them talking. "I'm done for Corine," says Phocion, "there's no curing me, my sweet. I love him too much, that man. I don't know what to do anymore, or what to say." "But Madame," says the pretty little one, "he will come around. You are famous for your booty!" "Ah, but what good is my booty if he sends me away?" "You must be patient, Madame." "Yes but where is he? What is he doing? What is he thinking? Does he love me? What will he decide?"

HERMOCRATE: *(Moved.)* Stop, Dimas.

DIMAS: I'm almost finished. "But what does he say to you when you speak with him, Madame?" "He scolds at me, and I get upset. He speaks wisely, and I try to do the same back. 'I pity you,' he says. 'I will change,' I tell him. 'Have you no shame?' he says. 'Will shame increase my chances?' I ask him. 'But your virtue, Madame.' 'Marry your virtue to mine, Sir, and *cure* me!'"

HERMOCRATE: I don't need to hear any more, thank you, that's enough.

DIMAS: Well I think you should cure the child, Master, by catching her illness and making *her* take care of *you*. If you never look at a woman, your…family tree will never grow. And that would be too bad. And along these lines, seeing as how even though I know everything I'm not going to breathe a word of it, could you put in a good word for me with that pretty little chambermaid?

HERMOCRATE: *(Aside.)* The final indignity. *(Aloud.)* Dimas, I am ordering you to hold your tongue. It would be devastating for…the person in question, if this story got around. I am going to send these women away. Order must be restored!

(Exit Hermocrate, sighing audibly. Léonide returns quietly.)

SCENE X

LÉONIDE: So, Dimas, what is he thinking?

DIMAS: He said, "Wardrobe must be restored." So he's sending you away.

LÉONIDE: I thought as much.

DIMAS: But then, I think he wants to keep you.

LÉONIDE: You've lost me.

DIMAS: What's worse, he seems to have lost himself. He can't make out what he wants at all. "Ah…" That was the last thing he said. All his philosophy has dried up, there's hardly any left.

LÉONIDE: Well what *is* left he'll surrender to me. He may be wise, but he'll fall into the same trap that caught his sister. Meanwhile I'm worried that Agis is avoiding me. I haven't seen him at all since he found out that I'm a woman. But look, I see him speaking to Corine. Maybe he's trying to find me.

DIMAS: You know him through and through—here he comes. *(He turns to go but hesitates and turns back.)* Madame, all this double-dealing—it won't leopardize my fortune, will it?

LÉONIDE: *(Smiling.)* No. Your fortune is safe.

DIMAS: *(From his heart.)* Thank you very much.

(Dimas leaves. Agis enters. Léonide turns to go.)

SCENE XI

AGIS: Aspasie! You run away from me every time I come near.

LÉONIDE: The fact is you ran away from me when last we spoke.

AGIS: I admit it. But I was troubled by something, something…disquieting. And it won't leave me alone.

LÉONIDE: Will you tell me about it?

(A long beat.)

AGIS: *(Haltingly.)* There is a person…I am very drawn to, but I cannot ascertain if what I feel is friendship or love. All this is so new to me—I must ask you again to advise me, to give me some…instruction.

LÉONIDE: I think I can guess who this person is.

AGIS: That couldn't be hard. You know that when you came here I had never loved at all. And since you've been here, I've hardly looked at anyone but you. So it follows, logically, that…

LÉONIDE: The person is…I.

(A beat.)

AGIS: Yes, it's you Aspasie. Can you tell me what I should make of it?

LÉONIDE: I can't help you at all. Maybe you can tell me what *I* should make of it. Because I am in the same…predicament. When I came here, *I* had never loved at all. And since coming here I've hardly looked at anyone but you. And I have changed, too.

(A beat.)

AGIS: You love me, Aspasie.

LÉONIDE: Yes, but what have we really learned from this? We loved each other first as friends, *then* we started feeling confused. Do we love each other now as we did first? Or in a different way? That's what we need to know.

AGIS: Perhaps we could figure it out if we told each other what we are feeling.

LÉONIDE: All right, let's see. *(After some thought.)* Did you have difficulty avoiding me just now?

AGIS: Immense difficulty.

LÉONIDE: This does not bode well. Did you avoid me because your heart was troubled by feelings you didn't dare tell me about?

AGIS: *(Delighted.)* That's it exactly! You understand me so well.

LÉONIDE: Well there you are. But I'm warning you, you're not necessarily going to feel *better* because of all this. In fact, from what I see in your eyes, the prognosis is less than promising.

AGIS: My eyes look at you with the greatest of pleasure—with a pleasure bordering on…excitement.

LÉONIDE: Well. That could only be real love. It isn't necessary to ask *you* any more questions.

AGIS: I would give my life for you. I'd give a thousand if I had them.

LÉONIDE: The case is closed. Love in your words, love in your eyes, love in your heart. This is real love if ever there was love, love as it ought to be…as it has always been.

AGIS: Or perhaps…as it has never been. *(A beat.)* So you can see, Aspasie, I love you not as I first did, but in a very different way. Now that you know what is happening in my heart, oughtn't I to know what is happening in yours?

LÉONIDE: Be careful Agis. A person of my sex may talk as much as she likes about her friendships, but must never speak of her love. Besides, you are already too full of tenderness, too…naked with tenderness; if you were to expose *my* heart's desire, things could get even worse than they already are.

AGIS: You were talking about my eyes, let's talk about yours. They seem to be telling me something new about your love for me.

LÉONIDE: I can't answer for my eyes. They may well tell you that my love for you has deepened. But I suppose I don't mind telling you that myself.

AGIS: *(Overwhelmed.)* Oh God—your words throw me into an abyss…of *passion!* Unfathomable! Incredible! You feel as I do!

LÉONIDE: Yes, it's true. I can't help myself. But to love as we love—it isn't enough. One must have the freedom to *live* one's love, and to be able to go on living it, and speaking it, forever. And Lord Hermocrate, who makes the rules—

AGIS: *(Interrupting her.)* I respect Hermocrate, and I love him, Aspasie, but I am beginning to learn that the heart cannot live by rules. I must see him immediately, before he finds you; he may already have decided to send you away, and we will need a little time to figure out…what we are going to do.

DIMAS: *(Appears upstage and hovers there, singing a warning.)* Tra la la la la.

LÉONIDE: You're right, Agis. You should go, quickly—but let's find each other again soon. I have so much to say to you.

AGIS: *(Exuberant.)* And I to you!

LÉONIDE: Go! Leave! When people see us together, I'm afraid they'll be able to read my thoughts, and see exactly who I am.

AGIS: *A bientôt,* my beautiful Aspasie. This time I am going to find Hermocrate, and convince him! *(He races away.)*

SCENE XII

DIMAS: *(Speaking hurriedly.)* By God, he's lucky he got away. The jealous one is here!

(He moves off quickly as Hermocrate enters.)

LÉONIDE: Hermocrate! Out of hiding at last. Couldn't you think of any other way to dampen my ardor than by *avoiding* me? And leaving me anxious and melancholy? Well your strategy hasn't worked; it makes me sadder, but no less loving.

HERMOCRATE: No, in fact something else kept me away, Aspasie. But I'm afraid your feelings are no longer at issue. Your presence here, from this moment on, is really…unmanageable. And it can only hurt you. Dimas knows who you are. Need I say more? He knows your…heart's desire. He overheard you talking, and neither you nor I can afford to count on the discretion of someone like that. So you must leave for your own good, to protect your honor.

LÉONIDE: Leave, Sir? Would you send me away in this state—a thousand times more confused than when I came here? What have you done to cure me? Is this the lesson in self-denial for which I sought out the wise Hermocrate?

HERMOCRATE: I hope what I have to say will end your confusion. You thought me wise. You loved me for that reason. But I am not at all wise. A truly wise and virtuous person would not be threatened by your presence. Do you know why I am sending you away? Because I am afraid that your secret will expose me, and make people think less of me. Because I am proud, and I fear that I won't *seem* virtuous—without troubling myself meanwhile to *be* virtuous. Because I am nothing but a vain and arrogant man, to whom wisdom is less important than the contemptible, deceitful mockery he has made of it. This, then, is the object of your love.

LÉONIDE: I have never admired it so much.

HERMOCRATE: You *can't* be serious.

LÉONIDE: Oh but I am, My Lord. That you can confess these things makes you even stronger—and me even weaker. You say you are not at all wise, and then you provide splendid proof that the opposite is true. This strategy isn't going to work either.

HERMOCRATE: Wait, Madame. You believed me capable of feeling all that love lets loose in the hearts of other men. Do you remember when you said that? Well, the least civilized soul, the most common lover, the most impulsive youth could not experience more upsetting emotions than those I have been feeling—nervousness, dread, rapture, jealousy. Is this a proper portrait of Hermocrate? The world is full of men who *want* to feel these things; any man picked at random is more suitable for this love of yours than I, Madame. *You must not feel it for me!*

LÉONIDE: But I do. You tell me to protect my honor: Could there be a greater honor than inspiring in you the feelings of which you speak? Or than that which you do me when you speak of them? *You* are protecting my honor! I no longer need ask you to help me find peace of mind; your confession has given it to me. I am at peace, I am happy. You have pledged yourself to me. We belong to each other.

HERMOCRATE: Then there's only one thing left to say—and I will end with that. If you stay, I will reveal your secret; the man you so admire will be disgraced; and his disgrace will reflect very poorly on you, and forever haunt your conscience.

LÉONIDE: And if I leave, my revenge will be certain—the love you feel for me will take care of that. I leave, and you run away from a love that could have been the sweet salvation of your life, and which will be the ruination of mine. I leave, and you delight in your sacred Reason, your relentless wisdom—fed by my unhappiness they will surely thrive. I leave, and you destroy my heart. I came to ask you for help in conquering my love for you, but you have given me no help at all, aside from admitting that you love me—an admission that redoubles *my* love. And after this, you send me away. Your so-called wisdom shores itself up at the expense of a young heart whose trust you have betrayed, whose virtuous intentions you have not respected at all, and which has served only as fodder to your rigidly held opinions and heartless theories. Surely my shame will reflect poorly on *you* and haunt *your* conscience!

HERMOCRATE: Lower your voice, Madame. Someone is coming.

LÉONIDE: *(Louder.)* You torment me, and expect me to keep my voice down?!

HERMOCRATE: *(Turning sharply to her, shouting her down.)* You move me more than you think! *(A beat. In a passionate whisper.)* But kindly *do not speak in a loud voice!*

(Harlequin enters, followed by Corine.)

SCENE XIII

CORINE: *(Running after Harlequin.)* Give that back to me! What right do you have to steal it? What are you *doing?!*

HARLEQUIN: What the devil do you *think* I'm doing? Would you make a mockery of my loyalty?! I am going to inform the master!

HERMOCRATE: *(To Harlequin.)* What is all this noise? What's the matter here?

HARLEQUIN: The matter here is one of some consequence to you, and only these devils know the details. However, since I have unmanned them, we'll soon know everything.

HERMOCRATE: Unmanned them?

HARLEQUIN: I just found this little fellow striking the pose of a thinker. He mused dreamily, he shook his head feverishly, he examined his manuscript intently. And I noticed he had at his side this shell, covered with green, yellow, gray, and white, where he dipped his pen. I sneaked up on him to see what document he was forging, but what a rogue! He wasn't forging words or letters, he was forging a *head!* And that head, Sir, was yours.

HERMOCRATE: Mine!

HARLEQUIN: Your very head, except for the fact that it was a lot less, well... *large* than the one you are wearing at the moment. Why just the *nose* that you normally have on is bigger than your entire face in this pretty little portrait! Is that legal? To belittle someone so? To cut him down to size? Look what this headshrinker has *done* to you—look at your *expression!* *(He thrusts the portrait at Hermocrate.)*

HERMOCRATE: *(Taking the portrait.)* Bravo, Harlequin. I don't blame you at all for being suspicious. Run along. I will look into this.

HARLEQUIN: Make them give you back the rest of yourself. You can't save face if you're missing most of it. *(He stalks off.)*

SCENE XIV

HERMOCRATE: *(To Corine.)* Why did you paint me? What were you after?

CORINE: I was glad to make a portrait of an illustrious man, and I would be proud to show it to people. It seemed a natural thing, Sir.

HERMOCRATE: You flatter me.

CORINE: And besides, I knew that this portrait would give pleasure to someone in particular, who would never have ventured to commission it.

HERMOCRATE: And who is that someone?

CORINE: Sir, I…

LÉONIDE: Hold your tongue, Corine.

HERMOCRATE: What's going on here? Aspasie?

LÉONIDE: Don't press her any further. Let's just pretend this never happened.

HERMOCRATE: *(Looking at the portrait.)* Yes but it *has* happened, how can I ignore it?

LÉONIDE: *(Sounding distraught.)* Let's not talk about it anymore. You are embarrassing me. *(She covers her face with her hands.)*

HERMOCRATE: *(Clutching the portrait.)* I can't believe what I am seeing. Or what is happening to me. *(Struggling to contain himself.)* *I don't know anymore what is happening to me.*

LÉONIDE: *(With passion.)* I don't know if I can endure any more of this!

HERMOCRATE: *(Overlapping her, confounded.)* This is…I am under a spell. I am being swept away.

LÉONIDE: Ah Corine, why have you *done* this?!

HERMOCRATE: Have you triumphed, Aspasie? Have you won the day?

(A beat. The women are beside themselves with expectation.)

HERMOCRATE: I *surrender!*

LÉONIDE: You are embarrassing me again, but I cannot hold it against you.

HERMOCRATE: Take the portrait back. It belongs to you, Madame.

LÉONIDE: I will not take it back unless your heart comes with it.

(They stand very close together.)

HERMOCRATE: It does. Nothing must keep you from having it. *(A beat.)* Take it from me.

(Léonide takes the portrait and hands it behind her back to Corine, who hands her a portrait of Léonide in its stead.)

LÉONIDE: *(Offering Hermocrate the portrait of herself.)* Then nothing must keep *you* from having *this. (A beat.)* Take it from me.

(Hermocrate takes it.)

HERMOCRATE: It is of you.

LÉONIDE: Show me that you cherish it.

(Hermocrate presses it slowly to his lips.)

HERMOCRATE: Have I humbled myself enough? I will not argue with you anymore.

CORINE: *(Studying Hermocrate's portrait.)* There's still something not quite right about it. But if the Master will stand very still for a moment, I can fix it straightaway.

LÉONIDE: Since we are alone and it will take only a moment, please don't refuse, My Lord.

HERMOCRATE: *(Standing very still.)* Aspasie, we are running a risk; someone could catch us together.

LÉONIDE: If as you say this is my moment of triumph, let's not throw it away—it's too precious. *(Backing slowly away.)* Your eyes look at me with a tenderness I would like to keep with me forever—so I can savor the memory. *(Moving out of Hermocrate's sight.)* You cannot see your eyes, Sir. They are enchanted. Quickly, Corine! Finish!

CORINE: Could you move your head a little to the side, Sir?

(Hermocrate turns his head, looking for Léonide.)

CORINE: No, toward *me*, Sir.

HERMOCRATE: Dear God, what are you reducing me to?

LÉONIDE: *(Close behind Hermocrate.)* Does your heart blush at what you would do for me?

HERMOCRATE: Do you wish it, Aspasie?

CORINE: Turn a touch to the right.

HERMOCRATE: *(In a hushed voice.)* Stop, here comes Agis! Go, Hermidas!

(Alarmed, they leap into action. Corine gathers her things and escapes. Agis enters.)

SCENE XV

AGIS: I was coming to ask you, Sir, to allow Phocion to stay with us for a while, but it seems that you may already have given your consent, and that my intervention is no longer necessary.

HERMOCRATE: *(In an anxious tone.)* You want him to stay then, Agis?

AGIS: I confess that I would have been annoyed to see him go, and that nothing could give me as much pleasure as having him stay on. To know him is to admire him, and friendship follows admiration naturally enough.

HERMOCRATE: I had no idea you were already so taken with each other.

(A beat.)

LÉONIDE: Actually, we hardly know each other.

AGIS: Apparently I am interrupting a private conversation. I beg your pardon.

(Agis withdraws.)

SCENE XVI

HERMOCRATE: Agis seems quite keen on your company. I'm not sure what to think. Since he has been with me, I've never seen anything interest him as much as you seem to. Have you told him who you are? Perhaps you're leading me on.

LÉONIDE: My Lord, you don't know what joy you give me! You said you'd been jealous, but I'd never *seen* you jealous—until now. I am so glad that you wrong me in this way. Hermocrate is jealous! He cherishes me! He *loves* me! He loves me at a price, but what does that matter? But still I must prove my innocence. Agis has not gone far, I can still see him. Let's call him back, My Lord. I'm going to speak to him *in front of you,* and you will see if I deserve your suspicions.

HERMOCRATE: No don't call him back. Aspasie, I see that I'm wrong. I give up. Your candor reassures me. And in any case, no one must know that I love you—yet. Give me time to arrange everything.

LÉONIDE: Take whatever time you need. Here is your sister. I will leave you together. *(She moves away. Aside.)* He is weak now. And I pity him. *(A beat.)* Heaven forgive my deception. *(She leaves.)*

SCENE XVII

LÉONTINE: *(Entering.)* Ah, here you are, dear brother. I've been looking for you everywhere.

HERMOCRATE: What can I do for you, Léontine?

LÉONTINE: Where do you stand with Phocion? Do you still intend to send him away? He does go on about you so, saying *such* nice things, that I promised him he could stay and that you would consent to it. Now I gave him my word—he won't stay long, so it simply isn't worth the trouble of going back on my promise.

HERMOCRATE: No Léontine, you know my esteem for you, and I will not go against your wish. Since you promised him, I have nothing more to say about it. He can stay as long as he wants, my dear.

LÉONTINE: Thank you for being so good-natured, brother. In fact, you know, Phocion truly deserves our…indulgence.

HERMOCRATE: I know. He does.

LÉONTINE: And moreover, I think he serves as a suitable distraction for Agis, who is at an age when he might easily rebel against his…solitary life.

HERMOCRATE: That could happen at any age.

LÉONTINE: You're right. We all have these feelings of…well, melancholy. *(A beat.)* I often feel quite…bored. I hope it's not wrong to say this to you.

HERMOCRATE: Wrong? Who wouldn't get a bit bored sometimes? Are we not made for society and mutual fellowship?

LÉONTINE: You know…it's a big step, to close oneself off from the world, in a retreat. We were perhaps quick to choose such a hard life.

(A beat.)

HERMOCRATE: Go on. I couldn't put all this into words as easily as you do.

LÉONTINE: But remember—what's done *can* be undone. One's…circumstances can always change.

HERMOCRATE: Indeed they can!

LÉONTINE: A man of your standing would be welcome anywhere, should he wish to change his circumstances.

HERMOCRATE: And *you,* who are lovely and younger than I—I wouldn't be concerned about you, either.

LÉONTINE: Indeed brother, few *young* men can hold a candle to you, and the gift of your heart would not be taken lightly.

HERMOCRATE: And I assure you that you could receive many such gifts without making the least effort.

LÉONTINE: Then, you wouldn't be surprised if I had…certain prospects?

HERMOCRATE: I've always been surprised that you had none.

LÉONTINE: Listen to you! And why couldn't *you* also have some?

HERMOCRATE: Well, one never knows. Perhaps I already do.

LÉONTINE: I would be *so* delighted if you did. After all, and I've thought about this carefully, is our beloved Reason greater than that of the gods, who thought up marriage in the first place? I mean, a married man is just as good as an unmarried one. *(A beat.)* Well, it's good to think about these things. We'll talk about it more another time. Adieu.

HERMOCRATE: I have some things to see to; I'll be along shortly.

(Léontine departs. Hermocrate reflects.)

HERMOCRATE: We both seem to be doing quite well for ourselves. *(He thinks.)* On whom could she possibly have set her sights? *(He thinks.)* I wonder if it's someone as young for her as Aspasie is for me. *(He thinks.)* Well, we must fulfill our destinies. *(A long beat.)* How weak we are. We are so weak.

(A beat.)

(Blackout.)

ACT III
SCENE I

(Léonide and Corine are discovered thinking.)

LÉONIDE: Come talk to me Corine! Would you ever have believed that you and I could have done this? Hermocrate and his sister have become obsessed with me, first one, then the other, and they are both actually planning to *marry* me. In *secret!* God knows what arrangements have already been made for all these imaginary nuptials! Everything seems to point to success. Well *I* never would have believed it—that love could reduce a famous rationalist to a passionate, jealous lover. That love could completely confound the minds of these oh-so-controlled paragons of reason and virtue. And I had to listen to every single word out of them, because I caught them as they fell…as I must continue to do until everything is settled, finally, with Agis. *(Sighing.)* Agis. I have to tell him who I am. And I dread it, but at least I know he wants to see me as much as I want to see him. He truly loves me as Aspasie, could he really hate me as Léonide?

CORINE: Take heart, Madame! After all that she's done for him, Léonide would have to seem even more lovable than Aspasie.

LÉONIDE: I'm inclined to think so, but his family—his parents—were destroyed by mine.

CORINE: Your father *inherited* his throne, he did not usurp it.

LÉONIDE: What's the difference to Agis? Oh Corine, I'm so in love…and I'm so afraid. Yet I must proceed as if I'm totally confident. *(A beat.)* Anyway, have you sent my letters home?

CORINE: Yes Madame, Dimas found me a messenger. You should have an answer soon. What is the plan?

LÉONIDE: I wrote Ariston to follow the messenger back here, and to bring my guardsmen and my ceremonial carriage with him. Agis must leave this place as a proper prince. I will wait here; come and tell me the instant they arrive. That will be the crowning moment, Corine. Thank you for all you've done for me.

CORINE: I'm off, but you're not through. *(Pointing offstage.)* She's back. *(Enter Léontine. Corine leaves.)*

SCENE II

LÉONTINE: A word with you, my Phocion. *(Confidentially.)* The die is cast. Our troubles will soon be over.

LÉONIDE: Thank heavens.

LÉONTINE: I have taken my life into my own hands. We will be wed, we will be together forever. I still think it's wrong to have the ceremony here, yet the other arrangements you've made don't seem...well, quite appropriate. You sent for a carriage to meet us, isn't that so? Close to the house?
(Léonide nods yes.)

LÉONTINE: But wouldn't it be better if, instead of leaving together, I left alone, went ahead to the city, and awaited you there?

LÉONIDE: Yes, yes, you're right. You should go on ahead, good thinking.

LÉONTINE: I'll go immediately and get ready to leave. *(She starts off but suddenly stops and looks around the garden.)*

LÉONTINE: Two hours from now I will no longer be here. Phocion, you will follow me soon?

LÉONIDE: *(Impatient.)* I can't follow until you've gone somewhere.

LÉONTINE: You should be grateful for my love.

LÉONIDE: Your love is...priceless. You shouldn't make light of mine.

LÉONTINE: You are the only person in the world for whom I would take this step.

LÉONIDE: It's not so big a step as you think. You run no risk. Now go get ready.

LÉONTINE: I love your eagerness. May it last forever!

LÉONIDE: If only you were as eager. This delaying makes me impatient.
(A beat.)

LÉONTINE: I'm sorry. Sometimes a sort of fear and melancholy come over me.

LÉONIDE: Isn't it a little late for that? I feel joy, only joy.

LÉONTINE: Oh don't be impatient, I'll go now.
(She turns to go, sees Hermocrate coming, and veers off in a new direction.)

LÉONTINE: It's Hermocrate! I just can't see him now!
(She escapes, as Hermocrate appears.)

SCENE III

LÉONIDE: So...Hermocrate. I thought you were busy arranging for our departure.

HERMOCRATE: Ah, my beautiful Aspasie, if only you knew how I...must battle my demons.

LÉONIDE: Ah, and if only you knew how tired I am of battling them with you! What does it all mean? I can never be sure of anything with you.

HERMOCRATE: Forgive this uncertainly in a man whose heart should be more resolute.

LÉONIDE: *(Pointedly.)* And more ardent. Well, you can be as uncertain as you like, but you really must get ready to leave. Unless you want to stay here and have Harlequin marry us.

HERMOCRATE: No no. *(A beat. He exhales his frustration.)*

LÉONIDE: Sighing won't hasten our departure.

HERMOCRATE: I have one thing yet to say to you—it's troubling me terribly.

LÉONIDE: You never stop, there's always one thing more to say.

HERMOCRATE: Aspasie. I have surrendered everything to you—my heart, my way of life, my volition. May I keep nothing of my own?

LÉONIDE: What would you keep?

HERMOCRATE: I have raised Agis since he was eight years old. *(Struggling with his feelings.)* I cannot give him up yet. Let him come.with us, let him live with us for a while.

LÉONIDE: I see…and who *is* he? Why is he so important to you?

HERMOCRATE: *(Hesitating.)* What concerns me must now concern you. So I will tell you his secret. You have heard of King Cleomones?
(Léonide nods yes. A beat.)

HERMOCRATE: Agis is his son. He was born in a dungeon. He was smuggled out of prison shortly thereafter. I am his guardian.

LÉONIDE: His secret is in good hands.

HERMOCRATE: Imagine the care with which I have hidden him, the love I have given him…and what would become of him if he fell into the hands of Princess Léonide. She is trying to find him, you know. Apparently she will not breathe freely until he is dead.

LÉONIDE: Yet she is widely considered to be generous, and fair.

HERMOCRATE: I put no faith in hearsay. She was born to blood that is neither generous nor fair.

LÉONIDE: They also say that she would marry the lost prince if only she knew where to find him. I mean, they are the same age…

HERMOCRATE: Even if she chose to pursue that course, the justifiable hatred Agis feels for her would certainly prevent it from happening.

LÉONIDE: I would have thought that forgiving an enemy was worth as much as hating her—or him. Especially if that enemy has done one no harm.

HERMOCRATE: If the price of such forgiveness were not a throne, you would be right. But forgiveness at that price… *(He pauses, and continues icily.)* …is not affordable. At any rate, it's not even a consideration.

LÉONIDE: I will welcome Agis and offer him my tenderest love.

HERMOCRATE: Thank you so much. He won't be with us for long. Our allies at court are rallying secretly against the Princess, and he will soon join them. Things are moving forward; we may soon see a complete turnaround at court.

LÉONIDE: Do they plan to kill the Princess?

HERMOCRATE: Avenge one crime with another? She is only the heir of the wrongdoers. No, Agis would not be capable of that. It will be enough to subdue her.

LÉONIDE: Well I think you have said what you had to say to me. Go get ready to leave.

HERMOCRATE: Adieu, beloved Aspasie. *(Looking around wistfully.)* These are my last hours in this place. *(After a moment he leaves.)*

SCENE IV

LÉONIDE: *(Peering about.)* Agis. Will he come to me now? I know he is waiting to find the right moment to speak to me. *(A beat.)* That he could hate me frightens me.

(Harlequin and Dimas arrive in high spirits.)

HARLEQUIN: Your servant, Madame.

DIMAS: Your obedient servant, Madame.

LÉONIDE: A little quieter, please.

DIMAS: Don't be suspenseful. We are alone.

LÉONIDE: What do you want?

HARLEQUIN: A bagatelle, Madame.

DIMAS: We're just here to strike a balance.

HARLEQUIN: To see what we amount to.

LÉONIDE: I'm feeling a bit anxious. I haven't time for idle chat.

DIMAS: So then, have we done a good job?

LÉONIDE: Yes, you've both served me well.

DIMAS: And the seeds we planted—they are sprouting?

LÉONIDE: *(Impatient, pointing offstage.)* I am waiting to speak with Agis, who is waiting patiently for me.

HARLEQUIN: Well if he's waiting patiently for you, you needn't feel anxious.

DIMAS: And we can talk business. Well, we've sold them short. We've taken them all in.

HARLEQUIN: We were rapscallions beyond compare!

DIMAS: We were deaf to the voice of conscience. It was hard. We were brave.

HARLEQUIN: Sometimes you were a boy, and it wasn't even true! Sometimes you were a girl, and I didn't even know it!

DIMAS: There were rendezvous—sometimes with *him,* sometimes with *her.* I had to give your heart to everyone, and yet give it to no one.

HARLEQUIN: There were portraits—to trap loving faces you couldn't have cared less about, faces that thought their likenesses had real value.

LÉONIDE: *(Unamused.)* You may now get to the point.

DIMAS: Your passion play is almost over. How much is the climax worth to you?

HARLEQUIN: Would you like to buy the dénouement? We are selling it for a reasonable price.

DIMAS: Bargain with us, or we'll ruin the ending.

LÉONIDE: But didn't I promise to make your fortunes?

DIMAS: We want ready money!

HARLEQUIN: Yes, because when one no longer has use for servants, one pays them badly.

LÉONIDE: Children. How insolent we are.

DIMAS: We have a right to be!

HARLEQUIN: Insolence agrees with us!

LÉONIDE: If you stand in my way, if you are indiscreet, I will see to it that you pay for your indiscretions in a dungeon. And I promise you, I have the power to make that happen. If on the other hand you keep your mouths shut, I will make good on all previous promises. What will it be? Prison? Or money? Now I *order* you to make yourselves scarce. You *might* redeem yourselves with prompt obedience.

(She glares at them. Dimas shrinks a little.)

DIMAS: *(To Harlequin.)* What do we do? More insolence?

HARLEQUIN: No, dungeons are cold. Let's go.

(They go. Agis enters.)

SCENE V

AGIS: I've found you, Aspasie, and we can talk. This whole situation has caused me such *distress!* I found myself almost hating Hermocrate and Léontine for all the affection they seem to feel for you. I was jealous! But who wouldn't love you? God, you are so beautiful, Aspasie. And how exquisitely sweet it is to love you.

LÉONIDE: And how it pleases me to hear you say that, Agis. You will soon know the real price of that love. Tell me…your love is so pure, so unquestioning—is there nothing that could take it away from me?

AGIS: Nothing. You will lose me only when I stop breathing.

LÉONIDE: I haven't told you everything, Agis. You don't know who I am yet.

AGIS: I know your beauty. I know your heart. I will adore you until my dying moment; nothing could break your spell.

LÉONIDE: Oh Gods, such love! But the dearer it is to me, the more I am afraid to lose it. I have kept it from you, Agis—who I really am. My name… *(A beat.)* It may shock you.

AGIS: But Aspasie you don't know who *I* am either! Or how daunted I am by the thought of burdening your destiny with mine. *(Crying out in pain.)* Oh cruel princess, I have so many reasons to hate you!

LÉONIDE: Who are you talking about?

AGIS: Princess Léonide, Aspasie. My enemy and yours.

(Agis sees someone coming and spins. Léonide looks to see who it is.)

AGIS: But someone's coming! I can't continue now.

LÉONIDE: Hermocrate! I *hate* him for interrupting us. *(Turning to Agis with great focus.)* Our future depends yet on a single word. You do not realize it, but you hate me.

AGIS: Hate you?!

LÉONIDE: *(A frantic whisper.)* There's no time now. See what he wants. *(Léonide exits quickly.)*

SCENE VI

AGIS: I can't imagine what she means. *(A long beat. Agis considers the state of his affairs.)* I don't know if I could forgive myself if I didn't tell Hermocrate what is happening to me. *(He paces back and forth animatedly.)*

SCENE VII

HERMOCRATE: *(Entering.)* Wait Prince, I need to talk to you. *(A beat.)* I don't know where to begin.

AGIS: What is troubling you, Sir?

HERMOCRATE: Something you probably never would have imagined, something I am ashamed to admit to you. But something I've decided, after much reflection, I must tell you.

AGIS: What is wrong?

HERMOCRATE: I am weak—as weak as any other man.

AGIS: What weakness do you refer to, Sir?

HERMOCRATE: The one we forgive in every man, the most ordinary failing, the weakness one would least expect to find in me. You know my views on that emotion called love.

AGIS: It seems to me they've always been a bit extreme.

HERMOCRATE: Yes, that could well be. But can I be blamed? A solitary man given to contemplation and study, a man who communes only with his mind and never with his heart, a man imprisoned by his own opinions is hardly in a position to pass judgment on certain...freedoms. He will always protest too much.

AGIS: There's no doubting it, you always were prone to excess.

HERMOCRATE: You are right, I agree with you! I said all kinds of things. That such intense emotion was ridiculous, extravagant, unworthy of a man of reason. I called it a delusion, and I did not know what I was saying. My words owed nothing to reason, or to nature, or to whichever god may have given us life.

AGIS: Because, deep down, we are made for loving.

HERMOCRATE: Indeed we are. Everything turns on this...love.

AGIS: One day it may turn on *you* for having held it in such contempt.

HERMOCRATE: It has already done so.

AGIS: Really?

HERMOCRATE: Ah, I suppose I must tell you the whole of it. *(A beat.)* I am about to change my...circumstances, and I hope you will follow me...if you love me. I leave today. I'm going to be married.

AGIS: And that is what was troubling you?

HERMOCRATE: It's not easy to go back on a lifetime of vows; it is a big change.

AGIS: Well I congratulate you. Perhaps you needed to learn the wisdom of the heart.

HERMOCRATE: I am certainly learning a lesson. And I will not delude myself anymore. If you knew what an abundance of love, what dedicated, even insistent passion this person has surprised me with, you would think poorly of me if I didn't accept them. Reason does not mean that we should be ungrateful, yet that's what I would have been. This person sees me a few times in the forest, takes a fancy to me, tries to forget this fancy but cannot, decides to talk to me, but is intimidated by my reputation for severity. So to avoid an unpleasant reception she takes on a disguise and changes her *sex,* becoming the most beautiful young man imaginable. She arrives here, and I recognize her from my walk in the woods yesterday. I ask her to leave. I even suspect that it is *you* she wants, but she swears that isn't so, and to convince me she whispers, "I love you." *(A beat.)* "You don't believe me? I give you my hand, I give you my fortune, I give you my heart. Give me yours in return, or else cure mine of this affliction. Submit to these emotions I feel for you, or else teach me to master them. Share my love, or else give me back my freedom!" And she says all this so beguilingly, and with eyes so…searching, and a voice so soft with love—she could subdue a savage!

AGIS: *(Disquieted.)* But Sir, this tender lover in disguise—have I seen her here? Did she come *here?*

HERMOCRATE: Yes, and she's *still* here.

AGIS: But only Phocion has come here.

HERMOCRATE: *(Delighted.)* She *is* Phocion! *(He sees Léontine coming. A sudden whisper.)* But don't say a word. It's Léontine.

(Léontine approaches. Agis hides his distress.)

SCENE VIII

LÉONTINE: *(To Hermocrate.)* Dear brother, I am going to make a short trip to the city.

HERMOCRATE: Indeed? And where will you be staying?

LÉONTINE: At Phrosine's. I've had news from her; she's asked me to come at once.

HERMOCRATE: Then we shall both be *in absentia*. I'm also leaving—in about an hour. I was just telling Agis.

LÉONTINE: You, too, dear brother? And where will *you* be going?

HERMOCRATE: I'm going to see Criton.

LÉONTINE: Heavens! To the city. Like me. It's…curious that we both have business in the city. Do you remember the subject of our conversation a while ago? Your trip doesn't by any chance have some secret purpose?

HERMOCRATE: Now the way you say that makes me wonder about *your* trip. You remember what you were hinting at when we spoke.

LÉONTINE: Hermocrate, let's speak openly. We see through each other. I'm not going to see Phrosine at all.

HERMOCRATE: *(With a smile.)* Well since we are speaking frankly, I will be no less candid with you. I'm not going to see Criton.

LÉONTINE: It's my heart that leads me where I'm going.

HERMOCRATE: And mine leads me.

LÉONTINE: And what is more…I am getting married.

(A beat.)

HERMOCRATE: Well...so am I.

LÉONTINE: Well that's wonderful, Hermocrate! Now that we have told our secrets, perhaps my...intended, and I, can avoid the expense of traveling elsewhere for the ceremony. He is here, and since you know everything, it's hardly necessary to sneak off.

HERMOCRATE: You're right. And I won't leave either. We will all four be married at the same time! Because she...the one to whom I have given myself...is also here.

LÉONTINE: *(A little perplexed.)* I haven't seen a woman here. *(A beat. Shaking off her hesitation and forging ahead cheerfully.)* I am marrying Phocion.

HERMOCRATE: Phocion!

LÉONTINE: Yes. Phocion.

HERMOCRATE: Well...now...you don't mean...the boy who came here to study? The one who wants to stay on with us?

LÉONTINE: I don't know any other Phocion.

HERMOCRATE: No wait a minute, wait. I'm also marrying him. We can't *both* marry him.

LÉONTINE: You're marrying *him?!* That's absolutely mad!

HERMOCRATE: It's absolutely *true.*

LÉONTINE: What can this mean? *My* Phocion, the Phocion who loves me with an infinite tenderness, the one who had my portrait made without my even knowing it?

HERMOCRATE: Your portrait? That's not *your* portrait, it's *mine!* And it was without *my* even knowing it that he had it made! *She!*

LÉONTINE: Are you sure you're not mistaken? *(Producing the portrait Léonide gave her.)* Look, here is his portrait. Do you recognize him?

HERMOCRATE: Oh my sister, I have one too. *(He produces his, looks at hers.)* Yours is of a man, mine is of a woman...
(They study the little pictures intently together for a moment.)

HERMOCRATE: But that seems to be the only difference.

LÉONTINE: *(Sadly.)* Oh heavens...has this happened?

AGIS: Oh, it has happened. And now I must speak. She didn't give me a portrait, but I am *also* supposed to marry her.

HERMOCRATE: What? You too, Agis? *(Grimly.)* What a very peculiar coincidence.

LÉONTINE: I am *outraged!*

HERMOCRATE: *(To Léontine.)* There's no point in grumbling. Our servants have obviously been bought, and I fear there may be more surprises in store. Léontine, let's go, there's no more time to lose. That girl must explain her deception. She must tell us the truth.

(Hermocrate leads Léontine off to find Léonide. Agis weeps.)

SCENE IX

AGIS: *(Through his tears.)* I have no hope.

(Léonide enters slowly and quietly, looking after Hermocrate and Léontine.)

LÉONIDE: So they're gone, the meddlers. *(Seeing Agis.)* Agis, what is it?

(Agis pulls away from her.)

LÉONIDE: Why won't you look at me?

AGIS: *(Furious.)* Why did you come here? Which of the three of us do you really intend to marry? Hermocrate? Léontine? Or is it me?

LÉONIDE: *(Gravely.)* Oh I see…I have been found out.

AGIS: Don't you have a portrait for *me*—like the others?

LÉONIDE: I wouldn't have given the others my portrait if I hadn't intended to give you my life.

AGIS: *Hermocrate* can have your life! Or Léontine! Good-bye, I am leaving. You have been…worse than false…*cruel*…I don't even know what to call it! Good-bye forever. You have killed me!

(Agis starts to leave. Léonide catches him.)

LÉONIDE: Wait! Listen to me!

AGIS: Don't *touch* me! Let me go!

LÉONIDE: I will not let you go, I will never let you go. If you refuse to listen to me, you are the most ungrateful of men.

AGIS: Me, whom you deceived? *Ungrateful?*

LÉONIDE: But I did it for *you,* it was for *you* that I deceived everyone. I had to. Every false word I have spoken is proof of my love. My heart's desire is honest. My love is true. You're wrong to insult me. And all the love you have for me—you can't see that now, but you *do* love me. And you will respect me. You will even ask my forgiveness. I *know* I will get through to you!

AGIS: I just can't understand how…

LÉONIDE: I did anything and everything I could to mislead them, to delude them, to seduce them. Because making them love me was the only way I could get to you, and you were the *only* object of everything I have done here. I was inspired at every turn by your eyes, your hands…your mouth…

AGIS: Ah, Aspasie, can I believe you?

LÉONIDE: Harlequin and Dimas helped me, they know my secret, they will confirm what I'm telling you. Ask them. I would even trust *them* to tell the truth about this!

AGIS: *(Still confused.)* Can it be possible that you are telling the truth? Aspasie…it was for love of *me?*

LÉONIDE: Yes. But that isn't everything. *(She pauses to gather her strength.)* The princess you just called your enemy and mine…

AGIS: Aspasie, if you *do* really love me you must know that she is trying to kill me. She will not spare the son of Cleomones.

LÉONIDE: *(Urgently.)* I know who you are. *(A beat.)* And I am in a position to put *her* fate in *your* hands.

AGIS: But I am asking only that we be allowed to decide our *own* fate.

LÉONIDE: *(Interrupting him urgently.)* Listen to me! Her fate *is* in your hands. *(She turns to face Agis. Her hand moves to her heart.)* The love in her heart…here…puts her at your mercy.

AGIS: Her heart… *(He realizes.)* You are Léonide, Madame.

LÉONIDE: I told you before that you didn't yet know how much I love you. Now you do. You have all my secrets and all my love. All my life.
(Agis, moved, falls to his knees at her feet. They both cry. Hermocrate and Léontine enter.)

SCENE X AND FINALE

HERMOCRATE: What is this? Agis on his knees? *(He approaches Léonide and produces the portrait she gave him.)* Of whom is this a portrait?

LÉONIDE: Of me.

LÉONTINE: *(Producing hers.)* And this one—you *impostor?*

LÉONIDE: That's of me, too. Would you like me to take them back, and return yours?

HERMOCRATE: *(Interrupting her.)* Stop it! I think your jest has gone far enough. Who are you? Why did you come here?
(Hermocrate stands facing Léonide. Enter Corine, followed by Harlequin and Dimas.)

LÉONIDE: I will tell you, but first…Corine?

DIMAS: *(Entering.)* Master, did you see? Horses! Soldiers! There's a gilded carriage at the bottom of the garden!

CORINE: Madame, Ariston has arrived.

LÉONIDE: *(To Agis.)* Come, Sire. Come, accept the tributes of your subjects. The royal guard awaits your word. It is time to go.

(Agis kisses Léontine and Hermocrate good-bye. Léonide gives money to Corine, who pays Dimas, then Harlequin. Agis rejoins Léonide.)

LÉONIDE: You, Hermocrate, and you, Léontine, who at first denied me your support—perhaps you are beginning to see the truth through my deception. I came here to return the throne to Agis. And to give him my heart as well. If I had come as a woman, as myself, I might have lost him forever. If I hadn't deceived the two of you, it all might have come to nothing. I had to be sure, you see. Hermocrate, you are certainly not to be pitied. I leave your reason in care of your heart. And you, Léontine. When I made love to you, I kindled something in you. Now that you know who I am, I expect that fire has died out. *(A beat.)* Or am I wrong?

(Léonide smiles at Hermocrate and Léontine, then leaves with Agis. Corine follows, Harlequin and Dimas move away. Hermocrate and Léontine remain onstage, each standing alone.)

(Fade to black.)

END OF PLAY

A MARIVAUX CHRONOLOGY

1643   • Louis XIV, aged five, becomes King of France.
                 • Playwright Molière (pen name of Jean Baptiste Poquelin) founds the Illustre Théâtre.

1660   • London theaters reopen after being closed for eighteen years by the Puritans.
                 • Actresses are allowed on English and German stages.

1640–
1665   • *Artists and writers active during this period include Bernini, Calderón, Corneille, Hobbes, Leibniz, Lully, Milton, Molière, Monteverdi, Rembrandt, and Velazquez; on the English stage: John Ford, Thomas Middleton.*

1673   • Molière dies.

1680   • Louis XIV creates the Comédie Française.

1684   • Playwright Pierre Corneille dies.

1688   • Pierre Carlet (Marivaux) is born in Paris.

1665–
1690   • *Artists and writers active during this period include Bayle, La Fontaine, More, Purcell, Racine, Schütz, Spinoza, Vermeer, Wren; on the English stage: Aphra Behn, George Etheredge, Thomas Shadwell, and William Wycherly.*

1694   • Philosopher and author François Marie Arouet de Voltaire is born.

1697   • Louis XIV exiles the Italian comedians from France for spoofing Madame de Maintenon.

1699   • Playwright Jean Racine dies.

1700   • Marivaux's leading actress, Silvia, is born.

1709	• Alain-René Lesage's play *Turcaret* is premiered.
1710	• Louis XV, great-grandson of Louis XIV and future king of France, is born.
1712	• Marivaux's first comedy *Le Père prudent et équitable* (*A Just and Prudent Father*) is published.
	• Philosopher, political theorist, and composer Jean-Jacques Rousseau is born.
1713	• Marivaux enters the literary life of Paris after studying law for three years.
1715	• Louis XIV dies; Philippe, Duc d'Orléans, rules as Regent for the five-year-old Louis XV.

1690– 1715	• *Artists and writers active during this period include Bach, Defoe, Handel, Locke, Pepys, Pope, Swift, Tiepolo; on the English stage: William Congreve, John Dryden, George Farquhar, John Gay.*

1716	• Pierre Carlet signs the name Marivaux for the first time.
	• The Regent recalls the Italian comedians to France.
1717	• Marivaux marries a wealthy woman, Colombe Bologne.
	• Antoine Watteau shows his *fête galante* painting *The Embarkation for Cythera*.
1719	• Marivaux's only child, a daughter, is born.
1720	• Marivaux's first success for the Italian players is produced— *Arlequin poli par l'amour* (*Harlequin Refined by Love*); his tragedy *Annibal* (*Hannibal*) plays the Comédie Française.
	• Marivaux is ruined in the collapse of John Law's disastrous financial scheme.
1722	• Working on *La Surprise de l'amour* (*The Surprise of Love*) Marivaux finds a muse in the actress Silvia.

1723	• Marivaux's wife dies. • The Regent dies, and the twelve-year-old Louis XV is ruler of France.
1731	• Marivaux's novel *La Vie de Marianne* (*Marianne's Life*) begins to appear in serialized installments.
1732	• The playwright Pierre Augustin Beaumarchais is born.
1734	• Another Marivaux novel, *Le Paysan parvenu* (*A Peasant Strikes It Rich*), starts serialization.
1739	• Tomasso Vicentini, Marivaux's only Harlequin, dies. • Literary cabals undermine Marivaux's success.
1740	• *L'Épreuve* (*The Test*) is Marivaux's last play for the Italian comedians.
1715–1740	• *Artists and writers active during this period include Bach, Canaletto, Chardin, François Couperin, Defoe, Fielding, Handel, Hogarth, Pergolesi, Pope, Rameau, Richardson, Domenico Scarlatti, Telemann, Vivaldi, Voltaire, Watteau; the London theater was dominated by Handel's operas.*
1742	• Marivaux is elected to the Académie Française in preference to Voltaire.
1744	• Marivaux moves in with his mistress Angélique-Gabrielle Saint-Jean.
1745	• Marivaux's daughter enters a convent.
1754	• Louis XVI is born.
1762	• The Italian comedians are absorbed into the Opéra Comique, and those who cannot sing are let go. • The Italian playwright Carlo Goldoni arrives in Paris (and later writes for the Italians).
1763	• Marivaux dies.

1740– *1765*	• *Artists and writers active during this period include Boucher,* *Burke, Chippendale, Diderot, Frangonard, Benjamin Franklin,* *Gainsborough, Gluck, Goldoni, Gozzi, Greuze, Guardi, Haydn,* *Hume, Lessing, Mozart, Reynolds, Rousseau, Smollett, Sterne,* *Voltaire, Walpole, Winckelmann. On the English stage: David* *Garrick, Oliver Goldsmith.*

1775   • Beaumarchais' *Le Barbier de Séville* (*The Barber of Seville*) is premiered.

1770   • The future king of France marries Marie Antoinette.

1774   • Louis XV dies and is succeeded by his grandson Louis XVI.

1775   • The American Revolution begins.

1778   • Voltaire and Rousseau die.

1783   • Great Britain recognizes an independent United States.

1784   • Beaumarchais' *Le Mariage de Figaro* (*The Marriage of Figaro*) is premiered.

1786   • Mozart's *Le nozze di Figaro* is premiered.

1789   • The French Revolution begins.

IN THE AMERICAS

The first five American presidents were born during Marivaux's lifetime. During this period there was intense development and negotiation in and among the thirteen colonies (and other American territories) and the European states that controlled or had interests in them. Marivaux's only connection with the Americas was his financial ruin in the collapse of a widespread but baseless speculation in Mississippi and Louisiana. The first playhouse in New York, by the way, was opened in 1750.

MARIVAUX'S PLAYS

1706   *Le Père prudent et équitable* (*A Just and Prudent Father*)

1720   *L'Amour et la verité* (*Love and Truth*)
        Arlequin poli par l'amour (*Harlequin Refined by Love*)
        Annibal (*Hannibal*)

1722   *La Surprise de l'amour* (*The Surprise of Love*)

1723   **La Double inconstance (*The Double Inconstancy*), translated here as *Changes of Heart***

1724   *Le Prince travesti ou L'Illustre aventurier* (*The Prince Disguised, or The Illustrious Adventurer*)
        La Fausse suivante ou Le Fourbe puni (*The Servant-Girl Disguised, or The Cheat Punished*)
        Le Dénouement imprévu (*The Unexpected Ending*)

1725   *L'Ile des esclaves* (*Slave Island*)
        L'Héritier du village (*The Heir to the Village*)

1727   *Les Petits hommes ou L'Ile de la raison* (*Mean Little Men, or The Isle of Reason*)
        La Seconde surprise de l'amour (*The Second Surprise of Love*)

1728   *Le Triomphe de Plutus* (*The Triumph of Plutus*)

1729   *La Nouvelle colonie ou La Ligue des femmes* (*The New Colony, or the Confederacy of Women*)

1730   **Le Jeu de l'amour et du hasard (*The Game of Love and Chance*)**

1731   *La Réunion des amours* (*Love's Reconciliation*)

1732   **Le Triomphe de l'amour (*The Triumph of Love*)**
        Les Serments indiscrets (*Careless Vows*)
        L'École des mères (*The School for Mothers*)

1733   *L'Heureux stratagème* (*The Successful Stratagem*)

1734   *La Méprise* (*The Mistake*)
        Le Petit maître corrigé (*The Fop Chastised*)

1735   *La Mère confidente* (*Mother and Confidante*)

1736   *Le Legs* (*The Bequest*)

1737   *Les Fausses confidences* (*False Confidences*)

1738   *La Joie imprévue* (*Unforeseen Happiness*)

1739   *Les Sincères* (*They Mean It*)

1740   *L'Épreuve* (*The Test*)

1744   *La Dispute* (*The Debate*)

1745   *Le Préjugé vaincu* (*Predjudice Overcome*)

1757   *Félicie* (*Felicia*)
        Les Acteurs de bonne foi (*Acting in Good Faith*)

THE ADAPTATIONS

This adaptation of *The Triumph of Love* is based on a translation by me and Nadia Benabid, and for the most part we adhered closely to the original French. I did change the gardener's way of misspeaking himself, and I allowed Harlequin some puns that are not always literal translations. Furthermore, as I could not imagine a performance in which Harlequin, compulsive wag and improviser, would not lapse from Marivaux's script, I have provided an intermezzo at the beginning of Act II, which is an adaption of an old *commedia dell'arte* scenario entitled "Harlequin in Love." I developed this scene in rehearsal with John Michael Higgins, the Harlequin of the first performance of this adaptation.

Changes of Heart is a freer adaptation of Marivaux in several respects. As Harlequin is the central figure in this play the issue of improvisation loomed even larger. I found I couldn't write his lines without constant interruption from him. Moreover, we know from reports of the first performance that there were several scenes in which the actors diverged from the script. So I let Harlequin interpolate occasionally, especially when he is on stage with Trivelin, another character with particularly strong ties to the *commedia* tradition. I have also made explicit a few things that are implicit in the French, or that are considered by many Marivaux scholars to be facts of the play— Lisette's love for the Prince, and Trivelin's for Flaminia. Lisette in the present version not only states her love objective clearly (in Act I) but also actually bargains with Silvia for it (in Act II); and I wrote a brief intermezzo for Trivelin and Flaminia at the top of Act III.

The only notable changes to *The Game of Love and Chance* are two new scenes—the end of Act I from the entrance of Lisette, and the second scene of Act II for Lisette and Dorante. I added both to explicate further the class issues and reflexes on which the play hinges. Also, I couldn't help imagining Harlequin and Lisette's first meeting, to which Lisette refers in Marivaux's original, or an encounter between Lisette and Dorante (which Marivaux neither referred to nor wrote). Both scenes slot into Marivaux's original with no real change to the plot or to neighboring scenes. The part of Orgon's valet, given one line by Marivaux, can easily be cut in performance. In the Huntington Theatre production we gave the substance of this line to Lisette.

In all three plays I took these and other measures to clarify and amplify themes or issues of style that I believe interested Marivaux. I frequently made small changes to bring to the surface certain social issues and responses that Marivaux's audiences would have understood tacitly but that are far from obvious in 1990s America.

PRONUNCIATION GUIDE

"Madame," in all three plays, should be pronounced *à la française*, with the stress on the second syllable.

Harlequin, a recognizable word in English, should be pronounced as such. French names are accented on the final syllable.

In *Changes of Heart*
>Trivelin   TREE-VE-*LA(N)*
>Lisette   LEE-*ZETT*

In *The Game of Love and Chance*
>Lisette   LEE-*ZETT*
>Dorante   DOH-*RAWNT*
>Orgon   OR-*GAW(N)*

>In I,1 Silvia talks about her neighbors:
>Ergaste   AIR-*GAHST*
>Léandre   LAY-*AW(N)DR(UH)*
>Tersandre   TAIR-*SAW(N)DR(UH)*

In *The Triumph of Love*
>Léonide   LAY-OH-*NEED*
>Phocion   FOH-SEE-*AW(N)*
>Aspasie   AH-SPAH-*ZEE*
>Corine   KOH-*REEN*
>Hermidas   AIR-MEE-*DAHS* (hard s)
>Dimas   DEE-*MAHS* (hard s)
>Léontine   LAY-AW(N)-*TEEN*
>Hermocrate   AIR-MOH-*KRAHT*

>In I,1 Léonide mentions Agis' father, whose name I have Anglicized:
>Cleomenes   KLEE-*AH*-MUH-NEEZ

>In III,1 Corine mentions a court functionary:
>Ariston   AH-REE-*STAW(N)*

>In III,8 Hermocrate and Léontine mention two friends:
>Phrosine   FROH-*ZEEN*
>Criton   KREE-*TAW(N)*

Marivaux

Three Plays

Smith and Kraus *Books for Actors*

GREAT TRANSLATIONS FOR ACTORS SERIES

Boulevard Comedies, tr. by Charles Marowitz
Chekhov: Four Plays, tr. by Carol Rocamora
Chekhov: The Early Plays, tr. by Carol Rocamora
Chekhov's Vaudevilles, tr. by Carol Rocamora
Ibsen: Four Major Plays, tr. by R. Davis & B. Johnston
Ibsen Volume II: Four Plays, tr. by Brian Johnston
Ibsen Volume III: Four Plays, tr. by Brian Johnston with Rick Davis
Arthur Schnitzler: 4 Major Plays, tr. by Carl R. Mueller
August Strindberg: 5 Major Plays, tr. by Carl R. Mueller
Villeggiatura: A Trilogy by Carlo Goldoni, tr. by Robert Cornthwaite

The Coffee Shop by Carlo Goldoni, tr. by Robert Cornthwaite
Cyrano de Bergerac by Edmond Rostand, tr. by Charles Marowitz
Emperor and Galilean by Henrik Ibsen, tr. by Brian Johnston
A Glass of Water by Eugene Scribe, tr. by Robert Cornthwaite
Mercadet by Honoré de Balzac, tr. by Robert Cornthwaite
The Sea Gull by Anton Chekhov, tr. by N. Saunders & F. Dwyer
Spite for Spite by Agustin Moreto, tr. by Dakin Matthews
The Summer People by Maxim Gorky, tr. by N. Saunders & F. Dwyer
Three Sisters by Anton Chekhov, tr. by Lanford Wilson
The Wood Demon by Anton Chekhov, tr. by N. Saunders & F. Dwyer
Zoyka's Apartment by Mikhail Bulgakov, tr. by N. Saunders & F. Dwyer

If you require prepublication information about upcoming Smith and Kraus books, you may receive our semiannual catalogue, free of charge, by sending your name and address to *Smith and Kraus Catalogue, P.O. Box 127, Lyme, NH 03768. Or call us at (603) 643-6431, fax (603) 643-1831. www.SmithKraus.com.*